LIQUIDITY AND INSTABILITY

LIQUIDITY AND INSTABILITY

By Courtney C. Brown
LECTURER IN BANKING
COLUMBIA UNIVERSITY

New York: Morningside Heights
COLUMBIA UNIVERSITY PRESS
1940

Foreign agents: OXFORD UNIVERSITY PRESS, *Humphrey Milford, Amen House, London, E.C. 4, England* AND *B. I. Building, Nicol Road, Bombay, India;* MARUZEN COMPANY, LTD., *6 Nihonbashi, Tori-Nichome, Tokyo, Japan*

MANUFACTURED IN THE UNITED STATES OF AMERICA

To

MARJORIE WARREN BROWN

who has helped me
in numberless ways

PREFACE

FOR MANY YEARS the term liquidity has been a subject of discussion among those interested in the field of banking. Exponents of various points of view have been classified broadly into two groups: the so-called currency school and the so-called banking school. The controversy between these schools, acrimonious at times, continues vigorously under the names of quantity theory and quality theory. There appears to be no prospect of a resolution of the argument. Surely the fact that the discussion has been carried through so many years by so many capable thinkers must indicate that elements of truth are to be found in both positions. Rather than attempt to review or extend the somewhat threadbare controversy, it is the purpose of this study to essay a fresh start.

One of the reasons for the inability to find common ground is the failure to define precisely the term liquidity. Liquidity is a quality of importance to substantially all assets, not merely to those owned by the banking system. In addition to possessing varying degrees of liquidity, assets are capable of maintaining value through time in varying degrees. A distinction will be made in this study between the problems concerned with the maintenance of liquidity of owned assets, on the one hand, and the problems concerned with the maintenance of value on the other. But liquidity is also a quality that attaches to corporate and individual persons. When so applied the term does subsume, as we shall see, the problem of value through time.

The reader may expect the argument to cover a wider range of ideas than is typically treated under the subject of liquidity.

After describing what we mean by liquidity, we shall attempt to discover the place the desire for more or less liquidity occupies in economic life in general. This necessitates a brief description of the institutional organization of wealth and titles to wealth. An effort will be made to appraise the importance of liquidity relative to other sources of economic change. This takes us into a discussion of various elements usually associated with business cycles in economic analysis. But the present study makes no pretense of setting forth an integrated theory of the business cycle. Rather, it is a work dealing with the problem of liquidity and its proximately associated phenomena—it is a description of liquidity and its place in economic theory.

The connotations of certain terms, as they are used here, will not be familiar to the reader. An effort will be made to define meanings clearly in cases in which they depart from customary academic usage. It is felt that a description of economic processes is facilitated by these occasional departures from established practice. The reader must judge for himself whether the method is justified. An example is the attempt to describe the factors related to business cycles without the use of the term money savings or of the term investment, in its usual meaning. The treatment of cyclical phenomena is presented entirely in terms of the receipt of money, hoarding, factors equivalent to hoarding in their repercussions, and the exchange of money for final new wealth output.

The discussion is limited largely to what appear to be dominant economic forces and characteristics. The meticulous reader may find exceptions to some of the generalizations. An attempt to deal with all the possible minor exceptions would too greatly burden the argument. Net forces, reflected through the whole economic group, rather than individualistic behavior, concern us for the most part.

Something will be said of price and interest theory, but no attempt at elaborate analysis of these elements and their integration in general theory will be made. Their treatment in the book is incidental and arises from their association with and significance to the description of liquidity. Moreover, in order to simplify the study as much as possible, no effort will be made to examine the influence of foreign economic relations on the problems of liquidity. The discussion is restricted to the institutions of the United States, without reference to the repercussions of foreign trade and international capital movements.

Many preceding authors have influenced these pages. It is as impossible to acknowledge the full extent of my indebtedness as it is to identify the many ideas and efforts that now combine to make possible so simple an operation as the turning on of an electric light. Those writings that have influenced me most specifically in the development of this work have been acknowledged in footnotes. In various stages of its preparation the manuscript has been read in whole or in part by Professors B. H. Beckhart, James C. Bonbright, and Arthur D. Gayer, by Dr. Eli Ginzberg, and by Messrs. A. A. Berle, Jr., C. Lowell Harriss, and P. B. Nortman. Their criticisms have been of great value. Professor Gayer has been especially generous with his time and advice. My chief debt is to Professor James W. Angell without whose meticulous guidance and patient encouragement the study might never have reached its present imperfect stage.

Mr. H. B. Bjorkman shared the burden of reading galley proof. Needless to say, full responsibility for the thoughts contained in this work rests with the author and not with these generous critics.

The John Day Co., Longmans, Green & Co., National Bureau of Economic Research, Inc., Harper & Brothers, Harcourt Brace and Co., Inc., Houghton Mifflin Co., The Ronald Press Co., The University of Chicago Press, E. P. Dutton & Co., and The Macmillan Co. have graciously consented to the reproduction of certain passages from their publications.

COURTNEY C. BROWN

New York City
October 1, 1940

cance to the description of liquidity. Moreover, in order to simplify the study as much as possible, no effort will be made to examine the influence of foreign economic relations on the problems of liquidity. The discussion is restricted to the institutions of the United States, without reference to the repercussions of foreign trade and international capital movements.

Many preceding authors have influenced these pages. It is as impossible to acknowledge the full extent of my indebtedness as it is to identify the many ideas and efforts that now combine to make possible so simple an operation as the turning on of an electric light. Those writings that have influenced me most specifically in the development of this work have been acknowledged in footnotes. In various stages of its preparation the manuscript has been read in whole or in part by Professors B. H. Beckhart, James C. Bonbright, and Arthur D. Gayer, by Dr. Eli Ginzberg, and by Messrs. A. A. Berle, Jr., C. Lowell Harriss, and P. B. Nortman. Their criticisms have been of great value. Professor Gayer has been especially generous with his time and advice. My chief debt is to Professor James W. Angell without whose meticulous guidance and patient encouragement the study might never have reached its present imperfect stage.

Mr. H. B. Bjorkman shared the burden of reading galley proof. Needless to say, full responsibility for the thoughts contained in this work rests with the author and not with these generous critics.

The John Day Co., Longmans, Green & Co., National Bureau of Economic Research, Inc., Harper & Brothers, Harcourt Brace and Co., Inc., Houghton Mifflin Co., The Ronald Press Co., The University of Chicago Press, E. P. Dutton & Co., and The Macmillan Co. have graciously consented to the reproduction of certain passages from their publications.

COURTNEY C. BROWN

New York City
October 1, 1940

CONTENTS

CHARTS

I

THE LIQUIDITY OF ASSETS AND PERSONS

ON OCTOBER 29, 1929, the New York *Times* carried spectacular headlines: "Stock Prices Slump $14,000,000,000 in Nationwide Stampede to Unload . . ."; ". . . Mob Psychology Big Factor[s] in Second Big Break." In the news article which followed, it was found that among other reasons, "Yesterday's far-reaching decline in stocks may be ascribed to a general loss of confidence." These pungent words were used by the New York *Times* to describe a particular phenomenon of the day. They serve equally well to introduce the subject of liquidity.

Headlines and news dispatches, by their nature, are more concise than accurate. To a certain extent, it is no doubt true that a general loss of confidence took place. This loss of confidence was accompanied by an *absence of conviction* that, in the future, owning one type of property would be more desirable than owning another. Such a state of mind may be expected to result in the sale of stocks and the acquisition of money. The holder of money is then better situated to acquire other types of property titles when a degree of conviction returns. But probably the chief motivation for such a flood of stock offerings at sharply declining prices was the *existence of a conviction* that money would gain in value relative to shares —which is the same thing as saying that there was a loss of confidence in the future value of shares relative to the value of money. This is quite different from saying that there was a *general* loss of confidence.[1]

[1] At the same time, there appears to have been a loss of confidence in the value of shares relative to the value of their associated corporeal wealth. Those shares of stock, the aggregate price of which had diminished by a staggering dollar amount

Another factor in this dramatic stock-market decline was distress selling. Creditors, having loans outstanding secured by shares, demanded payment of their loans in money or required additional collateral. Other creditors, observing the "flight to money," joined the procession by calling many of those loans the provisions of which would permit such action, more or less regardless of the type of the security behind the loans. Some debtors, losing confidence in the future money value of their assets, wished to dispose of them in order to pay debts which were fixed in terms of money. Probably the majority of debtors, ever hopeful, preferred to maintain their debts if possible, trusting to recoup their losses.

In essence, this convulsion in the share market seems to be interpretable in terms of one principal factor. There was a major change in public preferences for one type of title to wealth, namely money, over other types of titles, especially shares and debts. Underlying this change in preferences was (1) *the dominant belief,* on the part of some, that money was for the moment a more suitable means of storing value for the future than other types of assets; and (2) *a lack of confidence,* on the part of others, in any type of asset as a suitable store of value through time—a temporary diminution of conviction that the economic future is "guessable."

The desire to hold money rather than other wealth forms was thus motivated by two forces: *conviction* on the part of some that money would enhance in value relative to certain other types of assets, and uncertainty or *lack of conviction* on the part of others regarding the relative prospective value status of any type of asset whatsoever. The first of these motivations

---

in a single day, were legal instruments evidencing ownership in a large segment of the nation's productive resources. It cannot be argued that the worth of the productive resources thus represented had changed so greatly. Nor is it ascertainable or probable that the expectations of future worth of the underlying corporeal wealth had been so materially altered in so brief a time. The "general loss of confidence" expressed through "mob psychology" was not a sudden loss of confidence in the ability of productive resources to satisfy human wants through time, from which their worth is ultimately derived. It was rather a loss of confidence in shares, as such. People wanted to "get out of" shares and "into" money.

may be resolved into a problem of relative value prospects. The second takes the form of arranging one's assets in a manner permitting of quick change when some degree of conviction should be restored.

LIQUIDITY AND VALUE OF ASSETS DISTINGUISHED

Liquidity has long been considered a complex and confusing conception. One reason for this confusion is the tendency to think of it, when applied to assets, as subsuming two components: (1) the ability to effect a quick exchange into money, *and* (2) the ability to effect an exchange into money at an unvarying price—in other terms, marketability and stability of money value through time. Both aspects are concerned with money price. But the first of these components is concerned with money prices in more specific periods of time. In this sense liquidity is typically regarded as increasing with the *shortness* of the time interval in which a "reasonable" money price may be obtained. The second aspect, on the other hand, is concerned with money prices in indefinite periods of time. In this second sense, liquidity is typically regarded as increasing with the *duration* of the time period in which a given price may be obtained. But the two problems are unlike in nature and cannot be handled under the composite heading of liquidity without confusion. Both are phases of the study of value. But the first aspect comprises a specialized phase of the field of value analysis, whereas the second *is* the study of relative values through time per se. We shall accordingly associate the term liquidity, *when applied to assets,* with the degree of ease in exchanging wealth titles for money, and shall disassociate it from the question of the maintenance of money values through time.

THE LIQUIDITY OF ASSETS DEFINED

Many definitions of the term liquidity, differing in detail, have been given by previous writers.[2] The majority of them

[2] Berle and Pederson, *Liquid Claims and National Wealth,* give numerous examples in Appendix B.

are not fundamentally different, however, in that they refer chiefly to banking assets, and hence to debts in one form or another. A bank loan is generally held to be liquid if its maturity is no longer than the time normally required to sell the underlying asset which serves as its security. In any event, the maturity should not be over ninety days. But since our study of liquidity is concerned with *all* types of assets in the community, this form of definition is of little use to us. A more usable and suggestive definition is given by Professor Ray B. Westerfield in the *Encyclopaedia of the Social Sciences:*

> This term when applied to an article of wealth or a credit item denotes the possibility of raising cash upon it by selling it or pledging it as security for a loan; in reference to a business concern liquidity is measured by the availability of cash, whether direct and immediate or indirect and involving the conversion of some assets into cash to meet ordinary or extraordinary demands upon it. The assumption in both cases is that the conversion can be carried out expeditiously without sacrifice of values and with slight cost and disruption of operations.[3]

In this passage, in which the reference is to all assets in the first instance, and in the second, to all business concerns which own assets and owe debts,[4] we may note two points of significant importance. First, liquidity is concerned with the possession or availability of cash.[5] Second, the cash must be obtainable *expeditiously,* without sacrifice of the value of the previously held assets.

The time factor connoted in the second of these points must

[3] Westerfield, "Liquidity," *Encyclopaedia of the Social Sciences,* IX, 491–92.

[4] Otherwise there would be no ordinary or extraordinary demands to be met. More will be said of the liquidity of business concerns (corporate persons) in subsequent pages.

[5] Professor Westerfield makes the availability of cash a derivative of the sale of an asset or its pledge as the security for a loan. It is difficult to see how a prospective lender would feel economically justified in granting a loan to a borrower who held only titles to assets that were not salable in the present or in the foreseeable future, or assets, the services of which are not salable in the present or through time. Although borrowing against an asset may expedite obtaining cash, it may also result in the realization of a smaller amount of net cash. Since loans ultimately rest on the prospective sale of assets or the services they render, our subsequent analysis deals with the exchange phase of the problem for the most part.

be examined further before we can obtain a satisfactory and usable concept. Among the definitions given by Mr. Berle and Miss Pederson in their study of liquidity is the following: "liquidity is a quality inherent in an asset or supplied to it by a reasonably stable mechanism of society furnishing reasonable assurance that it can be converted into cash within a period of time recognized by the commercial community in which it moves as reasonably short." [6] Here the time factor becomes somewhat more conspicuous. But the emphasis is still placed on a period recognized by the commercial community as reasonably short. It is more valid to conceive of all assets as possessing varying degrees of liquidity. Those that can be converted into cash in shorter periods of time than others, *ceteris paribus,* are judged to possess a greater degree of the quality we call liquidity. But substantially all assets possess more or less liquidity; the term should not be restricted to those which can be converted into cash within any arbitrary period of time.

Convertibility into cash and liquidity are thus synonymous terms. Assets are converted into cash through sale or, as in the case of a maturing debt, through exercising the rights of contract. The time required to effect the conversion will depend on the nature of the market for the asset, if the conversion is made through sale. If the conversion results from contractual rights, the nature of the contract will determine in the first instance. It may be, however, that the debtor is unable to fulfill the terms of the contract. This inability of the debtor to meet his obligations may have resulted from his previous transactions in which sale of other assets, or voluntary exchange, played an important role. Thus the liquidity that attaches to an asset because of contract is conditioned in turn by the salability of other assets. Salability becomes the centrally important phenomenon in the study of the liquidity of assets.

Salability or unsalability of an asset must be distinguished from its depreciation or appreciation. Salability depends on the organization and condition of the market *and* on the amount

[6] *Liquid Claims,* p. 24.

that is to be sold. If there is by assumption no appreciation or depreciation, salability may be described "as the relationship between the selling price and the time which the seller must *wait in order to get it*." [7] General economic and business change proximately relate to appreciation and depreciation, rather than to salability, and are abstracted from the concept.

The liquidity of an asset thus becomes essentially a market phenomenon. Some markets, such as the stock exchanges, are organized to effect sales in brief periods. Others, such as the market for, let us say, rare tapestries, are not so organized. Extended periods may be required to find a buyer willing to pay a price, within a range of prices, that all who possess knowledge of rare tapestries and the market for them agree is fair or reasonable. The tapestry may be sold immediately at a price below this range. It may never be sold at a price above this range, unless the range itself moves upward in the course of time. But in estimating the liquidity of the tapestry, we are interested in the probable time required to find a buyer within the range of fair prices that exists at the moment. This range is set in highly organized and competitive markets by the spread of the bid and the asked prices.

When judging the degree of liquidity of any particular asset or type of asset, we should consider these elements: (1) the time that would probably be required to convert the asset into cash, and (2) the spread or the range of money prices, one of which may be expected in such a time period. If the spread remains unchanged, an asset is said to be more or less liquid as the typical time required to exchange it directly or indirectly for money is shorter or longer. If the time period is constant, an asset is said to be more or less liquid as the range of probable prices is smaller or greater. Generally speaking, an attempt to shorten the time factor below its typical limits is at the expense of price.[8]

[7] Makower and Marschak, "Assets, Prices, and Monetary Theory," *Economica,* V, new series (Aug., 1938), 280.

[8] Berle and Pederson illustrate this point with an interesting graph on which they have plotted a "liquidity curve." The shorter the time on the x axis, up to a certain point, the smaller is the price on the y axis. *Liquid Claims,* p. 29.

These several factors manifest themselves in the ability to exchange an asset for money in a ratio not greatly different from that anticipated after a survey of the market and within the limits of a period of time prescribed by the organization of the market. This *prospective* liquidity generally is what we mean in saying that a thing is a more or a less liquid asset.

The price at which an asset is acquired is sometimes made the point of reference in judging its liquidity through time. The owner of an asset may consider it liquid only if he can subsequently dispose of it at his purchase price or at a better price. In other words, he has a "reservation" price which he places on his asset. The purchaser of 100 shares of United States Steel stock at 100 may consider his holding illiquid if the price drops to 90. A bank officer may consider his Treasury bonds illiquid if he paid 105 for them in the open market and they are now selling at 100. This is not, however, the sense in which we are using the term liquidity here. True, holding the Steel Corporation shares and Treasury bonds as vehicles for conveying titles to wealth through time would have proved to have been disadvantageous during the period of possession; but the liquidity status of these securities would not necessarily have been changed by their price fluctuation. The time required to convert either of them into cash and the prospect of realizing a money price within an expected range of money prices (even though in a lower range) will not necessarily have been changed.[9]

Markets are described as "good" when bid prices and offer prices are not far apart, and when the size of the market is ample to accommodate relatively large transactions without great price changes. Now the decline in the price of the Steel Corporation shares and Treasury bonds may have reacted psychologically in such manner as to widen the spread between

[9] It may be that the liquidity status of the *purchasers* of the shares or bonds will suffer as a result of the depreciation in price, if they have money obligations of a fixed nature maturing or about to mature, but the liquidity status of the Steel Corporation shares and Treasury bonds will be unchanged unless the price decline has impaired the condition of the market. More will be said of this in subsequent pages.

the bid and asked prices. Likewise, the change in the level of prices may have resulted in a reduction in the size of the market. In each event the liquidity of the securities would be impaired. But this is not a necessary or even a usual result of price changes through time. Such impairment of markets is more frequently identified with *sudden* price changes which are of a temporary nature. The impairment of the liquidity of an asset is likely to be of a correspondingly temporary nature. When the sudden price movement has abated, the former liquidity status of the title will be substantially restored, even though at a different level of prices. As applied to assets, liquidity is a quality that is usually independent of a particular current level of prices. It is not proximately related to general business change of a cyclical nature.

Roughly speaking, the spread between bid and asked prices measures the range of prices within which an actual price may be realized in a period of time prescribed by the organization of markets. The bid and asked prices may be real or they may exist only subjectively in the minds of prospective traders. They are usually real in the case of securities traded on organized exchanges. They are more frequently subjective in the case of real estate and comparable transactions.[10]

Liquidity also varies with the size of markets—which is another way of saying that it varies with the size of an asset offered relative to the size of its market.[11] An increase in the amount of the asset offered may impair the degree of liquidity, either by lengthening the time period required to effect an exchange against money or by widening the spread of the expected range of prices. The size of the offering is thus implicit in a definition that describes liquidity in terms of typical time periods and of expected money prices.

Liquidity is a quality possessed by all economic assets in vary-

10 The subjective offer price to which we here refer should not be confused with a so-called reservation price on the part of a single seller. Rather it refers to prices that buyers may justifiably expect to be met immediately if they make the bid, or sellers may expect to be taken if they make the offer.

11 This is not the same as saying the size of the asset relative to the total stock of the asset.

ing degrees. Although the usefulness of short definitions is not always great, it may be said that *the liquidity of an asset is a quality that increases and decreases with changes in the ability to exchange the asset for money in general, but not for a specific amount of money*. This ability increases with a narrowing of the range of prices within which it is thought that the asset may be sold and with a shortening of the period of time within which a price can be obtained within this expected range of prices.[12] Conversely, the liquidity of an asset will decrease as the expected range of prices broadens and as the time required to obtain a price within this range lengthens. In the development of markets there has been a tendency for the time and spread factors to contract together, thus improving liquidity. But it does not follow that these two components of the liquidity of assets always contract and expand together, *pari passu*. Especially in short periods there may be an expansion or contraction of either without a corresponding change in the other.

These two factors measure the ability to exchange an asset for money in general, but not for a specific amount of money, which is a matter of the value of the asset through time. Liquidity is not a physical property that attaches to assets. Rather, it is a quality that assets possess as the result of the institutional organization of society and the play of public psychology upon those institutions.

THE USE OF THE TERM LIQUIDITY IN THE CURRENT BANKING CONTROVERSY

In this study we are interested in the degree of liquidity possessed by *all* assets. The term liquidity is not always used with this inclusive meaning. For years it has been considered implicitly a quality that applied more or less exclusively to

[12] It has been suggested that this might read "the shorter the period within which it is thought that a given expected *minimum* price can be obtained," or again, "within which the minimum price of the expected range of prices can be obtained." In organized markets this minimum would be the bid price. The period of time required to convert an asset into money at this price is simply a matter of the techniques of the market in question and does not necessarily correspond to the time required to obtain, through trading, a price other than the minimum in the expected range of prices.

bank assets. Hence most of the literature in regard to the subject treats of this aspect. This literature has concerned itself with a discussion of the kinds of assets suitable for a bank's possession and the reasons why they are so. A comprehensive review of this somewhat threadbare and inconclusive debate is provided by Mr. Waldo F. Mitchell.[13] The nature of bank assets is a phase of our problem to which we shall return in a later chapter.[14] At this point we may note that Mr. Mitchell finds in substance:

> There have been two theories of the liquidity of bank earning assets, as applied to an individual bank. First, there is what may be called the "orthodox" theory, which states that banks should lend only for short periods of time for commercial purposes, so that the maturity of the paper would complete the commercial transaction and liquidate the loans. The second theory may be called the "shiftability" theory. This second theory holds that experience shows that paper often cannot be liquidated at maturity; that when the paper can be liquidated at maturity, it may not be desirable to liquidate it; that when demand is made on the liabilities of an individual bank, the only reliance for liquidity in an emergency lies in the power to shift assets to other banks and get funds from the banks that still have available funds; and that when credit has been largely expanded and assets have been shifted until the reserves are practically exhausted in all the banks, liquidity in the banking system can be attained only by a slowing up of business or a lowering of the price level.[15]

These are not theories of liquidity so much as theories of how liquidity should be maintained. The shiftability thesis has been vigorously supported by a group of writers, among whom Moulton, Currie, and Mitchell himself have been conspicuous. Fritz Machlup, on the other hand, has denied "every existing theory of liquidity," and has held that even "short-term capital is never really liquid," saying,

> . . . short-term saving is liquid in so far as a new saver takes the place of the liquidating one. The substitution of one saver or investor for another can be expected in normal times. There is a continuous prolongation and turnover of the short-term loans and

[13] *The Uses of Bank Funds, passim.* [14] *Infra,* Chap. IX. [15] *Ibid.,* p. 3.

short-term investments. The individual owners, creditors, and debtors change but the volume of the capital is not reduced. If it is attempted to liquidate more short-term capital than the amount of new capital which is replaced, the creditors discover that their capital is *not liquid* and can only be liquidated successively according to the further supply of new capital or according to the shrinkage of production.[16]

These are conclusions similar to those we shall find in our subsequent study of debt. The term capital is an ambiguous one, and the exact sense in which it is used in this quotation is not clear. We suspect it is not unlike debt, however.

Perhaps the stanchest modern exponent of the "orthodox" theory was Professor H. Parker Willis. Liquidity to him was a concept that was applicable not only to assets and persons, but to the whole community as well. It meant more than the mere convertibility of an asset into money. It was a matter of clearance or offsetting of claims, regardless of their form or nature.

The liquidity of a community does not necessarily depend upon ability to convert into coin or into anything else. . . . Liquidity consists of the ability to meet claims in full when they are presented for payment—but such payments may consist in the presentation of similar, or offsetting claims of simultaneous maturity.

[In order to accomplish this the banking community and the central banks have a duty to refuse] credit to all except those who are unmistakably able to meet claims against them at maturity by the presentation of other claims. This in practice would mean a refusal to extend credit for any purpose that involved the use of funds for a longer period than the average in the community where the transactions were taking place.[17]

On this view, possession of the claims required for offsetting purposes results from the ownership of *current* claims to wealth derived from the production-consumption process.

Liquidity . . . is the power inherent in production and consumption operations to obtain titles to actual current wealth, as distinct from what may be produced in the future or may be derived from

[16] Machlup, "The Liquidity of Short-Term Capital," *Economica,* XII (Aug. 1932), 283.

[17] Willis, *The Theory and Practice of Central Banking,* p. 32.

later employment of productive capital in the turning out of goods that will be wanted by actual users at a later date.[18]

Applying these ideas to so-called credit or debt instruments, one is more or less compelled to conclude that the only suitable asset for banks is the short bill. Bills are typically used to finance the carrying of goods that are already in existence and owned. Notes, even though they are short-term, are more generally used to provide funds for the purpose of acquiring goods not previously possessed or even in existence.[19]

It may also be mentioned that the exclusive use of bills in banking operations is the only means of gearing bank "credit" to the often-cited "needs of business." In this event, the real wealth serving as the counterpart of the purchasing power resulting from the bank loan has come into being before the bank loan. But when banks grant loans on other than trade bills, the purchasing power may come into being *before* the real wealth which serves as its offset. This is true whether the credit instruments are short-dated or long-dated. But the orthodox theorist generally has not carried his reasoning to this rigorous conclusion. Rather, he has been content to advocate any type of short-term debt instrument for banks, so long as its maturity falls within the period in which the accompanying business transaction is expected to be completed.

In the above quotation, the ability to meet maturing claims with offsetting claims is made to depend upon possession of present claims in the form of "titles to actual current wealth." But titles to actual current wealth are not typically in the form desired by creditors and hence must be converted to money before presentation in satisfaction of a claim for money. We must thus arrive at the conclusion of the late Dr. Caroline Whitney, one of Professor Willis's able students, that: "liquidity depends ultimately upon the salability of goods." [20]

18 Willis, Chapman, and Robey, *Contemporary Banking*, pp. 296–97.

19 I am indebted to Professor F. Cyril James for this suggestion, made in the course of a seminar meeting of the School of Business, Columbia University, at which he was visiting lecturer.

20 Whitney, *Experiments in Credit Control*, p. 186.

It is true that the identification of liquidity with convertibility into cash may be abortive in a sense. Such is the case if cash is defined as specie or currency and there is an insufficient quantity of cash, so defined, to satisfy claims that are presented. Professor Willis's conception that the "liquidity of a community does not depend upon ability to convert into coin or anything else" overcomes this difficulty. Presumably cash would be used, whether specie or currency, to settle the unbalance appearing in the clearance of other claims. But the important point for our purposes is that the clearance of non-money claims is effected in practice, directly or indirectly, by first converting the claims into money *in one of its various forms.* Hence it appears that from the social as well as from the individual point of view liquidity is a question of convertibility into money.

We will defer our discussion of appropriate bank assets. Let it suffice at this point to stress the fact that liquidity is a question of convertibility into money. An asset is convertible into money *both* by sale (shiftability) and, if the asset is a debt, by previous contractual arrangement (redeemability). The first is a voluntary transaction on the part of the holders both of money and of the assets that are liquidated. The second becomes an involuntary transaction after the terms of the contract have been set. But its successful completion is not unrelated to the debtor's ability to pay money. This ability in turn may be increased or decreased by the liquidity and value characteristics of those assets owned by the debtor. In the ultimate sense, it then appears that liquidity rests upon the voluntary transaction of sale; the exchange of non-money assets for money.

THE MEASURE OF LIQUIDITY

By definition, money is the measure of the degree of liquidity possessed by all forms of wealth. Hence money possesses maximum liquidity. But to say that money is of maximum liquidity is *not* the same as saying that money is always the most desired form in which to hold a title to present economic wealth or a claim to future economic wealth. Cyclical or secular price rises are, in substance, an expression by the community of lessened desires to hold money units relative to other forms of wealth. This does not mean that money, because of the lessened demand for it relative to real wealth, has become less liquid. It may mean that the demand for liquidity by the community has lessened. More likely, it may mean that the community has changed its relative value expectations concerning money. Titles to wealth other than money can never attain the liquidity status of money so long as their own degree of liquidity is measured by money.

The measure of the liquidity of assets used in this study is the ability to exchange them for money. One does not say, when stretching a rubber band along the edge of a ruler, that the ruler reciprocally contracts and expands as one stretches and releases the rubber. The rubber has become longer or shorter relative to its linear measure, the ruler. Similarly, other forms of wealth become more or less liquid relative to their liquidity measure, a unit of money. The liquidity status of money, like the linear dimension of the ruler, is unchanged.

While it is possible to describe money as possessing maximum liquidity, it is difficult to grade other wealth-titles precisely according to their liquidity status. Various factors are responsible for this difficulty. Titles to wealth are held in various forms. These forms, as we shall see, are of great importance in determining the liquidity status of ownership, but the liquidity of ownership is frequently different from that of the ultimate wealth involved. Moreover, different segments of the same kind of wealth may be put to a variety of uses and these uses may change through time. Particular units or bundles of wealth may be placed in an indefinite number of different associations with other types of wealth, from which it may be easy or difficult to disassociate them. Again, the liquidity of a given asset may vary from time to time because of changed market conditions.

These are factors which result in a variable liquidity status for many forms of wealth. Certain characteristics of wealth forms and of titles to wealth forms, however, are discernible. These are sufficiently conspicuous to permit the business man, consciously or unconsciously, to make rough liquidity classifications in his daily life. A partial classification is as follows:

Highly Liquid	*Less Liquid*	*Least Liquid*
Listed bonds	Short-term personal notes	Long-term personal notes
Listed stocks	Standardized commodities	Unstandardized commodities
Acceptances	Bonds and stocks of close corporations	Real estate
Commercial paper (prime names)	Inventories	"Fixed" assets
Commodity contracts		
Time and savings deposits		
Insurance policies (cash value)		

A somewhat different view has been expressed by Mr. E. F. M. Durbin:

While I do not believe it is possible to arrange classes of goods into a general order of liquidity preference, it is obvious that some classes of things such as cash balances and credit balances are commonly regarded as more liquid than other groups of things.

In an accompanying footnote he adds:

For example, during a period of Trade Cycle depression fixed interest securities will be regarded as more liquid than equities or commodity stocks and will stand to the left of the series arranged in order of liquidity. But during a high inflation they will be regarded as less liquid and will stand to the right of them. This means that if confidence is further shaken during a depression the community will hoard fixed interest securities, while if it is shaken during a high inflation they will hoard real goods. There is therefore no general order of liquidity.[21]

It will be observed that in this passage Mr. Durbin is not using the term liquidity in the same manner that we are using it here. It is true that, in a depression, bonds, fixed in terms of money, are considered to be a more suitable type of holding than equities and commodity stocks. But this is not due to any

[21] Durbin, *The Problem of Credit Policy*, p. 106.

improvement in the liquidity status of bonds. Rather it is attributable to the recognized tendency of money prices of equities and commodities to decline in conditions of depression. Correspondingly, in conditions of "high inflation," bonds are regarded as less attractive than equities not because of an impairment of the liquidity status of bonds relative to money, but because of the expectation of higher money prices for equities and commodities. The fact that a loss of confidence during inflation is accompanied by a desire for real wealth is not due to any loss of liquidity by prime bonds or money. It is a result of questioning the prospective price of money in terms of real wealth, not of questioning the money price of money, which is an identity.

THE CONCEPT OF SOLVENCY; SOMETIMES USED TO DESCRIBE THE LIQUIDITY OF PERSONS AS CONTRASTED WITH THE LIQUIDITY OF ASSETS

One source of confusion in the use of the term liquidity has already been described, i. e., the tendency to associate changes in money prices of assets through time with the liquidity of these assets. Another source of confusion is the practice of applying the term "liquidity" both to assets and to individual and corporate persons, usually without realizing the dichotomy.[22] When applied to the status of persons, liquidity becomes substantially synonymous with solvency. It is more precisely synonymous with the *degree* of solvency. In this use, liquidity refers to the *money amount* of assets owned by a person relative to the *money amount* of debts owed. It also refers to the *liquidity characteristics* of his assets relative to the *maturity schedule* of his debts. How readily may the assets be exchanged for money? When do the debts fall due for payment?

Changes in relative values through time may substantially revise the liquidity status of persons by changing the *money amounts* of assets relative to debts, without changing the liquidity characteristics or maturities of either. Thus the liquidity

22 Willis went a step further and applied it to the whole community. See *supra*, p. 11.

status of *persons* is determined by a greater number of factors than is the liquidity status of assets.

The measure of the liquidity status of persons, individual and corporate, is found, in the first instance, in the liquidity status of the things they own. If they owe debts, a further measure is found in the money amount and the liquidity status of the things they own, relative to the money amount and the maturity schedules of the debts they owe. Unlike the situation in respect to assets alone, here the question of relative value prospects through time enters conspicuously. A person may revise his liquidity status either by changing the nature of his assets or liabilities, or by changing the money amount of his assets relative to liabilities. It follows that a change in his liquidity desires relative to his liquidity status may result in several courses of action. These will be examined in some detail in subsequent chapters. For the present we shall confine ourselves to matters of definition.

This distinction between the liquidity of persons and the liquidity of assets has been made by several writers in the recent past. Mr. A. M. Newman credits Professor Westerfield with pioneering the distinction in his article on "Liquidity" in the *Encyclopaedia of the Social Sciences,*[23] and proceeds to comment upon it in the following terms:

> . . . we must draw a line of distinction between the liquidity of *an asset,* or group of assets, and the individual liquidity of a person, or group of persons, which I shall call *individual* liquidity. The two types of liquidity are distinct, though in discussion they appear nearly always to be mixed.[24]

Several years prior to the publication of the *Encyclopaedia of the Social Sciences,* Mr. Glenn G. Munn had discussed the liquidity of persons.

> Liquidity. A term referring to that condition of an individual or business a high percentage of the assets of which can be quickly con-

[23] *Supra,* p. 4.

[24] Newman, "The Doctrine of Liquidity," *Review of Economic Studies,* III (1935–36), 82.

> verted into cash without involving any considerable loss by accepting sacrifice prices. Liquidity implies a high degree of currentness and financial solvency, i. e., that the value of the current assets is well above that of the current liabilities.[25]

This identification of the liquidity of persons with their degree of solvency is consistent with the use of the term liquidity in business parlance. A brief summary of certain simple accounting concepts, as they relate to the question of solvency, will serve to focus our attention upon the factors of importance in judging the liquidity of legal and natural persons.

Every active business enterprise and most natural persons are possessed of assets and liabilities. The liabilities of corporate enterprises are divided into two parts. On the one hand, the enterprise per se has a liability to its owners. On the other, the enterprise usually owes debts to outside parties who may or may not participate directly in its ownership.

Solvency is not a precise term. As commonly used in business circles, solvency means but one thing: ability to pay debts as they fall due. This is also the meaning in common law which "makes insolvency depend on inability to pay debts precisely when they mature." [26] Under the National Bankruptcy Act and its amendments this is not the case. Instead of referring to a point in time—namely, when debts fall due—the legal test of solvency is generally made on the basis of an appraisal of "the fair valuation of the debtors' property," which probably means the *prospective future value* of assets relative to the known dollar amount of liabilities to others than the owners. This is a highly significant difference in the treatment of the time factor, which, we have seen, enters as an element in the problem of the liquidity of assets.

The first important National Bankruptcy Act (1867) followed the common-law definition of insolvency. The law was repealed in 1878, and state law became applicable. A uniform Federal law regarding the treatment of insolvency was again

25 Munn, *Encyclopaedia of Banking and Finance,* p. 404. Quoted by Berle and Pederson, *Liquid Claims,* Appendix B., p. 224.

26 Bonbright, *The Valuation of Property,* II, 751.

drawn in 1898 to supplant the heterogeneous state laws. This Federal law established a definition of insolvency which differs from that common in business usage.

Under the National Bankruptcy Act a person (firm or corporation) is insolvent "when the aggregate of his property . . . is not, at a fair valuation, sufficient in amount to pay his debts." However, it may often happen that a person, firm, or corporation is forced to have its affairs reviewed by a court when the cash assets are not sufficient to pay debts when they become due, and under the laws of some states such a condition constitutes legal insolvency. So long as the National Bankruptcy Act is in effect, state laws relative to insolvency are not effective.[27]

Subsequent judicial interpretation of this definition has elaborated without clarifying its meaning. When Federal courts are called upon in reorganization proceedings, or on other occasions, to judge the solvency of an enterprise, the test is usually made on a basis of a reasonable appraisal of the total *prospective future* value of assets relative to the known undiscounted dollar amount of liabilities to others than the owners. Business practice provides a more severe test. If at any point in time the company is unable to provide money to meet its maturing debts, the company is considered insolvent as a going concern, and the court would in all probability be petitioned to take charge of its affairs. The time point of testing in the business case is the *present.*

Depending on the nature of the business, assets consist of various titles to wealth and combinations of wealth possessing a wide variety of liquidity characteristics. In other words, different time intervals are required to dispose of different parts of the total assets at prices within the ranges or spreads of expected prices. These different liquidity characteristics provide a basis for judging how long it *might* take to exchange various assets for money. In addition, it is expected that certain assets *will* be exchanged for money in given time periods in the regular course of business. Likewise, liabilities to others, expressed in money terms, mature at different times. Business practice

[27] Kester, *Advanced Accounting,* pp. 757–58.

deems an enterprise to be insolvent if money is not made available, by its prior possession or by acquisition through the pledge or sale of other assets, before debts fall due and are presented. To guard against this contingency, good managers attempt to arrange their affairs so that the part of their assets held in money or the equivalent, or readily convertible into money, will be more than sufficient to cover imminently maturing liabilities. The success of this effort will depend on two factors, the liquidity of the assets and the maintenance of their money value through time.

The money amount and due date of the liabilities are generally ascertainable with precision. Except for currency and bank deposits, the time and price features of assets are not determinable with equal precision. If the judgment of the manager in arranging his assets and liabilities has been incorrect, the enterprise will be unable to pay its bills as they are presented, and it may be unable to continue without court aid. The court may then be called on to decide whether the enterprise is insolvent, in the indefinite reasonable value sense. If so, a reorganization or a liquidation of its affairs will follow, the technique and outcome of which will depend in part on the court's previous ruling regarding legal solvency.

These characteristics of business operation provide still a *third* test of solvency. It is used to determine the *degree* of solvency or liquidity of a person or firm. For each asset or combination of assets owned by an enterprise, there is a price within a range of prices that *might* be expected to be realized within a period of time prescribed by the organization of markets. There is also the expectation that certain assets *will* be exchanged for money in a given period of time. The money amounts and the time periods involved in liabilities are in most cases known. Thus an array of expected prices and time intervals of assets can be set against the known amounts and time intervals of liabilities. Although this comparison does not prove solvency or insolvency in either of the first two senses, it reports tendencies toward financial strength or weakness.

Use has been made of this concept in the case of industrial and commercial firms. The accounting practice has developed of comparing the expected prices of those assets the estimated time factor of which is usually one year or less with the amount of those liabilities the known time factor of which is usually one year or less. Such items are called current assets and current liabilities. The difference between the two aggregates is called working capital.

> Current liabilities are, in accordance with standard practice, those which will mature within twelve months from the date of the balance sheet and for which no special provision for liquidation . . . has been made. . . .
>
> . . . it is possible . . . to define current assets, without specific reference to the period of their realization, as all of those assets from which current creditors expect, in the normal course of business operations, to secure liquidation of their claims. . . . Every business is organized to sell some commodity or service which has been bought, manufactured, or possessed for that purpose. . . . Its sale gives rise to claims against customers and when they are realized or collected, the trading cycle from cash, through merchandise and receivables back to cash is completed. It is usually to these assets, or rather to the cash realized from them, that current creditors must look for the liquidation of their claims. . . . Other assets . . . may be classed as current assets but must prove their right to inclusion with that group by showing a fairly short period—usually not to exceed twelve months—during which their realization in cash may reasonably be expected.[28]
>
> For determining solvency, the relation between current assets and current liabilities is the ratio used.[29]

This corporate accounting procedure has merely formalized the factors used in estimating the degree of solvency or liquidity of all persons, corporate and natural. As such, it serves to focus attention on those phases of a person's affairs to which he gives attention when a change takes place in his liquidity desires. It would be hazardous to hold that persons are always highly rational about the nice adjustment of their assets and liabilities with changes in liquidity desires. Economists once held that

[28] Kester, *Advanced Accounting*, pp. 27–28. [29] *Ibid.*, p. 735.

persons effected a rational balance between pleasures and pains. But it is true, nevertheless, that adjustments between assets and liabilities are the means available to persons to change their liquidity status, and that these adjustments receive attention with changes in attitudes toward liquidity.

SUMMARY

From what has been said it may be seen that the study of liquidity comprises two broad topics. First, it is a study of the characteristics of various types of assets or titles to wealth, and of the ease or difficulty of exchanging them for money in general, but not for a specific amount of money. This is a matter of the liquidity of assets per se. Second, it is a study of the nature and amount of titles to wealth owned by an individual or other economic unit relative to the nature and amount of debts owed. This is a matter of the liquidity of persons, both natural and corporate. The analysis of these two groups of phenomena and of their implications for other phases of economic life constitutes the broad focus of this study.

In a rigorous sense, the desire for liquidity of assets and persons springs from a lack of conviction, although the desire to hold more or less money, the most liquid of all assets, may be motivated by changed value judgments in addition to uncertainty. When people excitedly sell assets and buy money, there is typically said to be a loss of confidence. This is not so correct a description as to say that the decreased confidence in assets is matched by the increased confidence in money. Instead of a diminution of conviction, there is a shift of conviction. Both a diminution of conviction and a shift of conviction are significant to our problem.

The liquidity of an asset is not a physical property of the asset. It is a quality related to and measured by the ability to exchange the asset for money in general. If the asset is a debt instrument, it may be exchanged for money according to the terms of its contract in addition to sale. But since the ability of debtors to meet their obligations payable in money must depend ultimately upon sales at some stage in the economic process, in the last analysis liquidity depends upon the salability of assets.

A distinction has been drawn between the problem of the liquidity of assets and the problem of their value through time. It is not unusual to subsume both of these problems under the term liquidity. Confusion is the result.

A more justifiable inclusion of the factor of value through time in the definition and analysis of liquidity is found when it is applied to the concept of the liquidity of natural and corporate persons. Even in this instance, however, such an inclusion is appropriate only if the person owes debts. If a person who is free of debts owns 100 dollars of easily exchangeable assets, his status is no more and no less liquid than that of the man without debts who owns 1,000 dollars of assets exchangeable with equal ease. When used with reference to debt-owing persons, the term liquidity is hence roughly analogous to a measure of the degree of solvency. We shall study the term in its application both to assets and to persons.

A major phase of the liquidity problem is the repayment or the extension of debt. A change in liquidity desires manifests itself in two ways. First, a preference for one type of title to wealth over other types may occur. This, when it appears in the community at large, takes the form of a revision in the scale of preferences for all types of titles. Second, and in a sense a manifestation of the first phenomenon, there may be a desire on the part of creditors to transform their ownership of debts into money by demanding payment. At the same time, some debtors, wishing a higher degree of liquidity in their over-all position, may wish to pay their debts in addition to attempting to change the nature of their assets. Thus an individual owning assets of value 100, and owing debts of amount 50, owes 50 percent of the value of his wealth titles. If he obtains money for assets of value 25 and uses it to reduce his debt, his equity is still 50 but he now owes only 33 percent of the value of his remaining wealth titles. At a time when the liquidity desires of the community are increasing, he is likely, as we shall see later, to be more doubtful about the maintenance of the dollar value of his assets. Thus, in the parlance of business, he is a prudent man to reduce his obligations. In studying changes in the size of debt as an expression of a change in liquidity desires, we shall make an attempt to discover some of the implications of this tendency of debt to increase and decrease with changes in public psychology. The approach will be made from the standpoint of all debts, rather than from that of any particular debts or classes of debts, such as government debts and private debts.

It may be noted at this point that a widespread desire to exchange titles previously held for others that are more liquid, and the desire to reduce debt, are synchronous. Both result in a contraction of economic activity. Conversely, a general desire for less liquid titles and a desire to expand debt are also synchronous. Both result in an expansion of economic activity. The phenomena are reciprocally motivating and provide no corrective forces within themselves. These propositions will be developed later. Also, as we shall see, the operation of the banking system, instead of restraining these tendencies, functions in a manner which stimulates them still further.

II

LIQUIDITY PREFERENCES

OTHER THINGS EQUAL, individuals will always want as much liquidity in their assets as they can attain. But we know that desires for liquidity increase and decrease from time to time. More accurately, we should say that liquidity desires are modified by their interdependence with other variables such as personal wants, profit expectations from production, and expected changes in the price level and in the level of money incomes. Other things do not remain equal.

There are certain secular influences which seem to be working toward an intensification of the desire for liquidity in assets. Modes of life, forms of business organization, and the very existence of liquid titles themselves may be cited in illustration.[1] But the phase of our problem of chief interest is the variation in the desire for liquidity that takes place as the reciprocal of changes in cyclical phenomena, such as variable profit expectations and the like.

THE DESIRE FOR THE LIQUIDITY OF ASSETS AND THE DESIRE FOR ASSETS

It is incorrect to say that one's efforts to enhance one's claims to economic wealth always diminish with an increase in liquidity desires, or vice versa. An attempt to preserve or enhance claims to real wealth and an attempt to preserve or attain greater liquidity in one's assets may result in the same thing, namely money hoarding, or they may result in antithetical behavior.

[1] Conceive of the desire for liquidity if we should become a nation living in automobile trailers.

Suppose that some members of the community are "bearish." They have a conviction that a general sagging in prices is going to take place. Other members of the community are without conviction regarding the future. Their uncertainty will induce them to rearrange their assets in liquid forms, so that they may be in a flexible position to acquire the kinds of wealth-titles they want when a degree of conviction returns; they will probably hoard money. But those members of the community whose conviction is bearish will tend to hoard money also, for they expect the real wealth value of money to increase.

Suppose other members of the community are "bullish." Unlike the bears, they will attempt to preserve or enhance their claims by holding title, not to money, but to non-money assets. They anticipate an increase in the money value of real wealth. Their action is antithetical to that of those seeking liquidity.

When the community is inflation-minded and there is a "flight from money," the flight may be to a great variety of assets possessing widely different degrees of liquidity. In the summer and autumn of 1933 many farms that had not changed ownership for generations were acquired by "nervous money" which had previously frequented the haunts of Wall Street. More liquid refuges for those fleeing from money were such things as jewelry or trading contracts in standard commodities like grains and cotton. Even small and unfamiliar businesses were acquired for the ostensible purpose of preserving real values. But those participating in this activity were not doing so to preserve liquidity, as was said by some at the time. Rather, they were willing to surrender liquidity in order to protect themselves from what they believed to be an imminent depreciation of money in terms of real wealth.

But let us shift from the liquidity of assets to the degree of solvency of persons. If a person owes debts, his liquidity, or degree of solvency, is measured by both the quantitative and the qualitative aspects of assets and liabilities. If money prices are rising and he shifts from money to real wealth, the lessening of liquidity in the nature of his assets may be compensated by the greater personal liquidity resulting from the increased money amount of assets relative to liabilities. However, if he guesses wrong and prices fall, he will lose liquidity on both scores.

On the other hand, the person owing debts cannot increase his claim to real wealth by possessing money in a period of falling prices, unless his money exceeds the money amount of his debts. But, by shifting from non-money assets to money, he can improve his situation relative to what it otherwise would have been. The money amount of his assets will have been preserved and their liquidity status improved.

It is reasonable to suppose that everyone wants as much liquidity in his assets and personal affairs as is consistent with other purposes to which assets are put. Under conditions of falling prices, assets may be placed in money, and thus made to serve a profitable purpose from the individual's standpoint. At the same time, of course, the individual maintains his assets in the most liquid form. This is not possible in the case of rising prices, although here we find that personal liquidity may increase to compensate for the lessened liquidity of non-money assets held. But a shift from money to non-money assets is not the typical method used by persons to increase their liquidity status, or degree of solvency (although sometimes used by those of a gambling nature). It is too dangerous, and too easily subject to failure. In practice, the effort to increase liquidity is nearly always a matter of converting assets into money or wealth titles that approach money in their characteristics. If the stipulations of debts that are owed permit, all or part of the money received from the sale of non-money assets may be used to retire outstanding debt.

Short period changes in liquidity desires are chiefly important for their effect on money hoarding. But liquidity is not the only factor affecting hoarding. Hoarding may be motivated by the desire to acquire money as a means of storing wealth, without particular reference to liquidity. We have seen that such will be the case if one expects money prices to decline significantly. Moreover, an increase in liquidity desires is likely to result in money hoarding, though it need not necessarily do so. A person may improve his liquidity status by selling assets and acquiring money. Or he may sell one asset and buy another with greater liquidity qualities. Again, he may pay off debts with money he has acquired in one of several ways.

It has been a recent practice to identify an increase of liquidity preferences exclusively with an increased desire to hoard money. The identification seems to be partially true but not wholly true. It means this, but it also means more. Changes in liquidity desires result in a number of important kinds of economic behavior.

THE USE OF THE TERM LIQUIDITY PREFERENCE IN KEYNES'S "GENERAL THEORY"

No book of recent years has focused attention on the questions of liquidity so forcibly as J. M. Keynes's *General Theory of Employment, Interest and Money*. Unfortunately, Mr. Keynes is interested in the shifting desire for liquidity chiefly because of its alleged influence on the rate of interest. Little is said of other consequences of shifts in liquidity desires.

The discussion that has been stimulated by this provocative book is likewise concerned chiefly with the questions of liquidity that relate directly to the interest rate and its behavior. It is the thesis of this study that shifts in liquidity desires tend to affect business life in a cumulative manner, not so much through the interest rate, as Keynes would have it, but directly through decreases of purchasing power accompanying money hoarding, or its substantial equivalent, *and* through their impact on the expansion and contraction of the corpus of aggregate debt. It follows that much of the discussion that has accompanied the Keynesian interest-rate controversy is not pertinent to our purposes here.

A brief review of the recent use of the term liquidity preferences, however, may help us sharpen our own meaning. Several quotations from the *General Theory* will serve to illustrate:

> . . . the analysis of the motives to liquidity preference . . . is substantially the same as that which has sometimes been discussed under the heading of Demand for Money [page 194].
>
> The three divisions of liquidity preference . . . may be defined as depending on (1) the transactions motive, i. e. the cash for the current transaction of personal and business exchanges; (2) the precautionary motive, i. e. the desire for security as to the future cash equivalent of a certain proportion of total resources; and (3) the speculative motive, i. e. the object of securing profit from knowing better than the market what the future will bring forth [page 170].
>
> The concept of Hoarding may be regarded as a first approximation of the concept of *Liquidity Preference.* Indeed if we were to substitute "propensity to hoard" for "hoarding," it would come to substantially the same thing [page 174].

These quotations do not depend upon interest rate relationships for their consistency. They merely relate the concept of liquidity preference to the demand for money—or more accurately, to the propensity to hoard money. According to Keynes, actual hoarding cannot take place because all the money is now owned by someone, and the public has no means of increasing its supply without the consent of the bankers. Liquidity preference in these passages is not related to shifts in demand along the scale of assets of greater or less degree of liquidity. It is a desire to hold title to more or less *money,* a demand for idle money balances. Whether the desire for these idle balances increases in absolute terms or *relative* to the size of total assets owned is not clear.

While this appears to be the most conspicuous use of the term liquidity preference by Keynes in his descriptive passages, other authors have found other meanings, either implied or explicitly stated.[2] For instance, the term has been taken to refer to the preference of an individual for a certain average degree of li-

[2] For the remainder of the present discussion of this topic, I have leaned heavily upon Millikan's "Liquidity Preference Theory of Interest," *American Economic Review,* XXVIII (June, 1938), 247 *et seq.*, in which the author holds that "more than five separate and inconsistent meanings have been found explicitly or implicitly in the works of the doctrine's chief advocate, Mr. Keynes."

quidity in the assets he holds. This is substantially the sense in which we are using the term here, when its application is confined to assets as contrasted with persons. The acceptance of this meaning makes it possible for an individual to satisfy his desire for greater liquidity in his assets without hoarding money or, for that matter, indulging a desire to hoard money.

Formal definitions of liquidity preference given by Keynes are directly related to its alleged effect on the interest rate. These need not detain us here. Let it suffice to say that liquidity preference is in some instances described as the instantaneous total (or partial) demand for money as a function of the interest rate. This seems to assume that income is independent of the interest rate in short periods. Again, liquidity preference is the total (or partial) demand for money at different equilibrium levels of income, which correspond to various interest rates. As a general rule, the demand for business and precautionary balances seems to be related to the level of income and the demand for speculative balances to the interest rate. We shall have more to say of liquidity preferences and their influence on the interest rate. At the moment we are interested in clarifying the meaning of the term liquidity preferences, and this can be done best without relating it to its alleged influence upon the interest rate.

LIQUIDITY PREFERENCE REDEFINED

Among other things, attitudes toward economic wealth are influenced by personal wants, value judgments, and attitudes regarding solvency or liquidity. These various influences, of course, in turn are acted upon by other influences. For instance, personal wants are based upon habit, income levels, esthetic appeals, attitudes toward the future, and so forth. Value judgments of non-personal assets must subsume an estimate of physical productivity, as well as a guess of the trend of future money prices and shifts in human wants. Attitudes regarding solvency and liquidity are conditioned by certainty or uncertainty and the nature of expectations regarding the future, which are, of course, related to personal wants and value judgments. Here is another case of action and reaction being thoroughly intermingled.

An appraisal of the significance of the desire for liquidity, or degree of solvency, in this complex of forces is not easy. The answer will depend largely on the definitions used. We could accept the first of the above Keynesian concepts and identify a change in the desire for liquidity with a desire for greater or smaller cash balances. In this event, everything that retards the exchange of money for other wealth-titles becomes an increase in liquidity preferences.

Or we could accept the second of the above Keynesian concepts and say that a change in the desire for liquidity refers to a desire for a different average degree of liquidity in the assets held by an individual. A man with a house might sell it, buy American Telephone bonds, and rent an apartment with the income from the bonds. In this event there has been, in the case of this individual, an acceleration rather than a retardation of the exchange of money for other wealth-titles. This is not a necessary conclusion from the standpoint of society, for reasons which we will find later. But there has been a "bidding up" of the prices for more liquid assets and an "offering down" of less liquid assets.

Again, we could enlarge the concept of liquidity, as the business community has done, to include the degree of solvency of persons. We have seen that a change in the desire for liquidity, in the sense of degree of solvency, may lead to a revision of the nature of assets on the one hand and an expansion or payment of debt on the other.

Each of these three meanings is current and has significance. Hence when we use the term *greater liquidity* preferences [3] in this study, we shall refer to desires that will result in one or all of three things: (1) a retardation in the use of the available supply of money, (2) a bidding up of prices of more liquid

[3] Liquidity desires, or a shift in liquidity desires, seem to be less cumbersome terms that mean the same thing.

assets relative to less liquid assets, and (3) a decrease in the amount of outstanding debt. We hope to show in the course of the study that these three phenomena, when judged from the standpoint of society, logically take place together and are thoroughly consistent with one another in that they result from (1) a desire for more liquidity in one's assets and (2) a desire for a greater degree of solvency in one's affairs.

SUMMARY

Many considerations enter into the determination of how individuals will arrange their assets and their liabilities. The liquidity of their assets and their persons is but one. Individuals will always want as much liquidity in their affairs as is consistent with their other purposes and with their expectations. An increase or a decrease in liquidity desires thus may result from changes in a wide range of factors, among which are personal wants, profit expectations, anticipations of price-level movements, and changes in money incomes. In addition, secular changes in liquidity desires result from changes in the mode of living.

The desire to hold more or less money is one result, but only one, of an increase or a decrease in liquidity desires. In his formal definitions of liquidity preference, Mr. Keynes seems to make the desire for more or less money the exclusive result. Since the number of money units is held to be unresponsive to these desires, there will be a corresponding movement of the interest rate. Thus the interest rate becomes a function of changes in liquidity preferences. These are propositions which we shall return to examine.

A substantive definition, in contrast to the Keynesian formal definitions, relates liquidity desires to a change in the average degree of liquidity in the assets held by an individual. Although this broadens the concept, it is not inconsistent with the idea that shifts in liquidity desires are accompanied by changes in the desire to hold money. Money is the most liquid of all assets.

But a more adequate description of attitudes toward liquidity must broaden the concept still further.

A shift in liquidity desires will be reflected in any one or all of the following: (1) a desire to hold more or less money, (2) a desire for more or less liquidity in the nature of one's assets other than money, and (3) a change in the nature of one's obligations and in their amount, relative to one's assets. The first of these consequences is reflected in more or less hoarding, the second in relative price changes of more liquid and less liquid assets, and the third in an expansion or contraction in the community's debt.

III

THE INSTITUTIONAL ORGANIZATION OF WEALTH OWNERSHIP

A WANT can exercise an influence upon economic life only if the institutional organization of society provides a means of making the want effective. True, in the course of time the want will modify the institutions. Once changed to conform to the want, the institutions remain ready to make effective the expression of those wants. Such a want is the desire for liquidity. Along with other influences, it has encouraged the development of the corporate form of business enterprise, the growth of highly organized markets, and, to a lesser extent, the practice of financing with fixed income and fixed maturity securities. These are social institutions that have been carried to a high point of development. A brief survey of the extant institutional organization of economic wealth and of the titles to that wealth will help to make clear the *milieu* within which the problems of liquidity have become of greater importance.

CORPOREAL, INTANGIBLE, AND TOKEN WEALTH

Economic goods, which constitute the whole of economic wealth, we will define as *anything,* corporeal or intangible, which has been appropriated and which contributes, directly or indirectly, to the satisfaction of individual wants. When it ceases to be able to satisfy individual wants—to render a utility, in the nomenclature of the nineteenth century—we will say that the economic good is *extinguished.* Among the causes for such extinguishment are use, obsolescence relative to substitutional goods, and the physical or psychological properties inherent in the nature of the good itself. That part of wealth which exists in an amount beyond the point of satiety of its possessor, and of those capable of obtaining its possession, will also be defined as economically extinguished, in the sense in which we are using the term.

The whole of wealth consists of *corporeal* or material forms on the one hand and *intangible* subjects on the other. Title to this corporeal and intangible wealth may be held by individuals personally or collectively. Moreover, title may be held directly or indirectly. In the latter event the title passes from an individual, or group of individuals, through a legal instrument or instruments, and attaches to the corporeal or intangible wealth.

Substantive or corporeal wealth is a self-evident term. It consists of all material things, the use of which is desired by mankind. Unless scarce, however, no attempt is made to appropriate it to ownership. Hence when we speak of the ownership of corporeal wealth, we shall refer only to that wealth which is scarce and thus of interest to the economist.

Intangible wealth is less easily defined. It has no physical substance. Abilities of all descriptions, economic loyalties, and other such objects capable of being reduced to ownership make up the corpus of intangible wealth, as the latter term is used in this study.[1]

All wealth so defined is owned. If wealth is so abundant as to permit its appropriation without cost or effort, the ownership is implicitly held by the state for its constituents. If such wealth should begin to assume the characteristics of scarcity, because of natural or human causes, the state's ownership would become explicit, and apportioning measures would follow.

Scarce wealth is explicitly owned wealth. It may be owned by the state, by an association of individuals within the state, or by individuals acting alone. The state, as well as individuals, may own wealth directly, without an intervening legal instrument. It is not unusual for the state to own large bundles of corporeal wealth in this direct fashion, since the state holds im-

[1] A brief discussion of intangible wealth and its significance to economic life is contained in the Appendix.

plicit possession of all property that has not been specifically deeded. Direct ownership of corporeal wealth by individuals and associations of individuals is limited, for the most part, to personal effects: furnishings, clothes, trinkets, the current supply of food, and so forth. In contrast, the greater part of intangible wealth is owned directly by individuals.

But in the case of corporeal or material wealth, titles to the most significant amounts of wealth are indirectly transmitted from the personal owner through legal instruments to the object. We shall call these instruments *tokens*. Their use has permitted an organization of wealth-titles which has in part divorced the liquidity characteristics of ownership from the liquidity characteristics of the associated real wealth. The divorce has been far from complete. It is, nevertheless, a highly significant derivative of the institutional development of society.

Thus title to wealth may be direct to the wealth, or it may be to a token which serves as legal evidence of the title to the real wealth. Moreover, the title may be to a claim, or debt, which is the right to ask delivery of real wealth. The title to a claim also may be direct or indirect, through legal instruments or tokens. The holder of direct titles to wealth or claims seldom shares his title with another. Holders of indirect titles may or may not share such titles.

Our description to this point has dealt with direct and indirect titles to specific wealth or claims to specific wealth. As contrasted with titles to specific wealth, there is no such thing as a title to general wealth, unless we can conceive of an all-powerful individual. But there is such a thing in contemporary society as a general claim to wealth, title to which is held indirectly through money. More will be said of this latter proposition. The brief table on page 37 will help to clarify these several terms.

We may follow through an imaginary, but not unusual, business procedure to illustrate the use of tokens. An individual, let us say, owns 100 acres of land adjacent to a city and suitable for development into a residential community. His ownership is evidenced by a legal instrument, in this case a deed. This deed-

I

Titles to Wealth

A. Direct, without legal evidence
B. Indirect, through tokens
  (a) Specific
    (1) Undivided (deeds, and similar instruments)
    (2) Participated (shares, and the like)

II

Titles to Claims or Debts *

A. Direct, without legal evidence
B. Indirect, through tokens
  (a) Specific
    (1) Undivided (personal notes, and similar instruments)
    (2) Participated (bonds, and the like)
  (b) General (money)

* The terms "title" and "claim" have much the same meaning in common usage. In this study, however, we reserve the word title to mean legal ownership, whereas by claim we mean the right to acquire legal ownership in time. Title will pertain to present ownership of wealth, claim to the right to ask for delivery of wealth in the future, but not necessarily of wealth yet to be produced.

token evidences his specific title to that particular parcel of land. The liquidity characteristics of the deed-token are substantially those of the associated real property as a unit.

The owner, wishing to dispose of the land, decides that he must build roads before he can interest prospective buyers in building sites. In order to get the cash for this purpose, he decides to invite others to join him in the enterprise. Accordingly, he incorporates the X Y Z Development Company with 1,000 shares of stock. He transfers his deed, evidencing title to the real estate, to the corporation, in exchange for 500 shares of the newly created stock. Now the incorporated company owns the real estate, due in part to possession of the deed-token and in part to another legal instrument, its charter, under which the state grants permission to the company to own land, among other rights.

The other 500 shares of stock are sold for $50,000 to 50 different individuals, 10 shares to each. Suppose the $50,000 is entirely spent in building roads. Whereas we started out with one deed-token and its associated real property, we now have 1,000 different share-tokens superimposed upon the deed-token, the charter-token, and the real property, including the roads.

In the first instance, a single individual held title through a deed-token to a single type of corporeal wealth, namely land. Now a group of 51 individuals share title to two types of joined corporeal wealth, namely, land and a system of roads. In addition, some intangible wealth has been added in the form of new abilities flowing from the corporate form. Patently, there has been a revision of the liquidity status of both ownership and the associated real wealth, flowing from changes in their respective characteristics. But the liquidity status of the two has not changed in equal degree.

The original owner of the land is now able to divest himself of part of his ownership, without direct reference to the land itself. Formerly, it would have been necessary to dispose of at least a part of the land. Now he can simply dispose of a part of his total share-tokens. The immediate ownership of the land does not change as a result. The corporation continues to own the land. The only effect is to introduce a new participant among the shareholders' group.

While ownership has thus been made more divisible, the land itself, now possessed of a road system, is divided into parcels and the separate parts are more accessible. In addition to the inherent qualities of the land as such, namely, space, fertility, and so forth, the real estate is now possessed of another quality, namely, enhanced accessibility, the counterpart of mobility. So far, this simple illustration has shown us how the inherent liquidity characteristics of ownership and of real property are revised through time. The organization of wealth-titles and the nature of the real wealth serving as the object of these titles are both of significant interest in judging the degree of liquidity available to a community. This is the conclusion when we look at the matter from the standpoint of the nature of real wealth and its ownership.

Among assets owned are debts. But for every debt owned, a debt is owed. Debts owned are assets. Debts owed are liabilities. We have seen that in addition to the liquidity characteristics of assets owned, the liquidity status of a legal person is governed by the money *amount* and the *liquidity characteristics* of assets owned, relative to the *maturity schedule* and money *amount* of debts owed.

Our real-estate proposition may be developed further to show something of the place of debt in the liquidity problem. Suppose that after completing the roads, sales of parcels of property are not taking place as rapidly as expected. It is decided to put in a water system. More money will be needed for this, but the present owners do not wish to admit new participants to specific ownership. Accordingly, they cause a mortgage to be written, covering the real estate and roads. They then issue $25,000 face amount of bonds in $1,000 pieces, which they secure by this mortgage. These 25 debt-tokens are sold to 25 different individuals.

There are now 51 stockholders plus 25 debt holders, or 76 different people who own title to assets, the partial embodiment of which was, in the first instance, the single piece of real estate owned by one man through a single deed-token. A segment of the "equity" ownership may be transferred by the exchange of any one of 1,025 different tokens, 1,000 shares of stock and 25 bonds, without specific reference to the associated real wealth.[2] Likewise, if the mortgage will permit, the real estate, roads, and water system may be transferred in whole or in part without the transfer of any one of these tokens. Before the debt was created the 51 stockholders of the X Y Z Development Company owned unencumbered land and roads valued at $100,000.[3] They now have an equity of $100,000 in land, roads, and a water system which is valued at $125,000. The 25 owners of the $1,000 bonds claim the rest of the equity. Obviously, the liquidity characteristics of the original land and of the ownership of the enterprise have changed with its development. The liquidity characteristics of

[2] It is here held that a part of the equity ownership may be transferred by the exchange of a bond. This, of course, is not the sense in which the term equity is usually used. The equity of the stockholders is reduced by the amount of debt they owe. This diminution of equity reverts to the benefit of creditors by the fact of debt *ownership*. It is in this sense that we are using the term equity here.

[3] Using par value of the stock as a measure.

economic wealth in general, and of its ownership, have in similar fashion changed with the development of our highly complex system of production and exchange, which has been built in large measure around the corporate form of organization. The X Y Z Development Company as a corporate person has likewise undergone change, so far as its liquidity status is concerned. In the first place, the nature of its assets has been altered. In the second place, the introduction of debt has resulted in a change in the relationships of its assets to its liabilities.

We are now able to draw three main deductions from our illustration. First, the inherent liquidity characteristics of objects of wealth differ. The liquidity characteristics of any particular wealth object change as it is successively related to other objects—for instance, the land alone and the land in association with the system of roads. Second, the liquidity characteristics of real wealth on the one hand, and of its ownership on the other, are not likely to be similar in the present-day organization of society. Third, debt plays an important part in the determination of the liquidity status of legal persons.

With the evolution of present-day industrial and commercial society, there has been a great increase in the use of share-tokens and debt-tokens as a means of holding titles to real wealth. Estimates have been made by Mr. Berle and Miss Pederson of the growth of liquid claims (including a corrected figure for stocks and bonds listed on the New York Stock Exchange) relative to estimates of national wealth. The figures appear to be uncorrected for price changes, but they serve to show an unmistakable trend toward the increasing importance of tokens.[4] At the same time, the forms and combinations of real wealth have themselves been materially altered.

MONEY

Specific wealth may be owned directly without an intervening legal instrument or it may be owned indirectly through such

[4] *Liquid Claims,* p. 73. It is estimated that "liquid claims" increased from 16 percent of national wealth in 1880 to 40 percent in 1930.

an instrument. We have called these instruments tokens. They have been found to have different liquidity characteristics than those of their associated wealth. Hence the liquidity characteristics of much of the ownership of wealth differ from those of the wealth itself.

Other legal instruments are evidences of debt, and represent a claim to wealth in the future. The claim may be specific with reference to a particular segment of real wealth. These specific claims overlap the specific titles. Together the specific titles and claims more than encompass the total of wealth-forms. But there is still another form of wealth ownership. Certain claims to future wealth exist, without reference to any particular wealth. They are general rather than specific in nature. Such claims are money claims. The community thus continuously acts as though it possesses more wealth than it does in fact. The value of the sum total of specific titles, plus specific claims, plus general claims, exceeds the aggregate value of all wealth. This paradoxical situation can be understood only in terms of an analysis of debt, and more particularly, of money as debt. It is a situation made possible by the belief of holders of debt that holders of wealth-titles will surrender them at the debt holder's duly authorized request. When applied to money as debt, it is a situation made possible by the belief of holders of money that holders of wealth-titles and specific claims will surrender them at the money holder's option. It is the basic phenomenon that gives value to fiat money.

Money is a special but highly important variant of debt. As the term is used here, money itself constitutes debt in two respects. First, it is the debt of the issuer. In most cases, its owner may at any time demand from its issuer redemption in other tokens (including other units of the same money-forms), or in real wealth, depending on the provisions of extant monetary law and practice. Second, the real wealth value of money is a measure of the real wealth debt which the community at large owes to all the holders of money. Put in another way, the real wealth value of the money stock is equivalent to the amount of real wealth which all the holders of money wish to do without, but which they wish to be owed by the community. The use of debt as money is the cardinal principle underlying existing banking and financial organizations. H. D. MacLeod regarded this use as having produced a change in the fortunes of the human race.

If it were asked what discovery has most deeply affected the fortunes of the human race it might probably be said with truth—*The Discovery that a Debt is a Salable Commodity.*

When Daniel Webster said that Credit has done more a thousand times to enrich nations than all the mines of all the world, he meant the discovery that a Debt is a Salable Commodity or Chattel: and that it may be used like Money: and produce all the effects of Money.[5]

Parts of this community debt, very much like other forms of debt, are constantly being redeemed in non-money assets, but new parts take their place. Thus the total amount of money outstanding may change, but it is never entirely retired. This is made possible only by the fact that there exists a desire to hold general demand claims against real wealth and against other tokens, exercisable in the present or in the future.[6] Without this desire to hold demand claims on the future, our money systems would be strikingly different, and would probably take on the nature of elaborate bookkeeping to effect more or less immediate clearance. Certainly no one could want a credit balance of claims on wealth beyond the point of satiety, unless he also desired a general or a particularized claim on the future. A desire for a general claim to wealth in the future manifests itself in a desire to hold money. A desire for a specific claim to wealth in the future manifests itself in a desire to hold non-money wealth-titles.

Money provides the means for satisfying the desire for any future claim, not a particularized future claim. To the extent that men anticipate the nature of future wants, other forms of wealth would serve quite as well. Likewise, if the community were certain of being able to exchange other forms of wealth at a

[5] MacLeod, *The Theory and Practice of Banking*, I, 200.

[6] Since the present is but an instant in time, we may reasonably conceive this desire to be a desire for demand claims on the future, even though the future may be the next instant.

later date for a fixed amount of money, those other forms would serve quite as well. But in actuality, future wants are indeterminate for the most part, and the value and the interchangeability of other forms of wealth and money vary.

We have previously seen that titles to all economic wealth are held by individuals or by legal members of the community. These titles may be direct, or indirect through tokens, but in all instances they are specific. In addition, claims to specific wealth are held by the owners of non-money debt. At the same time, general claims to substantially *all extant wealth* are held by the owners of money.[7] Since all titles to economic wealth are subject to direct and indirect specific titles, and much of it is subject to being claimed by the holder of non-money debt, there seems to be an arithmetical contradiction in saying that money constitutes a general claim, in addition to the specific titles and claims. How can all wealth be subject to both specific titles and claims *and* to general claims at the same time, when the specific titles and claims more than encompass the whole?

The answer appears to rest on a psychological phenomenon. The owners of claims to specific wealth are secure in their belief that those who hold title to the wealth will surrender it, or money, in accordance with the terms of the contract. Hence they are willing to go without specific titles to wealth in the present which they might otherwise hold. In the same manner, the owners of money, secure in their belief that those who hold specific titles and claims will surrender them for money at the money owner's option, are willing to go without specific titles and claims to wealth in the present, which they might otherwise hold. Without this willingness on the part of its holders, money could not serve as a store of value. The aggregate amount of this value has been appropriately termed the *virtual wealth* of the society:

> . . . in a community, of necessity, the aggregate money, irrespective of its amount, represents the aggregate value of the wealth which the

[7] It may be held that some forms of wealth are not obtainable at any price, but this is difficult to know with certainty, especially if the price offered is sufficiently high.

community prefers to be owed on these terms rather than to own. This negative quantity of wealth I term the *Virtual Wealth* of the community because the community is obliged, by its monetary system and the necessity of having one, to act as though it possessed this much more wealth than it actually does possess.[8]

This concept is more familiarly described as the purchasing power of money, but it should be noted that it refers to the purchasing power of the aggregate stock of money at a point in time, and not to the purchasing power of a single unit of money. A concept, similar in most respects but restricted in its connotation to the *consumer's* preference for doing without wealth, is used by Keynes in his *Tract on Monetary Reform,* and is designated k and k^1.[9]

Underlying the cruder forms of the quantity theory of money is the proposition that the total stock of money has a fixed real wealth value, regardless of the number of units into which it is divided—that is, the proposition that what Soddy has called the Virtual Wealth is a constant. But it is not logical to hold that the total stock of money has a fixed real wealth value, regardless of the number of units into which it is divided. Changes in the demand for money as a means of exchange are offset by changes in its supply when used. In this capacity money appears to be substantially neutral, as held by the classicists. Changes in the demand for money as a store of value, however, are not correspondingly offset. If, because of revised liquidity desires or because of revised expectations of relative values, the desire to hold money as a store of value increases relative to the desire to hold non-money wealth-titles, then the real wealth value of the total stock of money will be increased, regardless of the number of units into which the stock is divided. With the same number of money units outstanding, each unit will be worth more in terms of real wealth. If fewer units are outstanding, each unit will be worth still more in the same terms. Conversely, if money is in less demand as a store of value, the purchasing power of

[8] Soddy, *Wealth, Virtual Wealth and Debt,* pp. 137–38.
[9] Keynes, *A Tract on Monetary Reform,* pp. 84–85.

the total stock of money is reduced. Each unit of money is worth less in terms of wealth, even though the number of units is unchanged. If the supply is increased, each unit will be worth still less. These are propositions to which we shall return in later chapters.

SUMMARY

It is plausible to believe that over a period of many years changing ways of living have increased the basic desire for liquidity. This secular increase in liquidity desires has contributed its part to the shaping of the institutional organization of wealth ownership. In turn, this institutional organization of wealth and its ownership provides the means whereby shifts in liquidity desires are made effective. The more a want succeeds in shaping the means of its gratification, the more effective will become the expression of the want. So it has been with liquidity desires and the institutions of wealth and its ownership.

Wealth may be corporeal or intangible. All wealth is owned by natural persons, associations, or the state. Title may be undivided or participated. It may be direct or indirect. Legal instruments, or tokens, serve as evidence of indirect title. They also serve as evidence of a claim to wealth. Titles always relate to specific aggregates of wealth. Claims may do so, but they do not always do so. Unlike titles, which are always specific, claims may be general as well as specific. Money serves as a general claim to all wealth exercisable at the option of the holder. The amount of wealth which may be claimed by a unit of money will vary through time.

This organization of wealth has resulted in significant differences between the liquidity status of wealth-forms on the one hand and of their ownership on the other. The tokens evidencing ownership are more liquid as a rule than the wealth itself. Nor is the liquidity status of persons necessarily analogous to the liquidity status of the assets they own. Debt enters as a consideration in the liquidity status of persons. The prevalance of specific claims in the community may result in changing the liquidity status of persons, without comparable changes taking place in the liquidity status of wealth or its ownership.

Another significant derivative of this organization of wealth ownership is the phenomenon of acting as though we possess, as a social group, more wealth than we actually own. All wealth is owned through specific titles. Yet much of this wealth is subject to specific claims, and the owners of the specific claims look upon their ownership as wealth. But a still further duplication occurs. Money is a general claim to wealth which its holders expect to be able to exercise at their option. Without this expectation, fiat money could have no value and metal money would have value only to the extent of the usefulness of the metal for non-money purposes. Money is also thought of as wealth by its owners. It is the most liquid form of wealth.

Within this institutional complex of corporeal and intangible wealth, titles to wealth, and claims to wealth, the desire for more or less liquidity is able to exercise a substantial influence upon the production and distribution of the material wants of society. The latter problem is of course, directly or indirectly, the chief concern of all economic inquiry. The manner in which this influence is exercised will occupy us for the greater part of the remainder of our study.

IV

THE CONCEPT OF FINAL BUYING

OVER 150 years ago Adam Smith observed that while a certain propensity of mankind to exchange and barter gives rise to a division of labor, this specialization of activity is limited by the extent of the ability to exchange—in short, by the extent of the market.[1] Presumably the great philosopher-economist was thinking in terms of long-period development. The broadening of markets that has since taken place has resulted in part from better transportation, communication, and trading facilities. It has been accompanied by the specialization of activity of more and more people, as foreseen by Smith.

THE EXPANSION AND CONTRACTION OF MARKETS

But in addition to this secular expansion of markets, since Smith's time the industrial-commercial world has been confronted with increasingly violent and comparatively short-lived expansions and contractions of markets. A century and a half ago, markets were limited and the division of labor was correspondingly limited. Today, for causes other than those of a physical nature, markets may become relatively limited within a period of months. But the degree of specialization of activity of mankind is decidedly a long-period development. It cannot be reversed in a period of time characterizing a business slump. And specialized labor without a market is unemployed labor.

Smith further observed that:

[1] Adam Smith, *The Wealth of Nations,* Everyman's ed., New York, 1933, I, 12–15.

When the division of labour has been once thoroughly established, it is but a very small part of a man's wants which the produce of his own labour can supply. He supplies the far greater part of them by exchanging that surplus part of the produce of his own labour, which is over and above his own consumption, for such parts of the produce of other men's labour as he has occasion for.[2]

The greater the degree of specialization, the greater will be the necessity for such reciprocal exchanges. These exchanges are a function of the size of markets. In extant society they are consummated chiefly by the use of money. An uninterrupted exchange of money against the surplus fruits of continuing productive activity thus becomes the *sine qua non* of the well-being of a community whose economic life rests on the principle of specialized activity and which produces and exchanges chiefly for money.

The desire for more liquid or less liquid titles or more or less solvency is one, but only one, of the factors occupying an important place in modifying the amount of money exchanged for real wealth. Conversely, the varying amounts of money exchanged for real wealth influence the desire for more liquid or less liquid titles or more or less solvency. Cause and effect, as is the case with so many problems in the social sciences, are inextricably entangled. It is possible to discover certain important elements in the problem, however, by studying the place in general economic behavior occupied by changes in liquidity preferences.

THE DESIRE FOR WEALTH

The desire for wealth is the desire for economic well-being in the present *and* in the future. Economic well-being may take the form of large consumption in the present or future, or it may take the form of acquiring economic power. Adjustments between current and future uses of wealth are in part a result of personal decision and in part are decreed by the nature and forms of wealth itself. The forms in which wealth are obtainable

[2] *Ibid.*, I, 19–20.

are the result of the state of techniques and resources and of a previous process of social selection.[3]

If, in the course of economic evolution, communities express a demand for wealth in uses involving a longer life than at an earlier period, this demand will be supplied within the limitations of natural resources. The industrial process with its increasing mechanization has expressed such a demand. As production has become more mechanized, an increasing proportion of the aggregate of all wealth has been allocated to the producing of more wealth. It is a proposition that cannot be proved or disproved, but it seems reasonable to say that the average life of that segment of total wealth which is devoted to further production is longer than the average life of that part used for personal enjoyment.

It is equally interesting to note that the average life of wealth not devoted to additional production is increasing. Professor Frederick C. Mills has found that the production of so-called durable consumers' goods expanded rapidly during the period 1922–29. There may have been positive retrenchment in the production of less long-lived consumers' wealth. To quote Professor Mills:

> The growing proportion of such goods (durable consumers' goods) in consumers' budgets meant that unconsumed utilities were being held in increasing volume by consumers. A decreasing proportion of the total production of the economy was being currently consumed, and an increasingly large "inventory" was accumulating in consumers' hands.[4]

This is admittedly a short-period sample from which to draw a long-period conclusion. But, it appears to be representative of a tendency extending back into the economic development of all highly organized nations. A recent study of post-war production notes:

> . . . In the case of consumer services and non-durable and semi-durable consumers' goods the trend of increase is low, amounting

[3] Durbin expounds this idea convincingly in "The Social Significance of the Theory of Value," *Economic Journal,* Dec., 1935, pp. 700 *et seq.,* especially p. 710.

[4] Mills, *Economic Tendencies in the United States,* p. 276.

for the group to approximately 3.8 per cent a year, whereas for each of the durable goods categories except residential housing it is appreciably higher, amounting for the group to approximately 5.4 per cent. . . . There is no comparable data to indicate whether the same type of change was going on before the war, but there is a presumption that the post-war trend is the continuation of a pre-war trend since agriculture which declined so greatly in relative importance was concerned primarily with the production of non-durable and semi-durable goods.

Contributing to the greater emphasis on durable goods is the continuing development of improved technology. Partly this takes the form of new commodities, . . . partly . . . the form of techniques or machines.[5]

This growth in the importance of durable consumers' goods, together with the greater proportionate amount of wealth used in production, contributes to a longer average life of all wealth.

Many, if not most, so-called consumers' goods preserve an element of future use through time concomitant with current use. Illustrations are provided in such familiar objects as a house, silverware, a motor car, furniture, and so forth. To the extent that an element of future use is preserved, the possession of a title to such consumers' wealth serves as a claim to future wealth. Thus among the factors entering the decision to acquire consumers' goods are (1) the desire to use the goods and (2) their prospective value through time.

Other types of titles relate to wealth that is entirely unassociated with current use by the possessor of the title. The owner of a share in the United States Steel Corporation cannot be deemed to use the corporation in the sense of consuming economic wealth. There must be an inducement other than the anticipation of use to cause the prospective owner of the share to exchange money for it. Such an inducement is provided by the expectation of preserving or increasing claims to future wealth. This is a matter of productivity and prospective changes in relative values.

The anticipation of use and the expectation of preserving or

[5] National Resources Committee, *The Structure of the American Economy,* Part I, 71, 73.

increasing claims to future wealth are the two principal motivating forces which induce people to exchange money for titles to real wealth. It is impossible to appraise the relative importance of these two motivations. It can be said that to the extent wealth-titles have acquired a longer life, the value-prospects motivation has increased *relative* to the motivation of personal use. This holds true, even for so-called consumers' goods. It follows that much of what is written regarding so-called producers' goods holds true for consumers' goods to an unsuspected degree. Moreover, it seems appropriate to place our emphasis on wealth as a store of value rather than on consumers' wants, because so much of consumers' goods, as well as producers' goods, are of a durable nature today. A third motivation to acquiring wealth may be a diminution of liquidity desires—this, in a sense, being a motivation of negative character. These motivations are inseparably intertwined, although one may predominate.

The acquisition of certain types of titles to wealth may accomplish both of the first two objects, in whole or in part. Even though use may be the principal purpose of acquisition, the claim to future wealth may be preserved in part through the continued usefulness of the object acquired. If the preservation or enhancement of a claim to future wealth be the principal purpose, the object to which title is acquired may perhaps be used in part without impairing this objective. But when money is exchanged for wealth which is to be entirely unassociated with personal use, the only motivations for its acquisition are (1) to preserve or enhance a claim to future wealth and (2) the negative motivation of a lessened desire for liquidity. These are questions that concern the value prospects and liquidity characteristics of various types of assets as stores of value. The two principal objectives that are desired from an asset as a store of value are that (1) it should preserve or enhance the original value and that (2) it should provide the means of easily converting the value into forms that may be desired in the future but which cannot be foreseen in the present. Several generalizations are possible regarding money and non-money wealth-titles when viewed as stores of value.

MONEY AS A STORE OF VALUE

Money as a conveyer of titles to future economic wealth has one outstanding advantage. Its possession provides the owner with a general, not a specific, claim to future wealth.[6] Insofar as future wants are not precisely determinable in the present, the possession of money offers the easiest means of satisfying those wants in the future. In other respects money may be a decidedly disadvantageous medium for conveying present titles to wealth to future claims. Title to money in the present constitutes a general claim to wealth in the future, but it is a claim to an uncertain future amount. This future amount is largely a matter of chance fluctuations in prices.

It has long been held that the personal decision as to whether to use wealth in the present or to retain a claim to future wealth is made on the basis of the prospective reward for abstinence. Other things being equal, a reward is less likely if a claim to future wealth is retained in the form of money than if it is retained in the form of productive real wealth. J. M. Keynes goes so far as to describe the holding of money as always being barren: ". . . it is a recognized characteristic of money as a store of wealth that it is barren; whereas practically every other form of storing wealth yields some interest or profit." [7]

Money is barren under certain circumstances, but it is not always so, and the exceptions are important. True, inactive money is always barren to the *community*. It will be just as barren to an *individual* if the prices of objects that are wanted in the future are constant. Money has no capacity to reproduce itself when hoarded. Nor can it, so long as it is unused, add to its owner's claims to future wealth in any possible manner as long as prices remain constant. If prices rise, however, not only will the owner of the hoarded money fail to increase his future claim, but his ability to command real wealth in the future will

[6] This future may be infinitely short or indefinitely long, depending on the period of time through which the money is retained.

[7] Keynes, "The General Theory of Employment," *Quarterly Journal of Economics*, LI (Feb., 1937), 215.

be diminished. But if prices sag, the owner of hoarded money will obtain an increased ability to claim wealth. This is the important exception to the Keynesian proposition.

Thus we find that there are two principal inducements to retain claims to future wealth in money: (1) uncertainty as to what kind of wealth one may want in the future and (2) the expectation of declining prices. The first of these inducements involves the comparative liquidity qualities of the particular wealth-forms that may be selected as alternatives to hoarding money. The second is concerned with relative values and may involve the liquidity status of persons as contrasted with assets.

WEALTH-FORMS OTHER THAN MONEY AS A STORE OF VALUE

Titles to wealth other than money also provide a store of value, but have different characteristics. The non-money title is specific with reference to a particular wealth-form or bundle of forms. In the absence of barter, it must be converted through money if it is subsequently found that other types of specific titles are desired. The ease or difficulty of converting specific wealth-titles to money—that is, of converting the specific title to a general claim—is determined by the degree of liquidity possessed by the specific title. This can never be so great as the degree of liquidity possessed by money. The lesser liquidity of non-money titles makes them compare disadvantageously with money, in this one respect, as a means of conveying present titles to future claims.

Although less liquid, the non-money title may have a decided advantage over money as a store of value. By converting one's titles to specific wealth that is used for the purpose of producing still greater wealth, it is possible to increase one's ownership of claims in the future. This is true when prices are constant. If prices are rising, the increase in the ownership of future claims will be still larger. If prices are falling, the increase will not be so large or there may even be a decrease. But in the long run the owner of non-money titles, if his titles are producing additional new wealth, is more likely to receive a reward than the holder of money. The amount of such reward is measured by the amount of the new wealth produced, if prices are constant.

But the choice is not limited to money on the one hand or titles to wealth used personally or in production on the other. Still another option is available. If the owner of a non-money title does not place his wealth in the production of new wealth, his prospects for future increases in his claims are substantially the reciprocal of the prospects for holders of money titles. No addition to his claim on future wealth will accrue as the result of the ownership of newly established wealth. His gain or loss will be determined solely by the chance movements of prices, less the amount of extinguishment taking place during his ownership. The liquidity qualities of this type of non-money title, for instance a commodity contract, are sometimes superior to those of titles to wealth placed in production.

Economic treatises generally divide real wealth into capital or producers' goods and consumers' goods. Various other classifications have been attempted on the basis of purpose, durability, or kind.[8] No attempt will be made here to extend the discussion. Let it suffice to say that all economic wealth that has not been extinguished in the past, or is not being extinguished at the moment, serves as a store of value. The possession of a title to extant wealth will provide its holder with a claim to future wealth to the extent that the present wealth is not extinguished. The worth of the claim at any time in the future, relative to its present worth, will be determined by the nature of the wealth, its relation to other wealth-forms including money, and the use to which it is put.

A loaf of bread may be purchased for the principal purpose of consumption, but unless it is entirely consumed at the time of purchase, a part of the loaf will remain as a store of value until it is completely consumed.[9] A house may be purchased for

[8] An excellent survey of the confusion accompanying the development of the term capital is contained in Irving Fisher's *Nature of Capital and Income*, pp. 53–65.

[9] It might be argued that even though the whole loaf is eaten, a store of value will remain until its nutritious physiological effects have been completely exerted.

personal use, but it may also continue to serve as a store of value for many years.

It may now be readily seen that the degree of liquidity possessed by a title to wealth (whether money or non-money) is by no means the only factor entering into the decision resulting in its acquisition. To put the matter conversely, the degree of liquidity desired in specific assets is by no means the only determining factor entering the decision to acquire specific wealth-titles. Of greater importance in the decision may be the prospective character of the title as a store of value through time. Another factor of greater importance may be the desire to use personally the wealth to which the title is a lien. The demand for titles derived from their prospects as a store of value is considerably more elastic than the demand arising from desire for personal use. The demand for titles, so far as it is derived from changes in the desire for liquidity in assets, appears to be highly sensitive and in large part conditioned by the other factors.

THE USE OF THE TERM INVESTMENT IN ITS USUAL SENSE

There has been an increasing tendency in economic writing to stress the importance of that part of the total exchanges of money for real wealth relating to capital goods and subsumed under the term investment.

For those beyond a subsistence income, there is usually a point at which individuals wish to retain titles to current wealth and claims to future wealth which are unassociated with their own consumption. In this event, the individual is free to choose without encumbrance the form of wealth in which he wishes to retain his title. He may hold money or he may acquire non-money titles. Investment is implicitly or explicitly disassociated from personal use. Most analyses of business-cycle behavior use this concept of investment as a key-point or determining influence. But there is no empirical reason or a priori basis for holding that investment, so defined, constitutes so highly important a factor in economic life. That part of the aggregate of money income flowing through this channel is relatively small, much smaller than that flowing into durable consumers' goods. Whether it is more variable in *absolute* amount than that flowing into durable consumers' goods, and thus more likely to disturb business equilibrium, is a matter which our present data are inadequate to show. It may be possibly contended, however, that in short periods the variability of investment in absolute amounts exceeds the variability of aggregate purchases of readily perishable goods by consumers. The data are highly uncertain, but the following figures may serve to give a rough idea of the relative importance of the size of the quantities.

NEW CAPITAL ISSUES, THE FLOW OF DURABLE GOODS, AND NATIONAL INCOME *

(The figures are in millions and are uncorrected for price changes)

Year	*(1) Flow of Producers' Durable Commodities*	*(2) Flow of Consumers' Durable Commodities*	*(3) Durable Commodities and Construction*	*(4) Corporate New Capital Issues Excluding Investment Trusts, Holding Companies, and the Like*	*(5) National Income Produced*	*(6) National Income Paid Out*
1932	2,019	3,806	9,235	324	40,089	49,296
1933	2,051	3,382	8,644	159	42,504	45,565
1934	3,138	4,686	11,562	159	50,611	52,057
1935	3,957	5,918	14,256	402	55,794	55,814
1936	5,429	7,342	19,470	1,202	65,226	64,207
1937	6,828	7,664	21,892	1,225	71,853	70,694
1938	5,164	5,410	17,727	867	63,993	65,021

* Columns (1), (2), and (3) are taken from Simon Kuznets *Commodity Flow and Capital Formation in the Recent Recovery and Decline, 1932–1938,* National Bureau of Economic Research, Bulletin 74, July, 1939, Table I. Column (3) includes columns (1) and (2), plus residential, business, and public construction.

Column (4) reproduces data compiled by the *Commercial and Financial Chronicle,* as reported in the *Survey of Current Business,* May, 1938, pp. 19–20; and May, 1939, p. 26.

Columns (5) and (6) are from the *Statistical Abstract of the United States* (Washington, 1939), p. 311.

The danger of attaching exclusive importance in business-cycle analysis to that part of the flow of national income which is wholly unassociated with personal use is that to do so may lead to fallacious analysis. The development of the Keynesian multiplier serves to illustrate the point. For Mr. Keynes, the aggregate national income consists of consumption plus investment. Investment includes only the acquisition of non-use articles, as it must, if by current investment is meant "the current addition to the value of the capital equipment which has resulted from the productive activity of the period."[10] Consumption must therefore be all the rest of the national income, which has not added value to the capital equipment. Durable consumers' goods seem to be included. Savings and investment are made to be equal. Thus no element of savings can possibly appear in the flow of money to durable consumers' goods. Now let us see how this nomenclature is used to make investment, operating through the multiplier, the main trigger-mechanism of economic change.

Mr. Keynes introduces his discussion of the motivation to exchange money for non-use wealth in seemingly innocuous but actually ambiguous terms.

> The psychological time-preferences of an individual require two sets of decisions . . . how much of his current income will he consume and how much will he reserve in *some* form of command over future consumption.
>
> But this decision having been made, there is a further decision which awaits him, namely, in *what form* he will hold the command over future consumption. . . . Does he want to hold it in the form of immediate, liquid command (i. e., in money or its equivalent)? Or is he prepared to part with immediate command for a specified or indefinite period, leaving it to future market conditions to determine on what terms he can, if necessary, convert deferred command over specific goods into immediate command over goods in general?[11]

Earlier in the *General Theory* the term consumption is defined in algebraic terms and the whole problem of durable consumers' goods is implicitly dismissed.[12] The result is that distinctions of value are lost. When *consumption is defined as one source of extinguishment, or loss of command over economic*

[10] Keynes, *The General Theory of Employment, Interest and Money*, p. 62.
[11] *Ibid.*, p. 166. [12] *Ibid.*, pp. 61–62.

wealth, the rate of consumption is determined by the extant forms of available wealth, as well as by personal decisions. When an individual wishes to defer consumption in this sense, he is confronted not with two but with three options: he may elect to hold money, he may elect to hold non-use wealth, or he may elect to hold durable consumers' goods. His prospects of retaining a claim to future wealth are capable of calculation with equal precision (or equal lack of precision) in each instance. The point to note is that a wide diversity of wealth-forms is available as a means of storing value. They range over many degrees with respect to productivity, usefulness, liquidity, and ability to retain value. If liquidity happens to be an important consideration, the decision may be between money and non-money wealth-titles. It may just as readily be among two or more non-money wealth-titles which differ in the degrees of liquidity which they possess.

That ambiguous terms are not innocuous may be shown by further examination of the Keynesian use of the term investment, and its complement, consumption. For this we return to the implications of the proposition that a relatively small part of the aggregate income flows through what is generally defined as investment. We shall first examine several additional passages from the *General Theory.*

Income = value of output = consumption + investment [page 63]. So far as I know, everyone agrees in meaning by *Saving* the excess of income over what is spent on consumption [page 74]. The fundamental psychological law, upon which we are entitled to depend with great confidence both *a priori* from our knowledge of human nature and from the detailed facts of experience, is that men are disposed, as a rule and on the average, to increase their consumption as their income increases, but not by as much as the increase in their income. That is to say, if Cw is the amount of consumption and Yw is income (both measured in wage-units) $\triangle Cw$ has the same sign as $\triangle Yw$ but is smaller in amount, i. e., $\frac{dCw}{dYw}$ is positive and less than unity [page 96].

From these propositions Keynes develops his so-called investment multiplier *k* (the units of measurement need not concern us at this point), which says that, depending upon the marginal propensity to consume, $\frac{dC}{dY}$, a given amount of investment I, will result in *k* times as much income Y (pages 114–116) when $1 - \frac{1}{k}$ equals the marginal propensity to consume.

$$\frac{dC}{dY} = 1 - \frac{1}{k}, \qquad \Delta Y = \Delta C + \Delta I,$$

$$k = \frac{1}{1 - \frac{dC}{dY}}, \qquad \Delta Y = \frac{1}{1 - \frac{dC}{dY}} \cdot \Delta I,$$

$$\therefore \Delta Y = k \cdot \Delta I$$

From these equations it may be seen that the closer $\frac{dC}{dY}$ approaches to unity, that is, the smaller the amount of new income saved, the more effective will be the multiplier; "if the marginal propensity to consume is not far short of unity, small fluctuations in investment will lead to wide fluctuations in employment" (page 118). But as the marginal propensity to consume approaches unity, new savings, as defined by Keynes, approach zero. Conversely, if savings increase, the marginal propensity to consume, $\frac{dC}{dY}$, becomes a smaller fraction and the multiplier becomes less effective. Now, if everything is "consumed" that is personally used, we get a very much smaller proportion of the national income devoted to "saving" than if we mean by consumption the loss of title to wealth. In other words, our estimate of the effectiveness of the multiplier hinges entirely on the definition of consumption which we accept.

The relative size of what we may call consumption has reciprocal effect on the relative size of investment, and in the Keynesian terms, correspondingly on the size of savings. If investment includes only the acquisition of non-use articles, then consumption (which together with investment equals total income) is a large quantity, including all durable consumers' goods purchased, as well as those extinguished in current consumption.

Only by definition are aggregate savings reduced by Keynes to a relatively small part of the national income. But it has been held that the smaller the amount of savings, in a given time period, the more effective is a unit of investment in multiplying income, while the greater the amount of savings the less effective will a unit of investment be. If income is divided, instead, into "current" consumption in the sense of extinguishment, on the one hand, and savings on the other, then savings are a very much larger element than is the case when income is divided into savings (which equal "production" investment) and consumption in its loose and larger connotation.[13]

It is no doubt true, as the doctrine of the marginal propensity to consume asserts, that there is a lag between changes in the national income and changes in the rate of actual extinguishment of wealth in current consumption. But it is not equally evident that a significant lag exists between changes in the national income and changes in the aggregate purchases of goods for current consumption *plus* durable consumers' goods. By excluding the purchase of durable consumers' goods from savings, that is, by putting them in ΔC, the aggregate of savings is made relatively small and the multiplier becomes a potent factor. But if the element in durable consumers' goods that retains a title to future wealth through time is *excluded* from ΔC, the marginal propensity to consume, or $\frac{dC}{dY}$, becomes a small fraction indeed, savings become a large faction of the national income, and the effectiveness of the multiplier itself approaches unity. The ambiguity of Keynes's use of the term consumption

13 Since $\Delta S = \Delta I$ and $\Delta C + \Delta I = \Delta Y$ by definition:

$$\frac{\Delta C}{\Delta Y} + \frac{\Delta S}{\Delta Y} = 1$$

As $\frac{\Delta C}{\Delta Y}$ approaches 0 the multiplier k approaches 1. As $\frac{\Delta C}{\Delta Y}$ approaches 1, the multiplier k approaches infinity. The size of the fraction $\frac{\Delta C}{\Delta Y}$ is entirely a matter of how we have defined savings, i. e., of the fraction $\frac{\Delta S}{\Delta Y}$. The larger $\frac{\Delta S}{\Delta Y}$, the smaller $\frac{\Delta C}{\Delta Y}$, and the less effective the multiplier.

has seemingly led him to attach more weight to changes in investment, as he defines it, than they deserve. "The marginal propensity to consume seems to lie . . . much nearer to unity than to zero" (page 118). It seems to be much more realistic to include durable consumers' goods, for the most part, in savings. This substantially reduces the significance of the multiplier.

In reviewing Mr. R. F. Harrod's *The Trade Cycle, An Essay*, in which that writer makes much use of the multiplier, Professor Hansen calls attention to the slippery nature of the terms consumption and investment.

Moreover, one needs to be careful in the use of the terms "consumption" and "investment." Unless one rigorously defines "consumption" to mean "current consumption" (that is, liquid or available output minus increases (or decreases) in stocks of liquid consumers' goods, as defined by Keynes in the Treatise—Volume I, pp. 127–28), one is likely to get into trouble. When one loosely speaks of "consumption" and "investment," into which of these categories does one place automobiles, electric appliances, furniture and the like? One gets distinctly the impression that Mr. Harrod has continually in mind producers' goods when he spoke of "investment." . . . If one included durable consumers' goods in "consumption," is there any evidence that consumption does not increase proportionally with income in periods of prosperity? Whatever the facts may be, I do not believe it is possible to give any precise theoretical formulation of the problem in hand without rigorously restricting the term "consumption" to "current consumption" as formerly defined by Keynes.[14]

Dr. Saulnier has provided an interesting critique of the Keynesian multiplier without direct reference to the definitional questions relating to saving and investment.[15] Citing Professor Pigou's suggestion of the importance of bank policy on the interest rate, he points out that the employment furnished by new investment,

. . . may serve to raise the interest rate because of the larger cash holdings which may be required as investment and employment increase in the face of a not too sympathetic bank policy, and because the method

[14] Hansen, "Harrod on the Trade Cycle," *Quarterly Journal of Economics*, LI (May, 1937), 521–22.

[15] Saulnier, *Contemporary Monetary Theory*, pp. 331–36.

of investment stimulation may cause a sharp increase in the liquidity preference schedule in the sense of a greater desire on the part of people to hold their wealth in the form of cash. Second, the marginal efficiency of capital may be reduced by virtue of a raising of capital equipment costs, and because of the development of less optimistic views concerning the prospects for yields.

Since the relationship of interest costs and prospective yields will determine the question of whether to invest or not invest, it follows that a new increment of investment *may* discourage further investment. Again, citing the work of Professor Haberler, who accuses Keynes of treating "relationships by definition as causal relationships," Dr. Saulnier concludes that the derivation of the formula for the multiplier precludes the determination of its value until "after the effect on income has been produced."

It may now appear to the reader that an analysis is too simple if based on the assumption that a new holder of money first decides whether to consume or to save, and if the latter, whether to hoard or to invest. The Marshallian principle of continuity runs through all of the possible courses of action. A dominant and highly significant phase of these possible courses of action that has not been adequately examined in theoretical economics is the purchase of durable consumers' goods. Whether such purchases are to be included in savings or investment is, for instance, a question of high theoretical importance in judging the significance of the multiplier.

Some forms of wealth are capable in part of meeting current consumption requirements, in part of serving as a socially unproductive store of value, and in part of serving as so-called capital goods, all at the same time. To illustrate, an individual may live in the house which he uses as his place of business. He may use his personal automobile for both pleasure and business purposes. In both cases he is consuming an element of his wealth, in the sense of deriving satisfactions from certain uses which are not productive of new wealth. An element of his house and automobile may be classed as capital goods, for they are used for productive purposes. As time and the use of the house and automobile diminish their future usefulness, a fraction of value is disappearing. But until completely extinguished, in the sense that their usefulness is ended, the house and the automobile serve as stores of value, though stores of diminishing value.

Consumption uses of wealth result in no replacement of value. If the owner of the house and the automobile is successful in his business, claims to new wealth will be acquired which more than compensate for that lost by using his property for business purposes. Wealth successfully placed in the productive system will result in the establishment of new wealth capable of providing still greater satisfactions. The value stored in wealth that is placed in production does not disappear as the old wealth is dissipated and the new takes its place, or as the form of the wealth is changed. Rather, it is transmitted to the new wealth produced. If the activity is successful, the value will be enhanced at the same time it is thus transmitted. In this sense, the placement and extinguishment of specific wealth in the production of more wealth is analogous to the use of wealth as a means of retaining or enhancing value, that is, as a store of value.

We found previously that there are two principal inducements to retain claims to future wealth in money: uncertainty as to what kind of wealth one may want in the future, and the expectation of falling prices. We now find that the inducements to retain claims to non-money titles are in part antithetical to these. First, there is the negative inducement of a lessened desire for liquidity, the antithesis of uncertainty. Second, there is the inducement of an expectation of rising prices, the antithesis of an expectation of falling prices. Third, there is an inducement to retain claims to future wealth in non-money titles which has no antithesis above. This inducement is the productivity of non-money titles. But still another inducement may be mentioned. When a claim on future wealth is retained in money, the holder of the claim is unable to derive any utility from its possession—except the utility of having liquidity. We have seen that many forms of non-money wealth may serve a dual or even a triple purpose, including personal use, provision of a store of value, and the production of new wealth. Hence our list of inducements to retain claims to future wealth in non-money titles would be incomplete if we did not include the anticipation of using wealth at the same time that it serves as the embodiment of a claim. This latter category encompasses the growing body of wealth-forms generally known as durable consumers' goods.

FINAL BUYING

Whether the stress of one's analysis is upon investment or not, all will agree upon the importance of an uninterrupted exchange of money against new wealth production in a society organized upon the principles of specialized activity. The point in question is whether the analysis of money exchanges is best cast in terms of consumption and investment, as mutually exclusive categories. The exchange of money that is of chief importance is not against any particular types of wealth. Rather it is against *all new wealth output.* This is the crux of the well-being of a community that produces and exchanges chiefly for money. All fluctuations in the exchange of money for wealth are important, but, as the argument of subsequent chapters may show, those against final new wealth output are of dominant importance.

An uninterrupted exchange of money against so-called capital goods alone will not suffice to support a given level of activity if the exchanges of money against so-called consumers' goods and labor (including the service trades, arts, and professions) are not equally continuous. The focus of our interest is not directed toward any one segment of the exchanges of money against final new output. Rather, it is upon the total of all money exchanges against final new wealth output of all descriptions. This is a concept not unlike that described as "final buying" by Myra Curtis and Hugh Townshend.[16] Mr. D. H. Robertson phrases the concept concisely when he speaks of a period

16 Curtis and Townshend, *Modern Money,* p. 66. The authors acknowledge their debt to Mr. A. H. Abbati for the term, which he developed in *The Final Buyer* (London, 1928).

in which "the stock of money changes once in final exchange for the constituents of the community's real income or output." [17] Final output may be described as new wealth at the stage when it has completed the flow through the several production processes (a difficult stage to determine, especially in the case of intangible wealth), or as successive *increments* of wealth added at each stage of production. In the latter case, the sum of the amounts of money exchanged once and only once for successive new *increments* of wealth is analogous, but because of time differences, is not necessarily equal to the amount exchanged once after the wealth has completed the total production process. In either event it is appropriate to describe the phenomenon as an exchange of money against final output. This exchange we shall call final buying.

If the number of money units is constant, the total amount of money *available* to exchange against new output of all kinds, corporeal and intangible, is equal to the amounts that have been paid out in the production-distribution process, plus or minus certain highly important correction factors. These correction factors will be studied in greater detail in a subsequent chapter. Briefly, they relate to (1) the changing size of what we shall term interstitial payments in the production-distribution process, (2) the varying amount of money used in exchanging previously existing property titles—that is, in the secondary circulation, (3) the use of money in making debt payments, and (4) the hoarding of money. Our interstitial payments correspond to what Curtis and Townshend call "pre-final" buying, and our secondary circulation roughly to their "post-final" buying. The aggregate of final buying and interstitial payments we will call primary circulation.

The focus of our problem is the amount of money exchanged against final new wealth output of *all* descriptions. This is the process that permits the maintenance or betterment of the economic well-being of the community. Without a constant amount of money exchanged at this point, no hope can be entertained

[17] "Saving and Hoarding," *Economic Journal,* XLIII (Sept., 1933), 399.

for an uninterrupted flow of money within the body of interstitial payments arising out of earlier stages of production. Neither will there be stable flows of money in the secondary circulation, which is not immediately associated with the production-distribution process.

This is not to say that if the amount of money exchanged for final new output of all descriptions is unchanged, autonomous changes in the quantity of money payments in other parts of the economy will not disturb the payments at the point of final buying. All the evidence indicates that they will. But without a stable rate of exchange of money for final new output, the hope of maintaining reasonably constant money exchanges in other parts of the economy diminishes to the vanishing point.

SUMMARY

The extent of markets limits the degree to which communities may specialize their activities. But the degree to which specialization has occurred is a matter of evolutionary change, whereas the extent of markets is subject to cyclical influences, in addition to those of a secular nature. The surplus products of specialized activity are exchanged for money. This exchange of money for the surplus products of new wealth output is the crux of material well-being in modern societies. But it is the variation of this exchange of money for new output that *is* the cyclical expansion and contraction in the extent of markets.

The desire for more or less liquidity is one factor, but only one, which modifies the amount of money exchanged for new wealth output. In turn, the amount of money exchanged for new wealth modifies liquidity desires. Individuals want wealth to use in the present or in the future, or to obtain economic power. The adjustment between present and future use, or possession, is in part a matter of personal decision and in part is determined by the forms of the wealth obtainable.

The average life of wealth appears to have been lengthened. This is true for two reasons. First, wealth used in producing more wealth typically has a longer life than that used personally by individuals. An increasing part of the aggregate of all wealth has been allocated to producing more wealth, as production has become more capitalistic. Second, that part of the total of wealth used by individuals for their own enjoyment has become more durable in nature. To the extent that an element of future use is preserved, wealth serves as a claim to future wealth, that is, as a store of value. This is true of so-called consumers' goods as well as producers' goods.

The use of wealth for personal enjoyment and as a store of value are the two chief reasons for exchanging money for it. Many wealth-forms provide the means of satisfying both of these wants in part. As wealth-forms acquire longer life, the demand for wealth as a store of value takes on additional importance. But money is also a store of value, albeit one with characteristics that differ from those of non-money titles. It is a general claim to an unspecified amount of future wealth. Non-money titles as stores of value are specific as to nature and must be converted through money to other forms of wealth that may be wanted in the future. Although less liquid, non-money wealth may be personally used or used to produce new wealth at the same time that it serves as a store of value. All forms of wealth, whether capital goods or consumers' goods, serve as a store of value until they are extinguished.

The chief components of the demand for assets are (1) a desire to convey present claims into the future and (2) a desire for personal satisfaction. The two are not mutually self-exclusive. The desire for more or less liquidity modifies both of these components of the demand for assets, even though it modifies the first of them the more.

Investment is a term typically applied to the exchange of money for assets that will not be used personally, rather than for assets that will convey present claims into the future. The variability of investment is the trigger mechanism in current business-cycle analysis. Perhaps investment in this sense is more variable in aggregate amounts than exchanges of money for perishable goods to be personally used. But it is doubtful whether investment in this sense is more variable than the aggregate of exchanges of money for assets which serve as a store of value *and* a source of personal use at the same time.

Investment and consumption are not mutually self-exclusive terms. To illustrate the inadequacy of a typical analysis developed from this assumption, we have tried to demonstrate that the effectiveness of the Keynesian multiplier depends wholly upon definitional questions. In other words, it depends upon the assumption of mutual self-exclusiveness of investment and consumption and the definitional allocation of all expenditures to one or the other. This is a procedure that cannot be supported by the facts of economic life.

The exchange of money for all new wealth output, rather than for any particular segment of it, is the focus of our interest. This exchange has been called final buying. Interstitial circulation is the term applied to exchanges other than final buying, made in the production-distribution process. The combination of final buying and interstitial circulation is called the primary circulation. Other exchanges, such as trading in previously existing assets of various kinds, take place without being proximately related to the production-distribution process. This we call the secondary circulation.

In a society of individuals organized to produce specialized forms of wealth, economic well-being depends upon the exchange of a constant or increasing amount of money for final new output of all descriptions. The present disposition in economics to focus attention on that part of the money flow exchanged for so-called capital goods has tended to obscure this essential proposition. Moreover, it has given rise to definitional difficulties. Categories of savings and investment or capital and consumption goods, although useful as analytical tools if their limitations are recognized, have assumed a precision of meaning far beyond that which they actually possess. We do not wish to minimize the significance of the traditional conceptual apparatus for many purposes. Nevertheless, we feel that for the purpose of studying the place of the desire for liquidity in economic behavior, a more useful concept is that all wealth-titles, until extinguished, contain a claim to other wealth. This, of necessity, must blur existing categories.

V

LIQUIDITY PREFERENCES AND CUMULATIVE CHANGE

IN THE FINAL ANALYSIS, the exchange of money against real wealth is motivated by but two inducements: the desire to use wealth personally and the expectation of increasing one's claims to wealth. The latter may be accounted in terms of money profits. If one does not wish to use wealth and does not anticipate money profits through an exchange of his money for wealth, there is no point in losing the liquidity which is provided by the possession of money.

The principal advantages of refraining from an exchange of money for real wealth result from the fact that future wants are indefinite, or that prices are expected to decline. These are the conclusions that apply to new wealth output as well as to wealth-titles in general.

LIMITS TO THE INTERDEPENDENCE OF CHANGES IN LIQUIDITY DESIRES WITH OTHER SOURCES OF CHANGE

The holding of money is the means of attaining the highest degree of liquidity. As wealth-titles become less comparable to money, their degree of liquidity tends to diminish. It cannot be said, however, that as wealth-titles become less comparable to money, their ability to provide personal satisfactions or to participate in the realization of expected money profits is enhanced *pari passu*. Except to the miser, the possession of money excludes the enjoyment of satisfaction provided by using real wealth. Only after the money has been exchanged for real wealth does the satisfaction result. But it cannot be said that the more illiquid the wealth, the greater the satisfaction. On the other hand, we have seen that when prices are declining the possession of money does not exclude the realization of money profits. Thus there is no close correlation between the degree of liquidity of assets owned and the money profits realized.

The exchange of money for productive or unproductive real wealth [1] involves a loss of liquidity. There is no close correlation between the degree of illiquidity and the anticipation of satisfactions or the expectation of money profits. But the anticipation of personal satisfactions and the expectation of productiveness to the individual expressed through money profits, are the only motivating factors that lead to the acquisition of illiquid titles.

In tabular form, the factors entering the decision to exchange or not to exchange money for real wealth are as follows:

I	II
Desire to Withhold Money from Exchange	*Desire to Exchange Money*
1. Desire for liquidity	1. Desire for real wealth to use personally
2. Desire to obtain money profit when price level is expected to fall	2. Desire to obtain money profit by holding real wealth, productive or unproductive in the social sense, when price level is expected to rise
	3. Desire to obtain money profit by holding socially productive real wealth regardless of price change

In addition to indicating economic behavior of an antithetical character, the factors listed under I, and II respectively influence each other. The relationships are not simple. As Marshall said of the relations between cost of production, demand, and

[1] The terms productive and unproductive must be elaborated. Wealth may be productive to society and unproductive to an individual if he is unsuccessful in increasing his claim to all wealth. Or it may be unproductive to society and productive to the individual if through its possession he succeeds in increasing his claim to all wealth. Here we are using the terms in the sense of productive or unproductive to society.

value,[2] their complexity makes a plain and simple statement difficult if not false.

The tabulation may be thought of as referring to the desires of more than one individual. It may deal with aggregates; with the desires of the community at large. A particular individual may desire a high degree of liquidity in his personal affairs, but this is of no great concern if someone else, with equally important affairs, wishes a correspondingly high degree of illiquidity. That with which we are here concerned is the dominant desire of the community. An accountant might call it the net desire.

The important factors with which we have to deal are the desires for satisfactions, for money profits, and for liquidity of assets and persons. The desires for future satisfactions in the form of consumption or economic power underlie the desires for liquidity and money profits. The desires for liquidity are essentially defensive in character, while those for money profits are aggressive in character.

The subsidiary consideration of continued use and value through time manifestly enters prominently into the decision to acquire particular types of wealth for personal use. Variations in the expectation of money profits will influence the decision to acquire greater or fewer titles to wealth for personal use, but not to the same extent that they influence decisions to acquire title to real wealth that will not be used personally. In the latter case it is the sole consideration.

THE PRICE LEVEL

We may abstract from the above table (1) changes in desire for wealth to use personally and (2) the social productivity of wealth, and hold these constant by assumption. Under these hypothetical circumstances it appears that liquidity desires, so far as they relate to the withholding of money, will vary with changes in the expectation of future price levels. If it is expected that prices will sag, liquidity desires will increase. If it is expected that prices will rise, liquidity desires will diminish. In our later argument

[2] Marshall, Alfred, *Principles of Economics,* (8th ed.; London, 1920), p. 368.

it will appear that desires to hoard money are related to a changing price level, both directly and indirectly, through the effect of such changes on the *aggregate* of money profits.

The price level as a concept is not precise and measurable. Yet it has a being which enters the consciousness of all who live in a commercial society. It may be defined, but not precisely measured, as a weighted average of the unit prices of all wealth exchanging for money in a given period. It is not especially important for our purposes that it be measured with precision. The important thing is not the changes that have taken place in the past in the price level but the *expectation* of future changes. Even though we might measure exactly past changes in the price level, we could not measure the nature or strength of these future expectations.

Such a description of a price level might be conceived for new wealth production entering the hands of final buyers. The prices of second-hand goods, tokens, and land (the secondary circulation) seem likely to follow prices of final new output. Likewise, prices in the earlier stages of production (the interstitial circulation) seemingly are set with an eye on final price. On this premise, the price level of final new output is of chief importance in determining changes in the general price level.

A somewhat different estimate of the influence of prices for second-hand goods is made by Miss Curtis and Mr. Townshend.

> . . . the price of new goods is necessarily affected by people's valuation of the old goods of the same kind which exist. . . . For there is always a stock of previously produced goods in existence, and this influences the market by furnishing a source of supply, actual or potential, alternative to new production.[3]

It would not be defensible to hold that the price of new wealth output is unaffected by the price of old goods in the second-hand market. In this sense Miss Curtis and Mr. Townshend are correct. But it is even more true that the price of second-hand goods is not unaffected by the price of new wealth. Moreover, the less organized second-hand markets are more likely to be competitive

[3] *Modern Money,* p. 204.

in nature, whereas in the new wealth output market, price is more likely to be fixed for extended periods by producers.[4] Being more flexible, the second-hand price will tend to fluctuate with reference to the fixed price of the new wealth against which it makes an alternative appeal.

A fall or rise in the price level may or may not lead to the expectation of a further movement in the same direction. Belief about the initial cause of the movement is important in determining the outcome. Let us suppose that the initial movement in the price level has resulted from arbitrary action on the part of the central banking authority or the treasury.[5] Suppose further that the price level falls without what has been called by Durbin, following Lavington and Clay, the distributional disadvantage of a moving price level.[6] In these highly artificial circumstances the public might believe that the decline can be, or will be stopped or reversed by opposite action on the part of the agency that originally provided the stimuli to change the price level. If, after a fall in the price level, the dominant expectation is that prices will stabilize or return to their former levels, there is no reason to expect liquidity desires to be stronger at the lower level than at the higher. They may be weaker.

If, on the other hand, a fall in the price level leads to the dominant expectation of further decline or to uncertainty, then liquidity desires will be stronger at the lower level. A cumulative series of deflationary actions and reactions is set up which is broken only by other forces. The fall in prices leads to the expectation of further decline, to greater desire for liquidity, to greater reluctance to exchange money for less liquid wealth-

[4] See Burns, *The Decline of Competition,* Chap. V, *passim.*

[5] The proposition that autonomous changes in the price level may be induced by changes in money quantities has a long and important intellectual history, ranging from the early formulations of the quantity theory by Jean Bodin and Locke to the more elaborate patterns of causation described by Wicksell, Mises, Keynes, and Hawtrey. Excellent surveys of the development of ideas concerning the influence of money on prices are found in von Hayek's *Prices and Production,* Chap. I, (Revised Ed., London, 1935); in Angell's *Theory of International Prices,* Part I, (Cambridge, 1926); and in Marget's *The Theory of Prices,* (New York, 1938), *passim.*

[6] Durbin, *The Problem of Credit Policy,* pp. 112–13.

titles, to further decline in prices. Obviously the system does not work so simply. But these are forces that will exert their cumulative pressures unless a price movement is unaccompanied by the dominant expectation of a further movement in the same direction. There is likely to be such an expectation unless the initiating source of the price movement is thought to be understood, and if understood, believed to have been removed.

THE PRICE STRUCTURE, A SUGGESTED INITIATING SOURCE OF CHANGE IN THE PRICE LEVEL

In addition to the concept of the price level there is the concept of the price structure, or the relations of prices, any one to all others. These price relations perform certain exceedingly important functions. They may relate the values of economic goods to one another in such a manner that all such goods that are offered for exchange are exchanged. That is, they may clear the markets by equating supply of and demand for wealth in its present forms. Also, price relations determine the distribution of the community's money income, which, in part, determines the nature of "tomorrow's" demand. To the extent that price relations do equate present demand and supply, and to the extent that they distribute the money income in such a manner that tomorrow's demand and supply may be equated, we can say that the price structure is in balance. It is a matter of degree, not of an absolute. Moreover, it is a matter of prices related to each other with reference to productive facilities and human wants, not of related prices *in vacuo*. We shall attempt to show that a significant lack of balance of the price structure in either of these two respects eventually will initiate a decline in the price level, independently of other factors such as money quantities.[7]

The substantial antithesis of the term price balance appears frequently in economic literature under various guises: price disequilibrium, maladjustment, distortion, disparity, etc. Professor Mills chooses the latter which he defines as

[7] It is not necessary to our purpose here that lack of what we have called price balance be the *only* initiating source of decline in the price level. It is sufficient that it be one of the initiating sources of change.

. . . the condition existing after a shift in price relations to which there has not been complete adaptation among elements of the economic system at large. We take the term adaptation in the above definition, to mean such adjustment in respect of the volume or character of production, allocation of man power, investment of capital, distribution of income, or disposition of other elements of economic life as may be necessary to *a working balance* of economic elements, with effective utilization of available production resources.[8]

Professor Slichter prefers the term maladjustment:

The breakdowns in exchange which we call depressions have a dual nature. For one thing, they are reactions to maladjustments which develop between supply and demand. The maladjustments may develop in a vast variety of ways. Naturally they all carry with them adjustments in the price structure. For business to pick up, these maladjustments must in some measure be corrected. This means that there must be changes either in the prices or in supply and demand, usually in both.[9]

In speaking of balance in the price structure we do not refer to a price structure characterized by an absence of long-period change in the relations among prices. Changing techniques, new forms of wealth, and revisions of the ultimate wants of people will necessitate price changes if a balance is to be maintained. Alfred Marshall has given us a neat exposition of why changes are necessary in price relationships.

The amount of the thing and its price, the amount of the several factors or agents of production used in making it, and their prices—all these elements mutually govern one another, and if an external cause should alter any one of them the effect of the disturbance extends to all the others.

In the same way, when several balls are lying in a bowl, they mutually govern one another's positions; and again when a heavy weight is suspended by several elastic strings of different weights and lengths (all of them being stretched) attached to different points in the ceiling, the equilibrium positions of all of the strings and of the weight mutually govern one another. If any one of the strings is shortened,

---

[8] Mills, *Prices in Recession and Recovery*, p. 34. Italics mine.

[9] Slichter, "The Economics of Public Works." In *Current Economic Policies*, ed. by J. B. Hubbard, p. 509.

everything else will change its position, and the length and the tension of every other string will be altered also.[10]

In a similar manner the problem of balanced prices is related to the many factors that may be respectively subsumed under the categories of demand and supply. The price structure may be said to be in balance when it does not retard, of itself, the rate of production and consumption. Such a condition involves first, an equating of present demand and supply through prices. Second, it involves a price structure that will distribute money income in a manner that will not so change the nature of future demand that the arrangement of production factors will not be able to supply it, but can supply something else instead. Perhaps a third requirement might be added. It may be said to involve *a degree of stability* among closely associated prices.

The prices of individual commodities, in their changes, stimulate or retard production and consumption and, in turn, reflect changes in production and consumption. So, also, the prices of individual services affect, and reflect, changes in the direction of human effort. But there exists a broader set of price relations, of importance equal to the specific connections between changes in the prices and quantities of individual commodities. These are the numerous relations, of varying degrees of intimacy, which tie all prices into a system.[11]

To mention several of these important close relationships among prices, it is desirable that there be a degree of stability in the relative prices of raw materials and finished goods, the prices of agricultural and manufactured goods, the prices of services, including wages, and corporeal wealth, the cost of government (taxes), and the national income.[12]

In the light of these three requirements, which might prove to be somewhat contradictory, the attempt to attain perfect balance in the price structure appears to be a phantom quest. The bal-

[10] *Principles of Economics,* p. 526. [11] Mills, *Behavior of Prices,* p. 31.

[12] There is another price relationship which might be included among closely related prices, namely, the relation of the price of debt, including money, to the price of real wealth. But this relationship is of such great importance that it has come to be differentiated from the price structure and called the price level. The distinction appears to be a highly useful one.

ancing of present demand and supply may result in a distribution of money income which will revise future demand. But changes in future supplies are limited by what Kaldor now calls the *specificity* of production factors.[13] Again, prices that may equate present demand and supply, and fortuitously result in a distribution of income that will not require significant changes in future supply, may be of such a nature that unbalance appears among closely related prices. Long-term contracts, including interest or wage contracts, are a typical source of unbalance in the price structure. But while perfect balance is seemingly impossible under existing conditions, the effort to attain a greater degree of balance is not a futile one. For there seems to be a wide margin of tolerance in the economy within which unbalance may exist without initiating a change in the price level. In other terms, it appears that considerable unbalance in the price structure is possible before it gives rise to the cumulative phases of business change that are related to liquidity desires through movement of the price level.

We have cited the influence of changing techniques and changing tastes that are independent of income to show that balanced prices do not imply unchanging relations among prices. Many price changes are necessary to meet the requirements of balance. But autonomous price changes that do not approximately reflect changes in supply and demand factors, or the failure of prices to change in response to unfettered supply and demand factors, will result in a greater degree of unbalance in the price structure. They may result in a subsequent fall in the price level.

Under conditions of perfect competition and perfect knowledge there could be no lack of balance in the price structure. Competition as the controlling agent in economic life would insure that all wealth produced would be wealth that was desired. Different forms of wealth would be priced at figures equating the cost of production to relative demands. A change in the composition of demand through time would cause no trouble for perfect

[13] Kaldor, "Stability and Full Employment," *Economic Journal,* XLVIII (Dec., 1938), 642–57.

competition implies complete mobility of all wealth, including human capacities, as well as complete flexibility of all prices.

Even the heated debates about under-consumption and over-production can be resolved into a question of balance in the price structure. It is held by those espousing these theories that the appearance of a divergence in the relative prices of human abilities (labor) and final corporeal wealth may result in a demand for wealth which differs from the forms of wealth that are produced. There may be too much of so-called consumers' goods produced relative to the effective demand for it. But in the perfectly competitive society, say their opponents, the interest rate acts as a price directing the demand for relative amounts of wealth going to satisfy personal desires on the one hand, and going into the production of still more wealth on the other. On this proposition it follows that even though differences appear in the relative prices of human abilities and corporeal wealth there will be an effective demand for the whole of new production. Different groups of people will express the demand but a full demand there will be in such a hypothetical state of society.

This question of balance, being a relative thing, may be looked at from the "goods" side as well as from the side of money prices. An additional and important function of the price structure is so to direct economic resources as to equate the production of particular goods and services with relative public demands. Economists have long ago shown convincingly that to the extent that markets are perfect, the pricing mechanism performs this intricate and complicated task. Equilibrium may be described as a condition in which all goods and services of all types coming on the market are purchased at prices representing, *in toto,* a compensation to all the factors entering into the production, the contribution of the factors being measured by their respective marginal productivities.

The phenomenon of deficiencies in purchasing power arising from withholding money from exchange presents no problem in this scheme of things. The allocation of money income between exchanges for final goods and services which are to be used personally and those which are to be put back into production is alleged to be adjusted by the interest rate, which is in turn a measure of the marginal productivity of new capital. If the demands of the community call for smaller additions to productive capacity, the interest rate presumably will fall, "money savings" will concurrently decline, and a greater part of current money income will be devoted to personal use. The converse is true with a rise in the interest rate. Thus the balance or equilibrium is supposed to be maintained. This is obviously an oversimplified statement of a very important body of economic doctrine, but it is enough to permit the development of the point that the problem of withholding money from exchange has no important place in it.

But perfect prices require perfect markets. Perfect markets require widespread knowledge on the part of buyers and sellers, completely elastic demand curves for individual sellers with their implication of smallness of each seller relative to the market, and the absence of all non-competitive practices and economic loyalties. The articles traded in perfect markets should have infinite divisibility and easy mobility. Much has been written regarding the progressive departure of the characteristics of markets from these and other requirements. Associations of corporeal and intangible wealth have resulted in much loss of mobility, divisibility, transferability, and convertibility for different uses. The use of tokens in part to overcome these handicaps, has resulted in less perfect knowledge on the part of the owners of wealth-titles. The very existence of intangible wealth itself impairs the validity of the assumptions of perfect markets.

There is nothing in the equilibrium analysis to cause one to expect a change in the price level as a result of a change in the price structure. A decline in the price of a good in the static equilibrium analysis may suggest a shift in demand to other goods. There is a decrease and an increase at the same time. Factors will *readily flow* from the depressed to the stimulated field. The concomitant price adjustments will change the price structure, but since presumably the same amount of business will be done as before, there is no reason to expect a change in the weighted average of all prices. But a change in the price structure under imperfectly competitive conditions, in which knowledge is less than complete and production factors are immobile, may give rise to a degree of unbalance and cause a change in the price level in a number of ways.

There are several ways in which we may look at this proposition. Let us start our analysis by holding constant all of the variables except the kind of goods that are produced—that is, the nature of supply. Suppose that with an unchanged composition of demand there is the expectation of a change, supply is modified to conform to these expectations and producers are subsequently disappointed. In such a situation it is fairly evident that a change in price relations will follow. Professor Watkins describes for us what its results may be on the price level.

The readiness of buyers to part with the available means of payment is conditioned no less by the qualitative aspect of the total offering for sale than by their volume. Here, however, the interrelationships of the various kinds of goods and services offered for sale become the major consideration. In other words, the quality of the total productive output of industry is primarily a function of the right proportions of the different varieties of products offered for sale. If, to take a very simple example, the quantity of hose offered for sale is wholly out of line with the number of pairs of shoes put on the market, the output of industry is to that extent unbalanced and *the price level, not simply the price of hose or shoes, will be affected* accordingly. For as the supply of each commodity constitutes ultimately a part of the demand for all other commodities, an impairment of the purchasing power of the suppliers of a commodity through forces affecting its price adversely cannot fail to react unfavorably upon the demand for and upon the price of other products. . . . In other words, the promptness and facility with which goods are exchanged against money and this money is again exchanged against goods, and thereby the price terms upon which these exchanges take place, are a function of the degree of correspondence between the composition of the total supply (volume of production) and the complexion of the aggregate demand. . . . The root of the evil is found in the development of "bad" relationships among different types of goods from which proceed price disturbances.[14]

[14] Watkins, "The Price System." In *Encyclopaedia of the Social Sciences,* XII, 373–74. Italics mine.

What Professor Watkins has not stressed sufficiently in this passage is the specificity of production factors. According to the static equilibrium analysis, the resulting reduction in the use of factors in the production of hose would liberate forces that would restore equilibrium. Especially would the decline in the cost of capital and labor induce their reëmployment in another segment of the economy. But this suggests that prices are flexible, that factors are mobile, and that knowledge of the composition of demand is better than is actually the case. The static equilibrium analysis describes an ideal case but one likely to happen only by chance. More probable, the necessary adjustments will take place slowly, if at all, with the result that the change in supply relative to demand will affect the amount of money exchanged for wealth, and hence the price level.

If it is true that a change in the nature of supply not compensated by a change in the composition of demand may result in a change in the price level, it is conversely true that a change in the composition of demand relative to supply will have the same result. We shall now assume supply to be constant and permit demand to fluctuate. The nature of present demand is in part the result of the manner in which the national income has been distributed in the past.

Suppose in a partly competitive and partly monopolistic society [15] the price structure is changed by the monopolist's raising his price. In the nature of the case there must now result either an increase in the price level or the monopolist's competitors must lower their prices. Let us say the price level is raised but demand continues as before. The monopolist will receive a larger money income (he has acted intelligently with reference to an inelastic demand curve) while the competitors will receive the same aggregate of money income as before.

Total money income of the community is thus increased in the first instance. But there will result a redistribution of income and

15 We use the illustration of a monopolist to simplify the case. However, as the reader progresses he will recognize that anything that changes the distributive *shares* of the money income without the necessary concomitant changes in production arrangements will be a source of trouble.

a changed composition of demand that *may* initiate a business decline and subsequent falling money income in a society in which competition is less than perfect and the factors of production are comparatively immobile. The relative distribution of the national income to various individuals as owners of wealth in its multifarious forms is determined by the price structure. It follows that a change in the price structure "today" will result in a different distribution of the national income and hence in a different composition of "tomorrow's" aggregate demand. More of some forms of wealth and less of other forms will be desired. But the composition of wealth-forms produced, or that might be produced, *does not change* as rapidly as the relative distribution of money income. As a result, there will be less than full employment of factors organized to produce wealth in forms, the demand for which will have been lessened by the shift in the distribution of income. The factors, including human abilities, that have been employed in the production of these wealth-forms will become unemployed.

When, as a result of an unbalanced price structure, unemployment of any of the factors of production begins to appear, lessened aggregate money income will be anticipated. This will be the case regardless of whether the price level has risen. It will be developed in the succeeding chapter that the aggregate of money profits of the community is determined chiefly by the price *times the quantity* of wealth exchanged for money. In all probability, the appearance of unemployment in any section of the economy will result in the exchange of a smaller aggregate quantity of wealth. It is increasingly evident that the factors of production are not mobile in short periods and they are unable to shift quickly to meet revised demands.

After unemployment of the factors of production in any particular sector has made its appearance, the cumulative phases of the situation may begin to operate.

. . . a breakdown in an individual industry may very well cause at least a temporary fall in the total demand below the level at which it would otherwise stand. Whether this will start a cumulative process of contraction or not depends first, on the magnitude of the disturbance and secondly on the general situation.[16]

Hoarding may first appear in those parts of the economy that have experienced the initial impact of unemployment, but it may soon spread throughout the economy. A fall in the price level may result and the cumulative factors making for lessened production and distribution may become operative. One of the initial or generative disturbances plausibly seems to be the appearance of unbalance in the price structure. Moreover, there is no reason to believe that the fall in the price level or in production and distribution necessarily will cure this lack of balance. Because of the different rates at which prices for unlike forms of wealth decline, the condition of unbalance may become greater.

> . . . although depressions are reactions to maladjustments, they are far from being simply corrective reactions. On the contrary, they are themselves a source of maladjustments, for the very drop in spending, which is the essence of depression, intensifies existing maladjustments and creates new ones.[17]

One phase of current economic organization is the extent to which certain prices lack flexibility. Statistical work in the past decade has indicated substantial differences in the degree of flexibility of different prices, as regards both frequency and amplitude of change. The imperfections of the markets, which are seemingly not as recent a development as many have supposed, result in some prices moving very much more slowly than others, and perhaps with a smaller amplitude of change. Such prices are described as "sticky" prices. It is a simple mathematical truth that if the weighted aggregate of all prices falls by a given amount—those prices which are not sticky must fall the more because of the presence of the sticky prices. Conversely, if the aggregate of all prices rises by a given amount, those prices which are not sticky must rise the more because of the presence of sticky

[16] Haberler, *Prosperity and Depression*, pp. 252–53.

[17] Slichter, "The Economics of Public Works." In *Current Economic Policies*, p. 509.

prices. The direction of economic resources in a manner equating the production of particular goods and services with the public demand thus may be rendered less perfect. The direction of public demand itself may be changed by these phenomena.

The resulting disequilibria are not restricted to the expansion phase of the cycle, that is, to new decisions allocating economic resources. They occur in the contraction phase as well. A changing price structure and price level may cause a commitment, perfectly directed at the time it was made to become thoroughly misdirected before it is completely extinguished. More study has been given to the misdirection of new production commitments than to the autonomous misdirection of existing commitments, arising out of the unbalance incurred in economic life as the result of contraction, but both are important.

The situation as regards the effect of changes in the price structure or the price level is not different in its results if, when our hypothetical monopolist raises his prices, the price level remains constant. In this instance, the prices of competitive wealth must decline by the nature of the case. But the competitor's cost of buying outside claims to his production may not correspondingly decline. Since production is for profit, marginal enterprisers may reduce their production or possibly cease their production. Unemployment of factors will appear with cumulative results similar to those described above. A like condition of unbalance will result if the monopolist merely maintains his prices while his costs of buying outside interest in his production are falling. The lack of balance in the price structure eventually may result in a decline in the price level.

Unbalanced prices may occur in many sections of the economy. Noncompetitive prices are typical in most markets today. Some of the conspicuous examples are old interest contracts, the prices of human abilities or wages in the broadest sense of the term, postage costs, finished goods prices in the so-called heavy goods industries, prices for public utility services, and prices of trademarked and branded goods.

INITIATING AND CUMULATIVE FORCES IN BUSINESS CHANGE

The foregoing analysis suggests that one of the important initiating sources of change in economic affairs is the appearance of an increasing degree of what we have called unbalance in the price structure. Among the effects of such an unbalance may be an eventual decline of the price level. If, after a fall in the price level, the public expects prices to remain stable or recover, there will be no increase in liquidity desires and no greater reluctance to exchange money for real wealth. It is even possible that the lower prices may seem like bargains, thus inducing a more rapid use of money. This is an assumption of the static equilibrium analysis.

But if it is believed that the decline in the price level was started by a lack of balance in the price structure which still continues or that the decline itself has given rise to a still more unbalanced price structure due to different degrees of flexibility in prices, then the public is more likely to anticipate further price declines. Hoarding and its equivalents will result with their consequences on the exchange of money for real wealth. This is the usual sequence of events. In all cases where a lack of balance in the price structure starts a price-level decline, or appears as the result of a price-level decline, the outcome seemingly will be a reduction in business activity and a fall in prices. Through the accompanying increase of liquidity desires it is highly likely that it will be followed by cumulative influences that result in a further reduction of activity and prices. It thus appears that the accomplishment of the objectives of full employment and distribution is substantially impossible unless some means are found to maintain *a degree* of balance in the price structure. Because of the different flexibilities of different prices, reasonable stability of the price level will aid rather than hinder the attainment of this essential purpose.

Changes in liquidity desires exert their influence on business life in a cumulative manner. They do not appear to become operative until an initiating source of business change has brought them into being. A large part of the remainder of this book will be given to a description of how liquidity desires, operating through hoarding, changes in debt, and the expectation of money profits, exert their cumulative influences.

The evidence of a change in liquidity desires, as defined in Chapter II, is found in (1) an increased desire to hold titles to money, (2) a shift in price relations in favor of more liquid titles, and (3) an expansion or contraction of the corpus of the aggregate of debt. In the present discussion of the place of shifts in liquidity desires in the exchange of money for real wealth, we have dealt only with the first of these. This has been for two purposes. It has helped simplify the analysis and focused attention on the crux of our problem, i. e., on the exchange of money for new output or final buying. Moreover, the second and third of the evidences of a shift in liquidity desires are important because of their influence on the exchange of titles to real wealth through money. More will be said of these in subsequent pages.

Again, in the present discussion, the net desire of the community to hold titles to money has been exclusively related to the expectation of future movements of the price level. By itself, the analysis obviously is incomplete. The inducements to part with money are (1) the satisfaction of wants and (2) the expectation of profits. The expectation of money profits is the only factor influencing the decision to acquire wealth not to be personally used, and it is an important factor in the decision as to whether or not to acquire wealth for personal use. From the standpoint of the individual, the expectation of money profits is conditioned, not only by expectations of price changes, but also by expectations of what we have called social productivity. But it is not the expected money profit of any one individual or corporate identity with which we are concerned. It is the aggregate of all money profits that are expected by all of the members of the community. This is a quantity that may be plus or minus relative to the recent past, according to the dominant expectations of the moment. The argument of this chapter, so closely related to changes in the price level, can carry conviction only if it can be shown that the aggregate of money profits tends to fluctuate with movements of the price level, not necessarily *pari passu* but in the same direction. We shall attempt to do this in the succeeding chapter.

SUMMARY

Liquidity desires are not something that can be isolated from the complex of economic forces with which they are associated, any more than price can be studied without reference to the factors subsumed under supply and demand. The sources of change with which liquidity desires are interdependently associated are the desire personally to use wealth and the expectation of money profits. These are the two basic inducements to exchange money for assets. If necessary, individuals are willing to sacrifice more or less liquidity in order to realize these wants. But it does not follow that there is a close inverse correlation between the degree of liquidity possessed and the realization of personal satisfactions or money profits.

Wealth may be productive to society in the sense of adding to the sum-total of the community's wealth. Without being productive to society, particular wealth-forms may add to the individual's *share* of the aggregate of community wealth. Thus the expectation of money profits is related to both the social productivity of wealth-forms and to price movements.

The amount of wealth demanded for personal use is also influenced by the expectation of money profits. To the extent that the wealth is durable, the expectation of general price movements will exert more influence on the decision to acquire it. Durable wealth serves as a store of value through time. Expected movements of the price level, that is, of the real wealth value of a single unit of money, accelerate or retard the exchange of money for durable wealth of all descriptions.

If we assume no change in personal wants or social productivity, the desire for more or less liquidity will vary with changes in the *expectation* of the future movement of prices.

In this connection the prices of final output appear to be more important than other prices. The effect of a change in the price level upon liquidity desires depends upon the effect it has upon expectations of future price movements. This may be a matter of opinion about the initial cause of the price change and whether it is felt that the source of change has been removed.

The relationship of all prices to each other and to basic wants and to a given arrangement of production factors is one source of change in the price level. This structure of prices has two important functions to perform: (1) to equate present supply with present demand in detail and (2) to distribute money incomes in a manner that will not so change future demand that specific production arrangements cannot supply it but can supply something else instead. To the extent that the price structure succeeds in the performance of these functions it is said to be in balance, to the extent it fails, out of balance. Balance is thus a matter of degree. Obviously, balance does not suggest unchanging price relationships since basic wants and techniques are in flux.

Because prices are not uniformly flexible a change in the general level of all prices will result in a different set of price relationships. The new situation may represent a greater or lesser degree of balance. But there is no certainty that a fall in the price level will automatically create an improved situation in this respect. If the lack of balance initiating the price level change has been aggravated rather than mitigated, expectations of further price decline will intensify liquidity desires.

We will attempt to show in the succeeding chapter that the *aggregate* of money profits tends to fluctuate in the same direction as the price level, although not *pari passu*. It follows that a price decline that leads to the expectation of still lower prices will be accompanied by the expectation of lower money profits, greater liquidity desires, and hoarding. Insofar as a price movement in a given direction leads to expectations of further change in the same direction, a set of *cumulative* actions and reactions become operative which contain within themselves no source of their own reversal. Whether a movement in one direction leads to the expectation of further movement in the same direction may depend on the dominant belief about the *initiating* source of change.

The movement of the price level is just as likely to aggravate as correct a price structure which is substantially unbalanced. The source of initial change will then remain. Hence, the expectation of further change in the same direction continues to exert itself through liquidity desires on the price level, money profits, and hoarding. In a later chapter we will see that fluctuations in the aggregate of debt enter into this complex in a conspicuous manner.

Initiating and cumulative sources of change in economic life have been differentiated. Changes in desires for liquidity are a component of these cumulative forces. To the extent that the institutions available for satisfying liquidity desires have increased in importance, the cumulative aspects of economic change are enhanced and the amplitude of business changes may be expected to be greater.

VI

AGGREGATE MONEY PROFITS

A NUMBER of difficult questions arise in connection with the determination of the source of and changes in the amount of the *aggregate* of money profits. Are money profits, as would be true under the definitions of J. B. Clark and Josef Schumpeter, nonexistent in conditions of perfect equilibrium? Is the sum total of money profits determined by the money value of the net increments to real wealth resulting from the excess of production and discovery over extinguishment? Is it determined by the complete distribution of new wealth coming into being, regardless of the amount of new output relative to extinguishment and regardless of the direction of change in the amount of its production? Is it determined by the direction of change, or the rate of change, of the amount of effective money—MV when V is the so-called income velocity? Is it determined by any one of these factors acting alone or by several of them acting jointly? Would it be theoretically possible for a community with a declining level of economic well-being to maintain a positive aggregate of money profits if all new wealth coming into existence were fully distributed?

Messrs. Foster and Catchings discerned some of these problems when they foresaw "such sources of trouble, for example, as the possibility of money profits without real profits, and real profits without money profits, and the impossibility of telling, on any given day, whether there are to be any profits at all." [1] Unfortunately, we have been unable to find these complex problems satisfactorily resolved in the subsequent work of these authors. Perhaps that is because they are substantially insoluble with our

[1] Foster and Catchings, *Profits,* p. 5.

present economic equipment. With diffidence, we shall have a try at the problems in what follows, in the hope that some clarification may result.

Theoretical answers to these questions are of interest to most economic analyses. The nature and source of changes in the community's aggregate money profits are of especial interest to this study, for a change in the aggregate will condition expectations. Changing expectations regarding money profits constitute one of the underlying motivations in changed desires for liquidity and in the exchange of money against real wealth.[2]

PRESENT CONFUSION REGARDING THE TERM MONEY PROFITS

For many years, in the development of economic theory, the terms profits and capital were closely related. Under the conditions of the eighteenth and early nineteenth centuries, ". . . it was natural to connect the income of the business manager with the ownership of capital, and in all the classical writings we find the word 'profit' used in this sense." [3] Again ". . . the classical economists included interest in profit as a part of the entrepreneur's return on the capital employed in production." [4] According to J. S. Mill, "As the wages of the laborer are the remuneration of labor, so the profits of the capitalists are properly, according to Mr. Senior's well-chosen expression, the remuneration of abstinence." [5] Abstinence is made the means of acquiring capital. Although in the above quotation capital and profits are closely identified, Mill had begun to get away from the earlier treatment of profits and interest as identical.

> The rate of profit greatly exceeds the rate of interest. The surplus is partly compensation for risk. . . . The gross profits from capital . . . must afford a sufficient equivalent for abstinence, indemnity for risk, and remuneration for the labor and skill required for super-

[2] This is not to say that aggregate profits are a cause of, or necessary to recovery. What is important is the dominant belief in future profits. Compare C. I. Barnard, *Fortune Round Table,* March, 1939, Appendix I.

[3] Knight, *Risk, Uncertainty and Profit,* p. 23.

[4] Foreman, *Efficiency and Scarcity Profits,* p. 7.

[5] Mill, J. S., *Principles of Political Economy* (Ashley ed.; London, 1929), p. 405.

intendence. And the three parts into which profit may be considered as resolving itself, may be described respectively as interest, insurance and wages of superintendence . . . the rate of profits depends on wages; rising as wages fall, and falling as wages rise.[6]

Marshall, as recently as 1920, held to the old association of profits and capital when he described profits as the net gain on capital in excess of interest at the current rate.[7] A number of excellent and detailed reviews of the early treatment of the term profit are available.[8]

In more recent years interest and profits have come to be distinctly differentiated, and interest alone has been treated as the remuneration of capital in the sense of the reward for abstinence. Profits are conceived to be a *residual* representing the wages of management, or payments for uncertainty-bearing, or both. But, generally speaking, there appears to be no great agreement among present-day economists as to the precise meaning of profits. Some fifteen years ago Professor Knight held:

. . . the theory of profit has remained one of the most unsatisfactory and controversial divisions of economic doctrine. It is, indeed, only within comparatively recent years that the existence of profit as a really distinct share has become established and the problem of its explanation given definite status.[9]

Some years later (in 1930) Professor Foreman apparently felt that little had been done to cure this deficiency in our economic thinking:

. . . there is as yet no settled method among legalists or economists in their analysis of profits. The residual surplus is today a conglomeration of unknown elements. In fact, it is the least understood of all the shares which go to make up the rewards of production, and yet it lies at the very heart of the great problems involved in the distribution of wealth.[10]

In an earlier passage Professor Foreman stresses the importance of a clear understanding of profits in these terms: "The danger

[6] *Ibid.*, p. 406.

[7] Marshall, *Principles of Economics*, p. 73.

[8] Special mention should be given Knight, *Risk, Uncertainty and Profit*, Chap. II; Ghosh, *The Theory of Profits*, Chaps. I–IV; and Foreman, *Efficiency and Scarcity Profits*, Chaps. XII, XIII.

[9] *Risk, Uncertainty and Profit*, p. 22.

[10] *Efficiency and Scarcity Profits*, p. 268.

and menace of commercial depressions rest in the profit making process, and the very heart of the problem lies in the obscure conditions and forces which affect the accumulation of profits." [11]

Conspicuously, there is need for precise understanding of the meaning of profits. Especially is this the case in the present study, which has assigned to the expectation of money profits a place as one of the important proximate motivations, if not the principal motivation, in *changes* in economic behavior.

PROFITS AS A RESIDUAL

First, let us consider the residual nature of profits. Nearly fifty years ago J. A. Hobson and J. B. Clark simultaneously pointed out that the laws governing rent were likewise applicable in the determination of all other incomes.[12] Contemplating the implications of such an extension of the law of rent, Hobson saw that all incomes are similar in the manner of their determination, and concluded that this similarity

> . . . completely destroys what may be termed the "residuary legatee" treatment of distribution. . . . Karl Marx found that capital was able to take all the product minus the wages of subsistence, which remained a fixed quantity and not a fixed proportion as the size of the product grew. Henry George, again, showing how interest and wages are fixed charges, placed the land owner in the enviable position of residual claimant. . . . Finally, General [F. A.] Walker plays the third and only remaining variety of change; for in his system it is rent and interest that are fixed charges, while labor holds the place of vantage and takes the growth of gain in higher wages.
> Whichever order we select, we shall be able to show that the claims of the first and second factors may be plausibly treated as fixed charges, and the third, therefore, takes all the remainder. . . .[13]

At the time this passage was written, it apparently had not become the universal practice to separate clearly profits and interest. Rent, wages, and profits at an earlier period had been conceived to be the sum-total of income, interest being subsumed

[11] *Ibid.*, p. 2.

[12] Hobson, J. A., "The Law of the Three Rents," and Clark, J. B., "Distribution as Determined by a Law of Rent," *Quarterly Journal of Economics*, V (1890–91), 263–318.

[13] *Op. cit.*, pp. 279–80.

under the latter. But Hobson was wrong in holding that the "residuary legatee" theory of distribution had been destroyed. As profits in the course of time became more clearly differentiated from interest and defined as wages of management, as contrasted with wages of labor, or defined as payments for uncertainty bearing, there has been an accompanying tendency to treat them as a residual. Contemporarily, we find Professor Foreman holding that "the residual surplus is today a conglomeration of unknown elements." [14]

Is there any more reason to consider profits a residual today than there was to consider interest, or rent, or wages a residual fifty or more years ago? In fact, does not the business community, from whom economics must ultimately draw its terms and problems, conceive of profits as accruing *through* interest, rent, or wages, or any combination of them? In addition, does not the business community know that the money profits of an individual may be increased by what have been called windfall profits or reduced by windfall losses?

REAL PROFITS

Few would disagree with the proposition that profits are the difference between income and outgo in a given period of time. Differences arise in defining what constitutes income and outgo, and in describing the sources from which income is derived and the purposes for which outgo takes place. It will be necessary for us to look more closely at the precise meanings of income and outgo before reaching a conclusion in regard to the proper meaning of profits. In doing so, we shall differentiate between real income and money income, on the one hand, and real outgo and money outgo on the other.

The real income of a community is identified with the creation of new economic wealth through additions resulting from natural or human effort.[15] This creation of new wealth is brought

[14] *Efficiency and Scarcity Profits*, p. 131.

[15] A still further classification of wealth may be useful to us at this point. We may think of all economic goods as consisting of *natural* resources, including personal endowments, on the one hand; and on the other hand of all goods, the

about by new discovery, or by rearranging various previous relationships of already existing store with previously known natural resources, of which personal endowments are a part. Implied in the phrase "creation of new economic wealth" is the placement of new wealth-forms in hands that will derive utility from the wealth. The method whereby this real community income is apportioned to, or appropriated by, various economic constituents of the community is not essential to the argument at this point. It is enough to say that in a given period of time new economic wealth is created.

Theoretically, this wealth might all be extinguished in consumption at the instant of its establishment. But even in this event it would still constitute real income to the community. Practically, it is not so extinguished, and at the end of the selected income period a part of the newly established store or newly discovered natural resources will remain unconsumed. This residue may be the result of deliberately abstaining from using wealth, the use of which would automatically cause its extinguishment, or it may be the result of necessarily doing without such wealth because of physical inability to place it in a position to be consumed in the given period. Again, it may be the result of a previous social expression of preference for the creation of economic wealth in forms which it is virtually impossible to extinguish through use in the given period. The community and the individuals therein may express a preference for doing without goods in any of these three ways. All retard the extinguishment of wealth. While in a reasonably short income period the

utilities of which are made available by *human action* of either productive or abstaining character. The objective manifestation or embodiment of these natural resources and deferred utilities may be either corporeal or intangible in nature. In the case of wealth other than natural resources, there is involved a doing without at some past time of satisfactions, the realization of which would have resulted in the extinguishment of the good. We may call this fund of voluntarily foregone satisfactions a "store" of wealth. It has accumulated as the result of man-made decisions in the past. In a somewhat similar sense, natural resources represent a store of utilities that may or may not be realized in the future. But they are the result of natural causes, not of man-made decisions. It is not possible arbitrarily to increase them at will. We can thus define wealth as consisting of natural resources derived from nature, plus store derived from past decisions to produce and do without.

creation of new economic wealth is likely to exceed the extinguishment of such new economic wealth, previously established wealth may also be extinguished, so that no net increase of wealth results; or this older wealth may be extinguished so fast that a net decrease results. Such might be the case in the event of a highly destructive war or a deep depression.

Now let us make an equally logical identification of real outgo (community or individual *spending*, in non-money terms) with the extinguishment of economic wealth. Real income has been described as the establishment of new economic wealth. It follows that community real profits, the difference between real income and real spending, are positive, zero, or negative in a given period of time, according to the relationship of establishment to extinguishment. This is tantamount to saying that real community profits are the *net* change in real wealth within a given period of time. They are the net changes, plus or minus, to real wealth. In terms of the earlier nomenclature, in a given period real profits are the net change in the aggregate of utilities available to the community between the beginning and the end of the period. From the utilities added through the increase of real wealth, if any, must be deducted those inherent in the natural resources and store that are extinguished by use during the period.[16]

We have seen that titles to all wealth of economic significance are held by individuals or their representatives. The measure of an individual's *real* profit in a given period of time is accordingly measured by the increase or decrease in his titles to real wealth; not, however, by a change in the *money* value of the real wealth to which he has title. It makes no difference whether he holds large or small claims, whether he directs large activities or merely uses his crude abilities in digging a ditch; if his title to economic wealth increases in a given period of time he has realized a real profit, in the sense in which the term is here

[16] It has been suggested that real profits as here defined might be likened to *net* additions to real capital, including durable consumers' goods. We refer, however, to all extant wealth and not to any segment of wealth, no matter how inclusive that segment may be.

used. Additions to an individual's real wealth-titles are acquired through appropriation. This appropriation is sanctioned by discovery and by the ownership of other wealth-titles, including the ownership of one's own labor, that participate in economic activity. Deductions from an individual's real wealth-titles result, among other things, from use of the wealth serving as an embodiment of the title, in the sense that it is extinguished. All this may be summarized as follows:

Individual real profits: the net change in titles and claims of an individual to wealth.

Assuming a constant rate of extinguishment in both production and personal use, individual real profits are obtainable by increasing beyond the rate of extinguishment the real wealth to which one holds title through: (1) new production, (2) discovery, (3) trading, (4) forcible appropriation (political coercion, thievery, and the like).

There is a substantial difference between this definition of real profits and the usual connotation, which connects the word with uncertainty bearing or wages of management. Our definition of real income is not greatly different from the more familiar concepts. In defining real outgo or spending, however, we have departed more markedly from traditional practice. Spending is a term usually denoting a money transaction. We use it in the sense of extinguishing, consuming, or using up real wealth. The exchange of money-tokens against other tokens, intangibles, and corporeal wealth to be personally used is usually called spending. As we have attempted to show earlier in the study, this is the most important of economic operations in a community of specialized activities. We have, however, preferred to conceive of money as the embodiment of a general claim on future wealth. Its exchange against other embodiments of wealth does not extinguish that claim. The claim has merely been transferred, to live on in the other embodiments until they are extinguished by physical, technical, or economic forces. It is only under the most unusual circumstances that all of the claim disappears at the instant of an exchange of money against another object. A gradual reduction of the title is more likely. We have identified "spending" with this extinguishment, and not with the exchange itself, which we call *buying.*

REAL SAVINGS

It may occur to the reader that our definition of real profits is equally applicable to real savings. This is quite true in our terms, although the identification is not always made. Saving consists of doing without economic wealth which might be extinguished in use. When the community increases its wealth, either by abstaining from using wealth which is extinguishable through use or by arranging the production of wealth in bundles the full use of which cannot be realized except through time, it expresses a desire to do without. But we have included in real profits elements not usually included in savings, namely, *additions* to natural resources from discovery, and the establishment of new store. The term real profits, as here defined, carries a connotation of relativity. It refers to the relationship *between* the establishment and the extinguishment of economic wealth in a given period of time. Savings, on the other hand, is a term usually connoting a failure to extinguish. In many cases it refers only to abstinence as the converse of use, without explicit reference to establishment—to an absolute reduction or lessening of outlay.

If the provision of economic wealth to the community be made the point of departure, much may be said for making real savings and real profits equivalent concepts. There appears to be no quantitative difference between abstinence and establishment in providing economic utilities. If, in a given period of time, establishment A, less extinguishment B, equals real profits C, real profits and real savings D will be equal if savings plus extinguishment are made the sum total of establishment. That is,

$$A - B = C,$$
$$B + D = A, \quad \text{hence}$$
$$C = D.$$

The point to note in this simple identity is that the term real savings has been used here in a sense that includes not only abstinence but establishment as well. To make the argument clearer, let us revive that man greatly abused by economists, Robinson Crusoe. When he arrived at his island he brought with him a small supply of wealth consisting of some crude tools, several pieces of clothing, and his previously acquired physical and mental abilities over and above his natural endowments. Being alone, the appropriation of the island's accessible natural resources caused him no legal difficulty. His immediate problems were two: to sustain himself and to prevent, if possible, a depletion of his store. This he did by bringing his store into association with the natural resources of the island, in such a way that his creation of economic wealth was sufficient to compensate for that which was extinguished through use and natural causes. Let us say that in this period (following the initial discovery of the natural resources) there were no real profits and no real savings—no increase in wealth. The extinguishment of economic goods was exactly balanced by their establishment.

Suppose that in a second period, either by (1) exerting himself more (which implies that there was less than full utilization of his factors of production in the first period) or (2) by placing his store in a more productive relationship to natural resources (which implies a changed technique of production in the second period) or (3) by reducing the extinguishment of his store by using less, he adds to his claim on economic wealth. In the first and second instances he adds to his store of wealth without extinguishing less. In the third instance the same purpose is accomplished without producing more. Quantitatively, all come to the same thing, a net increase in store. Unless we wish to limit the meaning of the term real savings to a decrease in the absolute amount of extinguishment, the distinction between real savings and real profits, as here defined, disappears. The usefulness of a concept that connotes *only* a decrease in the absolute amount of extinguishment is questionable. Moreover, what is of more importance, it is apparently dangerous. A necessary corollary is that the appearance of real savings would imply a reduction in the demand for wealth that is currently being extinguished in satisfying personal desires. This is actually true, on the real level of analysis, only if a constant rate of establishment is assumed.

Equally true is the proposition that, given a constant rate of extinguishment, society can save more only if it establishes more wealth. Thus the use of the term savings to refer only to a decrease in the absolute amount of extinguishment is valid only in the limiting circumstances of a full utilization of productive resources. But granting a theoretically full utilization of productive resources, the only manner in which real profits, as here defined, can be increased is through a reduction in the rate of extinguishment. Thus the terms real profits and real savings are again found to be equivalent. They will therefore be treated as identical concepts in that which follows. This is the only sense in which the term savings has precise meaning. Money savings is an ambiguous term and will not be used in this study. Connotations which attach to it are more adequately covered by the concept of hoarding.

MONEY PROFITS OF INDIVIDUAL ENTERPRISERS

Having given a definition of real profits, we are now ready to pass on to money profits. In the simplified state of affairs provided by Mr. Crusoe on the island, no problems arise relative to specialization of activity, the location of wealth, exchange, or money, the common denominator in exchange. In modern societies, economic activity involves all of these elements. Owners of titles to existing specialized store and natural resources permit a part of it to be brought into association with other wealth forms for the production of specialized new store. Ownership to the new wealth accrues in amounts and forms greater than are desired by the producer for current extinguishment in personal use. But this fact, of itself, does not result in money profits.

It may safely be said that anyone engaged in productive economic activity is possessed of natural resources, as the term has been defined above. It is difficult to conceive of one so engaged not possessing some store. The past act of acquiring this store has placed the owner in the position of an enterpriser. All that are productively engaged, whether they be laborers, artists, managers, or what not, are enterprisers in this sense of the term. The success of the enterprise in acquiring title to specialized forms of wealth in excess of personal requirements will depend on whether this wealth can be exchanged, through money, for other desired economic goods, equivalent in real terms to the cost of the acquisition. Following Marshall, we shall consider money a true measure of these real quantities. The money that may be realized for this surplus wealth must equal or exceed the money cost of its acquisition, corrected for time adjustments, in order to make the enterprise of acquiring it financially successful.

The case of a well-paid corporation lawyer will serve to illustrate the phenomenon. Embodied in his ability is a large element of store, established through time and measured by the money expense of acquiring his training. This training represents the production of specialized wealth; its form is intangible instead of corporeal. Others engaged in the enterprise of acquiring titles to wealth must pay money to obtain its use. Likewise, a laborer learning a trade at the sacrifice of money income that might otherwise be realized is an enterpriser assuming the risk that he will be able later to exchange his specialized ability for money in excess of the money cost of its acquisition. When we consider the case of an individual engaged in the enterprise of producing corporeal wealth such as shoes or corn, the picture becomes more familiar. On this showing *everyone* productively occupied is an enterpriser engaged in the establishment of specific titles to new specialized wealth in corporeal or intangible forms.

The lawyer has acquired the ability to render more legal service than he can personally use, the laborer knows how to make more pins than he needs, and the producer of shoes and the grower of corn do not personally want their entire output. Hence at the same time that everyone is an enterpriser in acquiring claims to specialized wealth, he is also in the position of attempting to dispose of the major part of his titles for money as an intermediate step to acquiring wealth-forms in amounts which he desires. The risk of converting surplus non-money titles into money must be borne by those who first acquire possession of such titles.

The quantity of new particularized wealth produced by any one economic unit is greater, except in unimportant cases, than that desired by the production unit or its constituents. It follows that the greater part of all new store must be moved and placed at points where it will find those who wish it and there be exchanged not for other wealth but for the common denominator of all wealth, money. Even the problem of real profits becomes twofold under conditions of specialization of activity. First, the establishment of economic wealth must exceed the extinguishment of such wealth in a given period. Second, members of the community receiving surplus specific titles to new wealth, embodied in the first instance in specialized forms, must rearrange such titles. In theory, this might be accomplished by barter. In practice, it is done by exchanging the specific titles to specialized store for the general claim, money. Money may then be exchanged for titles to other embodiments of wealth, in amounts which the claimant most desires. This latter phase of the problem is that of converting real income, including real profits, into money or through money into other embodiments of wealth.

We may make an additional proposition. In an exchange economy all new specialized goods not directly extinguished in use, or title to which is not passed by gift, must exchange at least once against money, in the course of time, or they become worthless and cease to be economic goods. The unimportant exceptions to this proposition represent the isolated instances of barter, of interest principally to the collector of oddities. Since the owners of money are free to choose the particular goods and services for which they will exchange money, or to withhold their money from exchange, it is essential (assuming prices to be unchanged) that the goods and services be produced in forms and quantities that will induce such exchange. Upon this depends the ability of those who have received surplus specific titles to new economic wealth of corporeal or intangible nature to change their specific titles to the general claim, money, and through money to other embodiments which they desire.

A cobbler, for example, owns a bundle of specific titles to corporeal and intangible wealth, suitable for the production of shoes, a specialized product. When his product matures, he exchanges it for money. This he uses to acquire other corporeal or intangible wealth, to extinguish in personal use and to replace the store and natural resources extinguished in producing the shoes. The point of interest in this simple case is that *in the first instance* the cobbler's titles to new wealth are in the form of shoes in an amount exceeding his desire for shoes. For practical purposes, it is necessary for him to change the embodiment of these new titles to money before he can obtain corporeal wealth and intangibles for his personal use, or supplementary wealth to replace that extinguished in production. In the first instance, his income is received in shoes. Only at the second stage does he obtain money.

In the absence of reserves, he must obtain money for his shoes before he is able to obtain supplementary wealth to be used in further production. This is true, whether he is replacing wealth extinguished or obtaining additional wealth to expand the size of his enterprise. Suppose he adds a helper. Embodied in the helper is a familiarity with the rudiments of shoemaking. This, we have seen, is a part of store. The cobbler, under the conditions of our exchange economy, must pay for this store in money. Thus the helper receives his claim to new wealth in the form of money in the period under consideration, even though at an earlier period he (himself an enterpriser) received it in the form of a title to shoemaking knowledge.

A corollary to this proposition is that those who supply supplementary store and natural resources in the form of goods and services, to be used in a particular enterprise or production process, receive claims to new wealth embodied in money. This is true whether the wealth supplied be managerial skill, selling ability, common labor, or needed corporeal wealth. To the extent that such money claims are paid, the equity of the paying agent or enterpriser (in claims to the new wealth produced) is diminished. The money required to make these payments may have been previously owned, borrowed, or obtained in exchange for new production as it matures.

The agents making money payments in the process of establishing new specialized wealth, no matter what their activity may be, in the first instance receive their new titles in the form of the new wealth itself. Enterprises operating at a money profit, in the sense that they are maintaining or adding to their money claims, must be able to exchange their new production for money in amounts not less than equal to the amounts they pay to supplementary suppliers of the store and natural resources needed in the production process *and* needed to replace previously owned wealth that is extinguished in production.

The latter is largely a matter of depreciation and depletion reserves. In the absence of discovery, the replacement of previously owned wealth is somewhat analogous to payments to supplementary suppliers. The chief difference is that such wealth may be and commonly is stored, and production may continue for extended periods without its replacement. Or, as is the case with some enterprisers producing services, the production process may not result in an extinguishment of the owned wealth at all. If previously owned wealth that is extinguished in production must be replaced, the money reserves set up for this purpose are in substance unrecoverable money outgo, in the same sense as payments to supplementary suppliers. This is so, even though title to the money reserves may still vest in the enterpriser. He may divert it to personal uses or to uses other than the replacement of the wealth extinguished in previous production, but it is still a proper cost in the theoretical or practical accounting of his individual money profits.

Professor W. C. Mitchell has defined profits as "the difference between the prices which an enterprise pays for all the things it must buy and the prices the enterprise receives for all the things it sells." [17] Somewhat the same concept of money profits is held by Mr. P. C. Ghosh.

[17] *Business Cycles, the Problem and Its Setting,* p. 183.

> The expenses of purchasing the claims of other people who have cooperated in the production or acquisition of [the] new production are called costs. If the value of the new wealth so procured is higher than the costs of acquiring all foreign interests in it, the excess is termed profit. So profit is the excess of the selling value of any deliberately acquired property over the price of its purchase from proprietors.[18]
>
> . . . both capital (in the economists' sense of capital goods other than "land") and labour, in the form of investment and enterprise, earn profits.[19]

To the costs of purchasing all foreign interests should be added the cost, if any, of replacing previously owned wealth, extinguished in production. Except for this qualification, the concept seems not materially different from ours.

Let us review individual real profits to demonstrate their contrast with individual money profits. An individual's *real* profits are his net change in titles and claims to wealth, not, however, a change in the money value of his titles and claims to wealth. He may acquire new titles in various ways, by production, trading, discovery, or force. These titles may be extinguished by their use in acquiring new titles *and* by personal use. They may also be extinguished by natural causes, without reference to use.

An individual's money profit is measured by the increase in *the money amount* of his titles and claims to wealth, less the money amount of extinguishment involved in acquiring the new titles, but *not* less the money amount of extinguishment associated with personal use. A man may receive large money profits but never become rich if his rate of extinguishment *in personal use* prevents the accumulation of real profits.

The increase in the money amount of titles and claims to wealth acquired in production or, better, in enterprising, may be measured before or after the wealth has been exchanged for money. Good accounting practice prescribes the latter. Adopting the accounting practice, the money profit of an individual is the difference between the unencumbered money received *in ex-*

18 *The Theory of Profits*, p. 342.

19 *Ibid.*, p. 340.

change for wealth acquired in production, discovery, trading, and so forth, and the unrecoverable money paid to the supplementary suppliers of store and natural resources necessary to obtain title to the exchanged wealth. It is also necessary to deduct the unrecoverable money paid out to replace the previously owned wealth that was extinguished in acquiring title to the exchanged wealth. Summarizing all this in outline form, we have:

Individual money profits: the net change *in money amount* of titles and claims to wealth, without reference to extinguishment in personal use.

Assuming prices constant, such profits are obtainable by increasing beyond the rate of extinguishment *in production* the real wealth to which one holds title, through:

(1) New production, discovery, trading, forcible appropriation.

Assuming prices falling, such profits are obtainable by

(2) possession of money and perhaps (1) above.

Assuming prices rising, such profits are obtainable by

(3) possession of real wealth and (1) above.

It can fairly be asked here why consistency does not require us to measure individual money profits by the difference between the money received in exchange for new production and the amounts paid to suppliers of *all* supplementary wealth—that extinguished in personal consumption, as well as in acquiring new titles. Although logically tenable, the adoption of this conception of money profits would, in substance, encompass the totality of money flows. Moreover, it would not fit the usage of business life. The loss of title to wealth which has been acquired for personal use is generally described as consumption, or the spending of previously received money profits. The diversion of replacement reserves to personal uses, for example, comes under this heading.

This reasoning is consistent with accepted business practice. Suppose that a corporation sells $1,000,000 worth of shoes in the period of a year. During the same period it pays $700,000 to supplementary suppliers of store and natural resources and sets aside $100,000 to replace its own extinguished wealth. A money profit of $200,000 is realized. But this does not necessarily mean that the corporation itself holds direct title to $200,000 more of wealth at the end of the year than at the beginning. The $200,000 may have been distributed in dividends to stockholders who spend it, in the sense in which we have used that term. Or, if the profit was not distributed, the corporation now holds additional titles to wealth embodied in various forms, of which money may be one, of value equivalent to $200,000.

The corporation may have exchanged a part or the whole of its money profits for additional inventory or machinery during the year, but the money profits remain in its profit and loss account. If sales were $1,000,000, costs of production $800,000, and a new machine was purchased at a cost of $100,000, then total money income was $1,000,000 and total money outgo $900,000. Money profits are not $100,000, however, but $200,000. Money profits of individuals are not the difference between total money income and total money outgo incurred in production-distribution activities. Rather, they are the difference between unencumbered money income and unrecoverable money outgo so incurred, including in unrecoverable money outgo the reserves set up for replacement.[20]

AGGREGATE MONEY PROFITS

In the above we have discussed the money profits of an individual enterpriser. But our chief interest concerns the expansion and contraction of the aggregate of individuals' money profits, and the factors contributing to change in this aggregate.[21]

[20] This definition is valid for the corporate form of organization only if we deduct from unrecoverable money outgo that outgo which is represented by dividend payments.

[21] As the description progresses, the reader will find a degree of correspondence between our aggregate money profits and the familiar concept of national money income produced, when this is defined as the money value of goods and services produced. Our aggregate money profits are (1) the money value of all goods and services produced or discovered *and distributed,* and (2) the money amount of the net change in price of existing assets that have been traded.

In order to examine the problem of *aggregate* money profits, we shall resort to an analysis of several hypothetical situations. To simplify the matter, we shall assume that costs arising out of replacement requirements are zero. We have seen that the real profits of a community are determined by the net increments to real wealth resulting from the excess of production and discovery over consumption and loss due to natural causes. Under conditions of specialized activity, the creation of new wealth entails its distribution in amounts and at places where it will provide satisfactions. Thus is determined the economic well-being of the community. Conversely, changes in the economic well-being of the community, thus defined, are a measure of the sum-total of its positive or negative real profits. It does not necessarily follow that changes in the sum-total of money profits are correspondingly determined.

Case I, *in which there are no money costs of production.*—Suppose that three individuals, A, B, and C, all enterprisers, produce respectively food, shelter, and clothing; A produces the food, B the shelter, and C the clothing. Each output consists of 15 comparable units of real wealth.[22] In the same period of time required to produce this total of 45 units of specialized wealth, assume that A, B, and C each consume 5 units of food, 5 of shelter, and 5 of clothing. Then there will be no real profit, as this term has been defined. Each man will wish to replenish his store of wealth in proportions corresponding to those existing before its consumption. For instance, each will attempt to maximize his satisfactions by acquiring 5 units each of food, clothing, and shelter. It would not be so satisfactory to any one of them to have 4 units of food, 6 of shelter, and 5 of clothing, or any other arrangement of their corporeal wealth. It should be noted that in this simple situation A has no competitor holding a surplus

[22] No satisfactory method of measuring real wealth has yet been devised. Alfred Marshall made money the measure of real economic quantities, but this procedure is not available to us here, since we are attempting to find certain reciprocal influences between money and real wealth. Physical quantities are useless in measuring relative values, unless money, the common denominator, intervenes. It seems that we must resort to the discarded Benthamic calculus and speak of 15 units of pleasures, satisfactions, or utilities, as provided by each production.

of food for disposal, B no competitor for his surplus shelter, and C none for his surplus clothing.

Suppose further that the three enterprisers incur no money costs in the production of their respective specialties, the only costs being those of personal efforts involving no money outlay. Each, as the result of his productive activity, is possessed of specialized wealth capable of rendering maximum satisfactions when equally distributed among the three. Relative to the products of the others, each desires but one-third of his total production. The problem here is patently one of distribution.

This distribution is usually accomplished through the medium of money. We may hence add to the assumptions of our hypothetical case by supposing that each enterpriser, in addition to holding title to specific specialized wealth in excess of his personal desires, holds title to money in the amount of \$5. The total stock of money is then \$15. The price level may be assumed as \$1 per unit of real wealth. A, B, and C meet to readjust their surplus specific titles. Are aggregate *money* profits possible under these circumstances?

A exchanges 5 units of food with B for \$5
5 units of food with C for \$5
receiving \$10
B exchanges 5 units of shelter with A for \$5
5 units of shelter with C for \$5
receiving \$10
C exchanges 5 units of clothing with A for \$5
5 units of clothing with B for \$5
receiving \$10

When these exchanges are completed, the wealth will have been readjusted so that each has a quantity of specific titles in the forms most desired. The surpluses arising out of specialized production will have been eliminated by distribution through the mechanism of money. Each enterpriser still has the same amount of real wealth, but now instead of 15 units of food or 15 units of shelter, his wealth consists of 5 units of food, 5 units of shelter, and 5 units of clothing. In the process of adjusting claims, each received title to \$10 and surrendered title to \$10, thus holding title to the same number of dollars at the end as at the beginning, namely, \$5. Title to \$30 was exchanged in all. There being \$15 owned by the three, the turnover velocity was 2.

Now let us see where money profits enter the situation. It will be recalled that money costs of production were ruled out by assumption. Since each enterpriser received and surrendered the same amount of money, namely, \$10, and ended with the same amount as he started with, namely, \$5, it might appear that there were no profits. The capacity of the real wealth to provide satisfaction has been increased substantially as the result of its distribution, but, in essence, this merely reinstated the utilities lost through consumption. No change in aggregate titles to real wealth has taken place. Correspondingly, no change in aggregate titles to money has taken place, nor has any one individual increased his particular title to money. There would accordingly seem to be no real profits or money profits, but, as frequently happens in economic theory, the most obvious answer is incorrect on closer observation. In our simple hypothetical case there have been *money* profits, even though there were no *real* profits. Money profits are not measured, either in practice or in theory, in terms of the number of money units to which an individual or the community has direct title.

Careful consideration of the illustration will reveal that money profits were here simply a bookkeeping or accounting phenomenon, based, in the first instance, on the flow of real wealth in distributive channels.[23] Enterpriser A, not desiring his surplus food for personal consumption, exchanges it for \$10, which he uses to purchase shelter and clothing. He enters in his ledger, under profit and loss account, receipts on sales, \$10; cost of pro-

[23] When we introduce money costs, money profits will also be seen to be associated with the flow of real wealth in what are generally described as productive channels. It will be recalled that we have conceived of all producers as enterprisers. This being the case, the money costs of production to one enterpriser are nothing more than the reciprocal of the distribution of specialized wealth by another enterpriser. Such specialized wealth includes labor, as well as other intangible and corporeal wealth.

duction, nil (since by assumption no money costs were incurred); money profit, $10. The same procedure will be followed by enterprisers B and C. Aggregate money profits of $30 result from the readjustment of specific claims. The purchase of shelter and clothing by A, of food and clothing by B, and of food and shelter by C requires the surrender of title to $10 in each instance. But this loss of title to $10 is not a deduction from money profits. It is rather a personal use of previously received money profits. We may conclude that if output, which has cost no money to produce, is distributed, money profits will ensue, regardless of whether there is a net increment or decrement to real wealth. Granting that prices are constant, it is evident that the aggregate of these money profits will depend upon the amount of wealth to be distributed and upon the completeness of its distribution.

Case II, *in which costs of production are introduced.*—What happens to money profits, in our hypothetical case, when we remove the assumption that there are no money costs of production? Let us suppose that the total of real wealth produced and consumed is the same as before, and that all other circumstances are also the same, except that A spends part of his time helping B to make shelter and C to make clothing; B does the same for A and C, and C for A and B. Each contributes proportionally to the others' activities, and receives a total money wage of $4 for his labor, $2 from each of his employers. Wage payments of $2 are received by A from B; he also gets $2 from C. The total wages he receives are $4; so likewise with B and C. The money cost of producing their specialties is now $4 for each of the three. This is unrecoverable money outgo, incurred in producing new wealth. In each instance, under the circumstances of our assumptions, the outgo is exactly matched by an unencumbered money income of $4 of wages received. When our simplified economic men meet to exchange their surpluses of specialized wealth, each will receive from his surplus corporeal wealth a money profit smaller than before by $4, which represents the cost of production. But the total money profit of each will have been enhanced by wages previously received.[24] From his enterprising activity relative to corporeal wealth, each now receives a money profit of $6 instead of $10, or a total of $18 for the three instead of $30. But each has previously received wages of $4 for his enterprising activity relative to intangible wealth (labor), or $12 in all. Thus for the entire production-distribution period, the sum-total of money profits is, as before, $30. But a change in the situation has occurred with respect to the turnover velocity of money. In the previous instance, there were $30 of money exchanges against real wealth. There being a total stock of $15 in all, we got a velocity of 2. In the present instance, we still have $30 of exchanges against corporeal wealth at the time of readjusting surpluses (the commodity price level is unchanged), but also $12 of previous exchanges against labor, another form of real wealth. There being a total of $15 in all, velocity is increased from 2 to 2.8 (42 ÷ 15).

If, instead of each man's receiving $4 of wages and sustaining $4 of costs, each received and paid say $8 in wages, the velocity figure would jump to 3.6 for the production-distribution period. Aggregate money profits would remain the same at $30, consisting of $24 of wages received and $6 from the production and sale of surplus corporeal wealth. Thus we may conclude, under our assumption of constant prices, that either changes in the organization of business life, which result in more or fewer money payments being necessary to bring a given output to final disposal, must be reflected in the volume of money exchanges, or else the aggregate volume of money profits will be altered. Money costs of production are in part a function of the organizational characteristics of economic life.

Case III, *in which the price level falls.*—If we retain our assumptions of a constant corpus of real wealth and complete distribution of specialized surpluses, but assume a decline of 50 percent in the price level, we get a marked effect on money profits and the velocity of money. We may first take the case

[24] Here we are tacitly assuming, for the purpose of simplification, that the acquisition of ability to labor is costless in terms of money, although this is not actually the case.

in which there are no money costs of production. Now each unit of real wealth exchanges for 50 cents. Each individual receives and parts with $5. Title to an aggregate of $15 changes in all. There being $15 outstanding, the velocity of money is now one instead of 2. Money profits are reduced from $30 to $15. But there has been no change in the production, distribution, and consumption of real wealth. Conversely, if prices are increased to $2 per unit, there will be a proportional increase in money profits without a change in the real wealth quantities.

The influence of price changes may be seen in another way. If each of our three men possesses a multiple-purpose tool, and if these tools are traded in circuitous fashion at rising prices during the production period, money profits will rise without reference to the amount or prices of our real wealth units. Again, money profits will decline if the tools, which are comparable to previously existing titles (our secondary circulation), are traded at declining prices. In the first situation, money profits might accrue, even though no new output were forthcoming. In the second, there may be no money profits, even though production and distribution continue. But normally there is new output coming along and, under conditions of competition, which we shall examine later, the prices of previously existing titles tend to be strongly influenced by the prices of new wealth production.[25]

When we introduce money costs of production into the situation, the only additional effect is, as before, on the velocity of money. If each individual receives wages of $4 in all and defrays a $4 money cost of production, velocity jumps to 1.8. Aggregate money profits remain at $15, of which $3 are realized from corporeal productive enterprising and $12 from labor. Changes in the level of prices thus have an immediate effect on the aggregate of money profits, which is independent of their influence on the production and distribution of real wealth (which of course they influence in actual experience).

Case IV, *in which aggregate real profits are introduced.*—

[25] *Supra,* pp. 73–74.

In the preceding hypothetical cases, we assumed a complete distribution of the surpluses of specialized wealth, and no change in the amount of its production relative to its consumption. We shall retain the assumption that distribution of surpluses is complete, but shall now drop the assumption that the number of units of wealth produced is equal to that extinguished. Let us assume that in a production-distribution period the rate of consumption remains constant, but that instead of 15 units of food, shelter, and clothing being produced by A, B, and C respectively, each now produces 18 units of his specialty. In other words, a *real* profit accrues to the three citizens of our hypothetical community during the period. Each of the three extinguishes 15 units of corporeal wealth and establishes 18 units during the period. The real profit is measured by the net increment of the 9 additional units of real wealth. Does the money value of the 9 additional units change the sum-total of money profits?

To make valid our assumption of complete distribution, it must now be provided that each of our economic men wants 6 units of food, of shelter, and of clothing, whereas 5 units sufficed him before. Of their respective specialties, each now retains 6 units for himself and exchanges 12 units for money. We may start, as before, with the assumption of no money costs of production. Each individual holds title to \$5 of money, and the price level is established at \$1 per unit of real wealth. When the individuals meet to exchange their surplus specialties,

A exchanges 6 units of food with B for \$6
6 units of food with C for \$6
receiving \$12

B exchanges 6 units of shelter with A for \$6
6 units of shelter with C for \$6
receiving \$12

C exchanges 6 units of clothing with A for \$6
6 units of clothing with B for \$6
receiving \$12

Each individual owns but \$5 when the trading begins. Unless these transactions take place simultaneously, or unless they take place concurrently in amounts of 5 real wealth units or less, a temporary extension of "credit" or debt will be necessary. More will be said of this phenomenon in a succeeding chapter on debt. We shall assume for the moment that the exchanges are accomplished in a manner that does not require the extension of debt.

According to the reasoning of the earlier cases, the aggregate money profit resulting from the distribution is now $36. There has been a net increase of 9 units of real wealth, of which 3 in all were retained by producers (one by each producer). It follows that, granted a constant price level and complete distribution of surpluses, money profits have increased concomitantly with real profits. But the *increase* in money profits is equal not to the money price of the entire net increment, but only to the money price of that part of the *new* increment of real wealth which is distributed. This is still quite different from saying that the sum-total of money profits is determined by the money value of net increments to real wealth. The velocity of money has increased from 2 to 2.4. The same conclusion regarding money profits is reached when we introduce money costs of production in these circumstances. Money profits from corporeal productive activity contribute $24 and wages $12, if each individual receives and lays out $4 in wages as before. In this case, money velocity increases to 3.2. Thus with constant prices and flexible money velocity, the aggregate of money profits fluctuates with the change in that part of real profits which is represented by *distributed new production.*

Correspondingly, if real profits had been increased by a reduction in consumption from 5 to 4 units while distribution remained at 30 units, as in Case I, there would have been no change in the aggregate of $30 money profits indicated in that illustration.

Case V, *in which money velocity does not respond.*—But what will be the result if, under conditions of increased production with no money costs, money velocity does not change, but remains at 2 as was the situation in Case I. There are now 36 units of corporeal wealth to be exchanged against money.

This can be accomplished only if the price per unit of corporeal wealth is reduced from \$1 to \$0.83⅓. If each individual exchanges 12 units of surplus wealth for \$0.83⅓, he will here realize a money profit of \$10—a total of \$30, not \$36. The aggregate of money profits thus remains the same as before the increment to real wealth accrued. In this instance, money profits bear no direct relation to the change in the corpus of real wealth. No increase in aggregate money profits results if an increase in real wealth is reflected in a proportionate lowering of money prices.

Let us now introduce a \$12 money cost of production into the situation in which real wealth surpluses increase from 30 to 36 units while money velocity remains at 2. In this event the price per unit of real wealth drops to \$0.50. Money profits now stand at \$18 instead of \$30—\$12 received in wages, and \$6 representing the difference between the price received for surplus corporeal wealth and the money cost of its production. Thus, in the absence of compensating movements in the velocity or amount of money, an actual decrease in money profits will result, in spite of the increase in the production and distribution of real wealth. The decrease results from a change in the organization of production without a compensating change in the rapidity of the use of money. The reader can now readily see for himself how, granting a rising price level, complete distribution, and an appropriate adjustment of money velocity, a money profit can be realized in the hypothetical illustration, irrespective of changes in real profits.

We may summarize some of the conclusions to be drawn from these hypothetical cases. Changes in the aggregate of money profits do not seem to be immediately connected with changes in the corpus of real wealth available to the community. That is to say, money profits and real profits, as we have defined the terms, do not necessarily fluctuate together. In practice, they are likely to fluctuate in the same direction. Money profits are positively influenced by the amount of wealth distributed and the money prices at which it is distributed.

The amount of money exchanged for new wealth output may be conditioned by many factors. Important among them are the changing number of money units available for use and the use of money for other purposes. There may be a revision in the organization of business life, requiring more or less money payments to bring new output to fruition—a revision in what we have called the interstitial circulation. Or there may be more or less money used in what we have called the secondary circulation, which includes transactions in previously existing titles such as land, securities, second-hand goods, and so forth. Or money may not be used at all, in which event it is hoarded.

Before leaving the question of the aggregate of money profits, we must look at the implications first of faulty distribution, then of competition. The latter raises the question of why there should be such a thing as money profits at all.

Case VI, *in which new output is not fully distributed.*—We return for the moment to the circumstances of Case I, in which 45 units of wealth are produced, of which 30 are available for distribution as unwanted surpluses. The price level is \$1 per unit of real wealth and there are no costs of production. Everything is as before except that B, who produces shelter, goes on a diet. He now wants only 4 units of A's surplus food, whereas under conditions of perfect distribution he wanted 5 units. Under these conditions the men meet to trade their surpluses as follows:

A exchanges 4 units of food with B for \$4
5 units of food with C for \$5
receiving \$9
B exchanges 5 units of shelter with A for \$5
5 units of shelter with C for \$5
receiving \$10
C exchanges 5 units of clothing with A for \$5
5 units of clothing with B for \$5
receiving \$10

Money profits, or the money receipts of each (there being no money costs of production), now total \$29 instead of \$30 as in

Case I. A finishes the period in possession of \$4, B of \$6, and C of his original amount of \$5. A has one unit of unwanted food. The velocity of money changes from 2 to 1.9 +.

It may be objected that this is not the way the thing would work out in practice—that A would lower the price of food until B was induced to give up his diet. This is not necessarily true, however. Under monopoly conditions A would rather reduce his production to 9 units as the lesser of two evils, if an effective inducement price fell below \$9 for the 10 units of his surplus food.

Let us next suppose that B can be induced to give up his diet if food is available at \$0.90 per unit. Then we return to a condition of complete distribution of surpluses of specialized production, but under somewhat different circumstances than those of Case I. Money profits would again total \$29 (as before, \$9 to A and \$10 each to B and C), but B and C would each have a \$9.50 money outgo, whereas they surrendered title to \$9 and \$10 respectively when A held the price of food at \$1 per unit. Our clothier, C, is the beneficiary of B's recalcitrance, followed by A's effort to effect a complete distribution of his surplus.

To say that B wants no more food at any price is to assume satiety of certain economic wants—always a dangerous assumption.[26] In the absence of satiety, B's failure to take 5 units of food at \$1 per unit implies that he prefers to use some of his money titles for other purposes, in the present or in the future. If the desire is to use the money titles for other purposes *in the present,* there may or may not be a compensating increase in the money profits of C, who produces clothing. It will depend on A's reaction to an advance in the price of clothing at a time when his money profits are declining. The situation is substantially that of a misdirection of production. The chances are that aggregate money profits will be reduced, as well as re-allocated. If B's desire is to use a part of his money titles for other purposes

[26] Professor R. T. Bye goes to some length to question the assumption, which he finds in H. G. Moulton's *Formation of Capital.* Bye, "The Process of Capital Formation and Its Relation to Inequality," *American Economic Review,* XXVI (Dec., 1936), 607–17.

in the future, there is a very definite reduction in the aggregate of money profits. This results in what we shall define in the next chapter as hoarding.

Case VII, *in which competition is introduced.*—It remains to examine the implications of competition. The tendency of profits to diminish with the intensity of competition is well recognized. At this point it will be necessary to complicate our hypothetical illustration slightly by assuming that in addition to A, B, and C, A^1, B^1, and C^1 respectively produce food, shelter, and clothing of comparable kinds; we shall also say in similar amounts. The assumptions of Case I will be continued, including that under which each individual is possessed of title to $5 at the outset. Hence there are now 30 units of money instead of 15. Six instead of three individuals now meet to exchange their surpluses of specialized production, two with a surplus of food, two with shelter, and two with clothing. None has sustained a money cost of production. All have sustained a psychic cost of production in the effort expended.

The prices at which they will offer their respective wares will depend on the prices which they anticipate paying for the surpluses of others. To each of them this will measure the value of money, that is, its purchasing power. Hypothetically, it would make no difference to A whether his money profit was $10 and the price of clothing and shelter $1 per unit, or $50 with the price of clothing and shelter $5 per unit. In real terms he is getting the same thing, 5 units each of clothing and shelter for his own use, in return for the effort expended in producing 10 surplus units of food. Factually, his attitudes are not so readily adjusted to price changes and he is likely to look to changes in the amount of his money profits rather than to changes in their purchasing power.

But in the long run, the value of money relates the *psychic effort-cost* of each of our hypothetical men to the amount of money profits necessary to make it worth while to produce a given surplus. The money profits of any one of the six cannot drop below this point long without resulting in a diminution of his output. Under conditions of perfect competition, the aggregate of money profits, working through the value of money, will be just sufficient to overcome the psychic cost of a given output. When our six economic men meet, no one will for long offer his surplus at a price below this point. Should he do so, he will find that when the exchanging is finished the ultimate fruits of his economic activity were not worth while. Should he offer his surplus at a price above this point, he would not be able to dispose of his wares at all.

The *ultimate* determinant of the aggregate of money profits is thus the psychic resistance to production reflected through the purchasing power of the profit realized, or the price level. But this resistance to production is of a sluggish nature, changing slowly with techniques and habits.

The more immediate determinants of changes in the aggregate of money profits are the amount of new output (not the amount of real profits, which are quite a different thing), the extent of the distribution of the new output, and the price level at which it is distributed. That is to say, aggregate money profits fluctuate with the amount of new output of all kinds distributed and the price level at which it is distributed. And the amount of new wealth distributed will depend upon two factors, the amount of new wealth produced and the extent to which this new wealth is distributed.

It is additionally true that money profits might fluctuate through trading previously existing wealth at increasing or decreasing prices. Practically, the prices of previously existing wealth seem to be more determined by prices for new output than determinant of new output prices.[27] It follows that variations in money profits from trading in old wealth will tend to change in the same direction as money profits from new output.

The most variable of the determinants of aggregate money profits and the one which will concern us for the most part is the changing value of money itself. Given a constant state of

[27] *Supra*, pp. 73–74.

technological development, changes in the psychological resistances appear to be evolutionary in nature. Changes in the value of money and concomitant changes in the sum-total of money profits are more volatile.

PROFITS AND PRODUCTION

When money profits are so defined that they may accrue to individuals as the result of productive use of or dealing in wealth in any of its multifarious forms—abilities, land, and other types of corporeal and intangible wealth—they are found to be associated with economic phenomena additional to pure production and the so-called capital goods that underlie it. They are found to rest *ultimately* on the psychological resistance to production. But the proximate and significant cause of their variation in the aggregate is the changing level of prices. This is an integral part of the problem of distribution quite as much as of that of production.

Money profits, as the term is used in this study, are approximately associated with distribution or exchange, even though they ultimately rest on the resistance to production. Real profits, on the other hand, are proximately associated alike with production, distribution, *and consumption.*

John Stuart Mill apparently had real profits in mind when he wrote that profits arise not from the incident of exchange, but from the productive power of labor.

> If we look more narrowly into the operations of the producer, we shall see that the money he obtains for his commodity is not the cause of his having a profit but only the mode in which his profit is paid him.
>
> The cause of profit is that labor produces more than is required for its support. . . . The reason why capital yields a profit, is because food, clothing, materials, and tools last longer than the time which was required to produce them; so that if a capitalist supplies a party of laborers with these things, on condition of receiving all they produce, they will, in addition to producing their own necessaries and instruments, have a portion of their time remaining, to work for the capitalist. We thus see that profit arises, not from the incident of exchange, but from the productive power of labor; and

the general profit of the country is always what the productive power of labor makes it, whether any exchange takes place or not.[28]

Even though Mill, in the term "general" profit, may be referring to what we have described as real profits, his definition seems to be deficient in the rejection of exchange as a contributing factor. We have seen that under conditions of specialized economic activity, the economic well-being of a community is determined not only by the relation of establishment to extinguishment, but is supplemented by the distribution of existing wealth in amounts and at places where it will provide the greatest satisfactions. The cobbler is not able to derive satisfaction from the shoes he produces over and above his personal wants until he has exchanged them for other titles to wealth of a character which he desires. This, we have seen, is in practice accomplished through money. Again, Mill overlooks the fact that an "incident of exchange" takes place when the capitalist contracts for his labor.

A very different view of profits than that given us by Mill is held by Mr. Ghosh:

> The difference of profit from other incomes cannot be discerned . . . in the . . . process of production. From the viewpoint of society, the peculiarity of profit lies in the . . . *method* of this income, and not in the nature of the services that help . . . to turn out a product. Profit is not the result of the "industrial process," it is rather the result of the mercantile process.[29]

We conclude that changes in the aggregate of money profits are not *immediately* the result of changes in new wealth production. Nor are they *directly* related to changes in the economic well-being of the community—what we have called positive or negative real profits or real savings. It has been seen that money profits can theoretically accrue, even though no new wealth is being produced.

As a practical matter, new corporeal and intangible wealth is always being produced, and under competitive conditions the price level of this new wealth, times its quantity at the point of

[28] *Principles of Political Economy*, p. 416. [29] *The Theory of Profits*, p. 12.

final buying, is most important as a determinant of changes in the aggregate of money profits. The prices of second-hand goods, tokens, and land, all of which are subsumed under our secondary circulation, tend to follow final new wealth prices. Likewise, the prices at which interstitial payments are made in the production process are influenced by final prices, though the *number* of such payments is not.

The reason for the appearance of such a thing as money profits at all rests in the psychological resistance to production. The value of money relates this psychic effort-cost to the amount of money profits necessary to make it worth while for enterprisers to produce a given surplus. In practice, the situation is not as neat as this. Enterprisers do not look at the value of money and then decide how much specialized wealth they must produce in order to obtain a money profit sufficient to satisfy a predetermined want. Enterprisers anticipate more or less money profit and adjust their production to such expectations without very much, if any, reference to the probable cost of satisfying their future wants—which are vaguely determined at best.

THE ALLOCATION OF MONEY PROFITS

We may now consider the allocation of this changing aggregate of money profits to persons in the community. Let us return to have one last look at our hypothetical men, who now compete with each other in their specialized fields. It may be that A^1 incurs no great psychic cost in producing food, while A finds it a struggle. Soon A^1 will be producing more, and A less. Since they both receive the same price, it follows that the one becomes a rich man receiving larger money profits, the other a poor man receiving smaller money profits. But there need be no change in the aggregate money profits of the two taken together. Likewise, possession of an improvement in technology, whereby a given amount of psychic effort-cost will produce a greater quantity of real wealth, will provide its owner with a greater *share* of the aggregate of money profits. It does not necessarily follow that the introduction of the improvement will result in an increase in the aggregate of money profits.

The introduction of money costs into the situation merely advances the situation to an earlier period. Those receiving money wages will compare them, through the value of money, with the psychic resistance to work. Under conditions of perfect competition in the labor market, the supply price of labor is thus established. Those paying money wages will add them to a quantity measured by the money value of their own psychic effort-cost in order to get the supply price of their surplus output.

Another factor enters into the allocation of the aggregate of money profits. This concerns the holders of money as a class and the holders of real wealth as a class. A changing price level not only varies the aggregate of money profits, but changes the distribution of the variable aggregate. The allocation of a changing aggregate of money profits to individuals of the community is not necessarily proportionate, *pari passu,* to their respective productivities. Substantial disparities between productiveness and proportionate allocations arise from changes in the price level, even though changes in price relationships may reflect reasonably competitive conditions.

The changing real wealth value of the total money stock is a function of changes in the total supply of real wealth itself, and of changes in the amount of real wealth which people are willing to do without in order to hold title to money. The changing real wealth value of a single unit of money is a function of these two factors plus a third, the changing number of units into which the total money stock is divided. It would take us too far afield to attempt even an approximate determination of the modifications in the relative status of holders of money and of real-wealth titles which arise out of price-level changes. All that can be said here is that (1) the aggregate of money profits rises and falls with movements in the price level, and that (2) rising prices are beneficial to holders of real wealth and injurious to holders of money. The position is reversed when prices fall. When holders of real wealth exchange it for money in a period of rising prices, they are said to have realized a windfall money profit. When holders of money exchange it for real wealth in a similar period, they are said to have realized a windfall money loss.

If the price level is stable, the holders of wealth may receive a money profit from the exchange of new wealth production which they sell, while the holders of money receive no money profit. If the price level is rising, the holders of wealth receive their profit from the exchange of new production *plus* a windfall money profit, while the holders of money sustain a windfall money loss. If the price level is falling, the holders of wealth receive their profit from the exchange of new production but will sustain a concomitant windfall money loss, while the holders of money receive a windfall money profit. If prices fall rapidly enough, production-distribution profits may be wholly appropriated by the holders of money. The expectation of falling prices, it will be recalled, has been mentioned as a motive underlying the desire to hold money that frequently is stronger than the desire for liquidity per se in the assets owned.

SUMMARY

The historical development of the term profit has led to as much confusion as enlightenment in regard to the forces making for an increase or decrease in the aggregate of money profits. Not until the time of J. S. Mill was there an explicit distinction made between profit as interest and interest as a part of profit. In the course of time, interest has been removed from the category of profit, leaving payments for uninsurable risks or payments for superintendence, or both, as profit. But these shares are now considered residual payments, just as profit receivers in the old sense were once made the residual legatee in distribution theory. In their due turns, rent and wages came to occupy this enviable position, so that, in a sense, the circle is now complete. This is true, in spite of the fact that nearly fifty years ago it was pointed out that the laws of rent are applicable to all incomes and that none may be treated as a residual, any more than the others.

We have approached the question of changes in the aggregate

of money profits through a study of income and outgo. Whose income and outgo, and what kind of income and outgo are questions essential to the problem. The first has been answered by saying that everyone engaged in economic enterprise, of which the producing of goods and services is the most significant phase, will be a recipient of profits if his enterprising is successful. Profits are not limited to any particular group or groups in society.

The real profit or loss of a *community* is measured by the net change in its material well-being, that is, by the difference between real incomes (additions to economic wealth from whatever source) and real outgo, or spending (the extinguishment of economic wealth). An *individual* in the community will realize a real profit or loss as his titles to real wealth increase or decrease. This does not refer to a change in the money value of his titles to real wealth, which is quite a different thing. Real profits and real savings are identical, but it should be noted that, in this sense, increased saving does not imply necessarily a lessening of extinguishment in personal use, except in the limiting circumstance of full utilization of production factors.

The real profits and savings of an individual vary with the relationship between establishment and extinguishment. But the money profits of an individual vary with the relationship of establishment, on the one hand, and *only* that extinguishment incident to establishment, on the other. Although deductible in measuring individual real profits, extinguishment in personal use is not a proper deduction in the case of individual money profits.

Every enterpriser in the community may obtain money profits. Most enterprisers are productively engaged. Their profit is received in the first instance in the form of a specialized good or ability, in an amount exceeding that which they wish to use personally. Because the owners of money are free to choose particular goods and services, enterprisers must assume the risk of converting their surplus goods and services into money at a rate that will make their enterprising worth while. If a profit is realized, the money received must exceed the amount paid to supplementary supplies of store and natural resources used for production and replacement.

Individual money profits are thus the difference between unencumbered money income and unrecoverable money outgo incurred in enterprising activities, of which production-distribution activities are by far the more important. Other forms of enterprising are discovery, forcible appropriation, and trading against price movements. If the money amount of one's titles to wealth changes as the result of enterprise in any of these activities, a money profit or loss will be realized. This is irrespective of what may have happened to the aggregate money amount of one's titles to wealth, which is a quantity that is affected by extinguishment in personal use, as well as by one's enterprising activity.

If prices are constant, changes in the *aggregate* of the community's money profits will be proportional to the amount of surplus wealth made available for distribution through production and discovery, and the completeness of the distribution of such surpluses. But this is not to say that changes in the aggregate of money profits are proportional to changes in real profits, even under conditions of constant prices. Again, it is incorrect to say that aggregate money profits are determined by the money value of all new increments to wealth. If prices are constant, aggregate money profits will change proportionately with that part of new wealth output which is distributed. But if prices are not constant, changes in money profits will bear no direct relation to changes in the amount of new wealth added to the corpus of wealth. Money profits and real profits do not necessarily fluctuate together, but are likely to fluctuate in the same direction.

Changes in the costs of production may result from changes in price relationships and from changes in the interstitial organization of economic institutions. Since all enterprisers are potential profit receivers, an increase or decrease in total costs of production will not change *aggregate* money profits, if there is no change in the amount of new wealth output and if the new situation is compensated by an adjustment in the amount of money or its use so as to keep prices constant.

If other things are equal, there is a proportional increase or decrease in aggregate money profits with a change in the price level. But it does not follow that under constant prices there will be no change in money profits. If the supply of new goods and services fails to coincide with demand in detail, aggregate money profits may decline, owing to faulty distribution. The difficulty can be overcome in a perfectly competitive society by a readjustment of price relationships within a constant price level, in which event there will be a reallocation of money profits without a change in their aggregate amount.

Under perfectly competitive conditions, the aggregate of money profits will be reduced to a point at which they will be just sufficient to make enterprising worth while. The sufficiency of this aggregate will be measured by its purchasing power, as reflected in the price level. It thus appears that the ultimate determinant of the aggregate of money profits is a psychic resistance to enterprising, reflected through the purchasing power of the profit realized. The immediate determinants, on the other hand, are the amount of new output, the extent of its distribution, and the price level at which it is distributed. But changes in the amount of new output alone do not determine the changes in aggregate money profits. Money profits are proximately related to more than pure production and its associated capital goods.

We may now attempt answers to the questions presented in the initial pages of this chapter. Unless money profits are treated as a residual, there appears to be no reason to conclude that they would be nonexistent in conditions of perfect competition. Nor is the sum-total of money profits seemingly measured by or proportional to the new increments to real wealth resulting from the excess of production and discovery over consumption. But money profits are decidedly influenced *by the money value* of new increments of wealth resulting from the production *and* distribution of wealth in all its various forms. The money value of these increments we have seen to be a function of the extent of the new output distributed, as well as of the price level.

While increments of wealth may be realized from the productive system, consumption may be going on at such a rate that net decrements to the economic well-being of the community will result. But this does not mean that the aggregate of money profits would be negative. Hence we conclude that it is theoretically possible for a community with a declining level of economic well-being to experience an unchanging or even an increasing aggregate of money profits if (1) new increments of surplus wealth are resulting from production, if (2) distribution is reasonably thorough, and if (3) the price level behaves appropriately.

The extent of distribution of new wealth production has been cited as *one* of the contributing elements in the maintenance or expansion of aggregate money profits. The *expectation* of money profits, on the other hand, was cited in Chapter V, "Liquidity Preferences and Cumulative Change," as a factor of outstanding importance in determining the disposition of people to exchange money for real wealth, hence in determining the extent of distribution. A part of the production of surpluses of specialized wealth is desired for personal use. A part is desired for use in producing still more specialized wealth. A third and probably less important part is desired for holding as a store of value through time, without reference to use or production. Variations in the aggregate demand for wealth to be added to the productive capacity of the community appear to be roughly correlated with the dominant expectations of money profits. Variations in the aggregate demand for wealth to be personally used appear to be less closely correlated with the dominant expectations of money profits, but nevertheless appear to move in the same directions.

It follows that if the extent of new output distribution is one of the determinants of money profits and if the expectation of money profits is one of the determinants of the extent of distribution, an adverse development in either may start a cumulative series of actions and reactions between the two. We have seen that changed desires for liquidity are also a factor tending to accelerate or retard the exchange of money for real wealth. But liquidity desires increase with falling profit expectations. Both tend to decrease the amount of new output distributed. Conversely, liquidity desires decrease with rising profit expectations. Both tend to increase the amount of new output distributed. Here we find another of several relationships associated with liquidity, in which the forces act in a cumulative fashion to amplify and extend a given direction to business movement. The discussion in the preceding chapter related liquidity desire to changes in expectations of the drift of future prices. It was also held that liquidity desires are related to expectation of money profits. It was recognized that the argument relating liquidity desires to expectations in regard to price could carry conviction *only* if money prices and the aggregate of money profits tend to fluctuate in the same direction. This we have attempted to demonstrate in the present chapter.

We may now turn to a closer examination of the circumstances surrounding the exchange of money for real wealth.

VII

HOARDING[1]

WHEN THE AGGREGATE AMOUNT of money is constant, the total amount of money *available* to exchange against new production of all kinds is equal to all the payments that have been made in the production and distribution process and which have not yet exchanged for wealth again. This is nothing more than a restatement on the money level of analysis of J. B. Say's well-known law that supply creates its own demand. But the total amount of money *available* to exchange and the amount *actually* exchanged are not necessarily equal. The total actually exchanged is the amounts that have been so paid, minus or plus an amount representing hoarding, dishoarding, or their equivalents. Hoarding thus becomes a matter of outstanding importance.

HOARDING DEFINED

There is an implicit time factor in all hoarding. Except for the negligible amount of money inadvertently lost or destroyed, no hoarding is associated with eternity. On the other hand, possession of money under any circumstances implies possession through a time interval; it cannot be merely instantaneous. Therefore, all money is in a sense hoarded for a period. We will describe the elongation or contraction of the *average* period of holding money as an act of hoarding or dishoarding. The sub-

[1] Throughout this chapter we shall assume that the amount of all debt, including money, is constant. Later, when studying debt, we shall continue to assume that the amount of money is constant, but shall permit debt other than money to vary in amount. When we are finally ready to bring the banking system into our analysis, we shall remove the assumption of constant money.

stance of the concept of hoarding under conditions of a constant amount of money is found in a time lag—in the direction and rate of change in the average time interval elapsing between one exchange of money against non-money assets and the next exchange.

Hoarding has at times been used to refer to an accumulation of larger money balances by the public as a whole. E. F. M. Durbin appears to fall into this error in defining the term as follows:

> . . . if the public as a whole decides to hold a larger sum of money in the form of bank notes . . . it *hoards cash.*
>
> The second and less obvious form of hoarding is *deposit hoarding.* In this case . . . certain individuals decide to accumulate larger bank balances.[2]

Perhaps Mr. Durbin refers to a *desire* for more bank notes relative to bank deposits, or the converse, within the limits of a constant stock of money made up of interchangeable bank notes and deposits. But his accompanying text does not indicate this to be the case. It seems to indicate that the public can acquire title to a larger aggregate of money in the form of either bank notes or deposits when it desires, the form depending on the preference of the moment. To the extent that the public can control the amount of money, such a concept might be appropriate. Since the public cannot exercise this control except in a perverse manner, however, as we shall see later, and since title to all extant money is already vested in someone, the concept is actually abortive. It is held to be so by J. M. Keynes:

> . . . if we mean by "hoarding" an actual increase in cash-holding, it is an incomplete idea—and seriously misleading if it causes us to think of "hoarding" and "not-hoarding" as simple alternatives. For the decision to hoard is not taken absolutely or without regard to the advantages offered for parting with liquidity;—it results from a balancing of advantages, and we have, therefore, to know what lies in the other scale. Moreover, it is impossible for the actual amount of hoarding to change as a result of decisions on the part of the public, so long as we mean by "hoarding" the actual holding of cash. For the

[2] Durbin, *The Problem of Credit Policy,* pp. 92–93.

amount of hoarding must be equal to the amount of money . . . ; and the quantity of money is not determined by the public.[3]

Keynes goes on to say that the only thing that a desire on the part of the public to hoard can accomplish is to raise the interest rate to a point at which the aggregate desire to hoard becomes equal to the available cash. In a subsequent article he elucidates the proposition still further:

> It is precisely because the facilities for hoarding are strictly limited that liquidity preference mainly operates by increasing the rate of interest.
>
> . . . I am convinced that the monetary theorists who try to deal with it (the propensity to hoard as a factor operating to reduce the "velocity" of money) are altogether on the wrong track.
>
> When . . . liquidity preferences are sharply raised, this shows itself not so much in increased hoards—for there is little, if any, more cash which is hoardable than there was before . . . as in a sharp rise in the rate of interest. . . . A rise in the rate of interest is a means alternative to an increase of hoards for satisfying an increased liquidity-preference.[4]

Keynes appears to be correct in holding that a desire on the part of the public for more money to be used as a store of value will not be accompanied by an increase in its supply. That he is right in holding that a desire to hoard will leave the amount of money and its velocity unaffected, and will evidence itself solely through a rise in the money rate of interest, appears highly debatable. As will appear later, a desire on the part of the public to hold titles to more money for a longer period of time is more than likely to be accompanied by an absolute decrease in the amount of money available for holding. This is evidently the case when demand deposits are included in the supply of money. Moreover, the tendency of the amount of money and its velocity to increase and decrease together seems to indicate that the desire to hoard money is accompanied by a retardation in its velocity. We shall return to these points later.

[3] Keynes, *The General Theory of Employment, Interest and Money*, p. 174.

[4] Keynes, "The General Theory of Employment," *Quarterly Journal of Economics*, LI (Feb., 1937), 210–11.

Building on the earlier work of D. H. Robertson, Professor J. W. Angell has developed a more useful concept of hoarding. Robertson, on the assumption that no money income can be disposed of at the instant of its receipt, divides the course of monetary circulation into theoretical periods, in which money can pass from hand to hand once but not twice.[5] Any one of these periods he calls a "day." An individual's money stock on any one day is his money income on that day plus the unspent money with which he starts the day. His money stock on any one day becomes his disposable income on the next day. Now hoarding, as defined by Robertson, takes place when a man takes steps to raise the proportion between his money stock and his disposable income. He feels that this definition makes the term equivalent to a decrease of the velocity of money against final output[6]—sometimes described as income velocity—as contrasted with exchange velocity or transactions velocity.

Instead of using Robertson's indefinitely short period, postulated as a day, Professor Angell resorts to average time periods in describing these phenomena.[7] The total stock of money is made up of two quantities, idle balances and active balances. Idle balances are money held by an individual or a business enterprise longer than what is for that individual or firm one normal maximum income-expenditure period (in our terminology, an income-purchase period). Active money is that part of the total money stock which at any given moment has been in the holder's hands for a period of time less than his habitual or normal maximum income-expenditure period.[8] An individual is hoarding if his idle balances, thus defined, are increased. The

[5] Robertson, "Savings and Hoarding," *Economic Journal,* XLIV (Sept., 1933), 399 ff.

[6] *Ibid.,* p. 401.

[7] Angell, "The Components of the Circular Velocity of Money," *Quarterly Journal of Economics,* LI (Feb., 1937), 224–71 *et seq.* Also see his more extended treatment, "The General Dynamics of Money," *Journal of Political Economy,* XLV (June, 1937), 289–346.

[8] It should be noted that money in Professor Angell's financial circulation is included in idle balances. The "expenditure" is therefore that on goods and services and not on titles and claims to old assets.

community is hoarding if the aggregate of idle balances, thus defined, is increased.

When the amount of money is assumed to be constant, its velocity may be changed by (1) a revision of normal payment habits or (2) a change in behavior relative to normal payment habits. The first of these factors, which implicitly rests on extant forms of business organization as well as on the mass psychology of an era, appears to be a more or less stable quantity in short periods. The second of these factors affecting velocity is simply equivalent to a short-period change in the proportions between what has been defined as active and idle balances—in short, hoarding and dishoarding. Thus, given a constant amount of money, a change in velocity may reflect other factors in some degree, but its greatest significance is that it reports an increase or decrease of hoarding in this meaning of the term. This definition of hoarding and dishoarding is substantially equivalent to that presented earlier in this chapter, namely, an elongation or contraction of the *average* period of holding money.[9]

The infinitive, to hoard, is sometimes given the same meaning as the infinitive, to hold. It is not at all unusual to hear of a holding of gold or silver, or of any form of wealth for that matter, referred to as a hoard. Accordingly, there is ample justification for using the term with this broad connotation, if that be desired. It will be more useful for our purposes, however, to restrict the meaning to possession of title to money for more than one average or normal period. By an increase of hoarding will be meant an increase in the period of time during which the average unit of money changes hands once. A decrease of hoarding will refer to a shortening of the period.

FACTORS SUBSTANTIALLY AKIN TO HOARDING

Even though there be no variation in the period of time during which the average unit of money changes hands, and hence

[9] If we drop the assumption of a constant number of money units, we must say this somewhat differently. Hoarding and dishoarding then describe the expansion and contraction of the typical time in which a unit of money exchanges against non-money assets.

no hoarding per se, it does not follow that the amount of money exchanged for final output is likewise unchanging.

In any one period of time, title to certain money units does not change hands at all. Title to other money units changes hands in forwarding goods from the raw material to the finished state. Such payments are a part of our interstitial circulation. Title to still other money units changes hands in dealings which are not immediately connected with the question of new wealth. This is the so-called secondary circulation, which includes transactions in all previously existing property titles. Money that is not exchanged for any type of title to wealth in a normal time period is hoarded money. A further examination must now be made of money in the secondary and interstitial circulations that is neither hoarded nor used in final buying.

The crux of the matter, as we have seen, is the steady flow of money against final new output. Factors that interrupt this flow, whether they result from hoarding or from changes in the amount of money used for purposes other than final buying, are sources of disturbance. Professor W. C. Mitchell made the point well when he wrote: "The flow of money must be kept adjusted to the counterflow of goods [and services] offered for sale, in detail as well as in gross." [10]

The flow of the money payments that result in final buying is not simple. Many interstitial transactions occur and result in a total volume of transactions which far exceeds the value of the finished goods and services distributed. As the aggregate of such payments increases or decreases, in consequence of changes in business organization, payment habits, or changes in the number of economically employed factors, the requirements of what we call the interstitial circulation, and of what Keynes has called the industrial circulation,[11] are altered.

Still other money payments are associated with trading in previously existing wealth-titles, without specific reference to the movement of wealth through the productive and distribu-

[10] Mitchell, W. C., *Business Cycles, the Problem and Its Setting,* p. 139. "And services" added by the present author.

[11] Keynes, *Treatise on Money,* Vol. I, Chap. XV, *passim.*

tive system. For the most part, these previously existing property titles consist of securities, used or second-hand goods, and titles to non-reproducible wealth such as land. The absorption of more or less of the flow of money payments by the secondary circulation may be at the expense of the interstitial circulation, or of what we have called final buying, or of both. If so, it may be the substantial equivalent of hoarding in reducing the velocity of money against final new output.

With an amount of money which is constant in the aggregate of its uses, changes in the amount exchanged for other than final new output thus will affect the rate of final buying in a manner similar to hoarding. The character of the vertical and horizontal organization of business influences the number of interstitial money payments required in the universe of economic activity. The size of business units relative to markets is a phase of this same thing. An expansion of the number of independent firms induced by the prospect of profits (an aspect of what Hawtrey now calls the widening of capital equipment) [12] likewise affects the requirements of interstitial payments. Changing techniques of production or methods of distribution, requiring an increase or reduction in the number of money payments, are similar in their effects. Lastly, increased production at a fixed price is analogous to these several factors in increasing the interstitial requirements of the total money circulation. Thus the nature of the flow of money payments to final buying is found to rest in part on the organization of business and business firms and the habit of trading in previously existing titles to wealth.

THE TIME PERIOD OF THE PROCESS OF FINAL BUYING

Cutting across these factors, the flow of money payments to final buying is influenced in another way by the institutional organization of titles to wealth. This is a phenomenon associated with the organization of wealth-titles into marketable

[12] Hawtrey, *Capital and Employment,* p. 36.

tokens, a topic described at some length in Chapter III, "The Institutional Organization of Wealth Ownership."

The desire to hoard is the desire to hold money either because of lack of conviction regarding the future, or because of a conviction that money provides a more suitable means of conveying titles to wealth into the future than other types of titles. To the extent that the desire to hold money reflects uncertainty, the desire to hoard and the desire for more liquid assets are analogous. But other means than the acquisition of money are available for satisfying the urge to acquire more liquid titles, depending on the degree of intensity of the desire for liquidity. The acquisition of some types of non-money titles involves a longer time lag in the flow of money to final buying than others. Hence changed liquidity desires may change the rate of final buying, either by causing an increase or a decrease of money hoarding or by inducing the purchase of certain types of non-money titles rather than others.

The procedure by which money is exchanged for that part of final new output which is to be used in further production is lengthened by the use of tokens. Money may exchange for tokens not once but many times before it ultimately exchanges against final new output. If changed liquidity desires express themselves in a greater demand for non-money marketable tokens relative to direct investment, a more circuitous journey of money to its final exchange against wealth will result. A direct exchange for final new wealth is an instantaneous exchange of money and is what we have previously defined as final buying. An indirect exchange through tokens may involve a substantial period of time. An individual may exchange money for a bond, passing the money to a dealer. The dealer may pay the underwriter, the underwriter may pay the issuer, and the issuer may finally exchange the money for real wealth or he may hold it as a cash reserve for an indefinite period.

On the other hand, the existence of tokens may be beneficial in another respect. The owner of money may not wish to part with it at all, if a readily marketable token is not available in lieu of a direct purchase of wealth. All tokens have been designed to increase liquidity. Some, such as short-term debt, accomplish this purpose so successfully that they are as satisfactory, or nearly as satisfactory, as money proper. But they are unlike money in that their acquisition may make money available for ultimate exchange against wealth. It may be argued that tokens, to the extent that they may provide a high degree of liquidity *and* a means to final buying at the same time, exercise a beneficial influence on the economy. In this respect the institutional arrangement of wealth-titles permits the satisfying of moderate liquidity desires without recourse to holding money. The continued exchange of money against final new wealth, so important to the economic health of the community, is thereby expedited.

If the share market is for practical purposes unavailable to a corporation wanting new assets, it may resort to the sale of thirty-year bonds; if the long-bond market will not take the issue, it may resort to the sale of a five-year note. In any of these events the corporation secures money, for exchange against wealth, which might not be available for exchange if the original owners of the money were confronted with the alternative of exchanging it directly for real wealth or withholding the money from exchange. In these several ways changes in liquidity desires, working through the institutional organization of property titles, influence the time-duration of the flow of money to exchange against final output and thus change the volume of hoarding or its equivalent.

The average length of the journey of money to exchange becomes unimportant when once established, but changes in its length constitute the equivalent of a change in the amount of hoarding, if the amount of money and its aggregate velocity in its various uses is constant. Changes in the length of the journey may or may not follow a moderate change in liquidity desires. There is no basis for assuming that the journey through the acquisition of more liquid short-dated debts is longer than that through the acquisition of less liquid long-dated debts. On the contrary, because of the tendency to earmark the use of funds when granting short-dated loans, the length of the journey, when this type of paper is acquired, may be the shorter.

In addition to the absorption of money in the process of trading in tokens and the different time periods of the journeys of money through tokens to final buying, there is still another way in which the existence of tokens may influence the flow of money to final buying. We have seen that tokens may possess inherently different liquidity characteristics than the wealth with which they are associated—they are impersonal, divisible, mobile, and traded on highly organized markets. A lack of precise knowledge of the status of their associated property is one evidence of market imperfections. Hence extant appraisals of tokens tend to fluctuate around the ultimate values of their associated properties. The creation and subsequent correction of these dispersions exercise an important psychological effect on the community's expectation of future money profits, both upward and downward, and hence tend to encourage or discourage final buying.

HOARDING AND LIQUIDITY DESIRES

We have previously seen how Keynes has related the concept of liquidity preference to the demand for money—or more accurately, to the propensity to hoard money.[13] He has also been interpreted as identifying the term with shifts in demand along the scale of assets of greater or less degree of liquidity. But the former concept is much the more explicit in Keynes's work. Of the two, the second, which identifies changes in liquidity desires with shifts along the scale of assets of differing degrees of liquidity, or more exactly of differing degrees of likeness to money,[14] seems to be a more realistic description of economic behavior. Moreover, it does not exclude a propensity to hoard money—that is, to hold title to money as a store of value for a

[13] *Supra*, pp. 28–30.

[14] An asset becomes the more like money the greater the degree of liquidity it possesses and, second, the more likely it is to maintain a value stable in terms of money.

longer than normal period, since money may be thought of as one of the various types of assets available.

All titles to wealth are owned by someone, and changes in public desires cannot immediately change the character of such titles. Through time, their character can be and has been changed materially. But, in periods for which changes in dominant liquidity desires are important (it may be a matter of weeks or months), non-money wealth-titles are comparatively inelastic as to supply. Corporeal wealth is usually more elastic as to supply than intangible wealth and tokens. But liquidity considerations play a less significant part in the decision to acquire corporeal wealth than is typically the case with tokens.

An important exception must be made to this proposition. We shall see in succeeding chapters that the supply of short debt, including money, does fluctuate readily with changed liquidity desires. But it fluctuates perversely, decreasing in supply with an increase in its demand as a store of value.

Since a change in liquidity desires expresses itself in a revision in the scale of preferences for all types of titles to wealth as well as for money, an alteration in the price structure, as well as in the price level, is likely to occur. The full nature of such alterations is too complex to be even approximately determined. They may be different at different times, depending on the strength of liquidity desires and the extant organization of wealth-titles. The more readily marketable the title and the less its tendency to fluctuate in money price, however, the greater will be the relative demand for it and the higher its relative money price when liquidity desires rise. Among other changes, short-term bonds will be preferred to long-term bonds, with a resulting increased spread between short and long interest rates.

The literature on the question of relative fluctuations between long and short rates is not very enlightening.[15] One reason

[15] Discussions of this subject may be found in Hawtrey, *Capital and Employment*, pp. 197–99; Hawtrey, *A Century of Bank Rate*, Chaps. V, VI; Hicks, "Mr. Keynes and the 'Classics': A Suggested Interpretation," *Econometrica*, V (1937), 154–55; Lavington, "Short and Long Rates of Interest," *Economica*, IV (1924), pp. 291–303; Pigou, *Industrial Fluctuations*, pp. 275–77; Riefler, *Money Rates and*

for this is that the relative behavior of long and short interest rates is intimately related to the peculiar characteristics of the money markets within which they happen to be quoted. A full discussion of the behavior of interest rates must await a description of the behavior of debt and the characteristics of our extant banking system. We may suggest at this point, however, that the controlling factors can be subsumed under (1) the demand for debts to own (which is another way of saying the supply of money to loan) and (2) the supply of debts to sell (which is another way of saying the demand for money to borrow). Old debts are bought and sold. And new debts are created and paid. Both operations influence the movements of interest rates.

Buyers of old debts and makers of new loans are substantially free to select the kind of debt instrument compatible with their then existing liquidity desires. Sellers of old debts and new borrowers of money are not so free. Especially in the case of new loans is the type of debt instrument decreed by (1) the disposition of the lender and (2) the purpose for which the money is acquired, and, to a lesser extent only, it should be noted, by the liquidity desires of the borrower. We may conclude that the demand for old and new debts to own is a stronger controlling factor than the supply of old and new debts to sell, in determining the relative movements of long and short interest rates. The demand for debts to own responds, as the demand for any other type of asset, to changes in liquidity desires. The stronger the liquidity desire, the greater will be the demand for short-dated debts relative to long-dated debts. *Ceteris paribus,* the short rate will decline relative to the long rate.[16] In

---

Money Markets in the United States, Chap. I and *passim;* Sayers, *Modern Banking,* pp. 151–56.

[16] There is a qualification to this proposition which is highly important historically. It is not so important at present, although it may become important again. If the banking system is "completely loaned" and there ensues a period in which business commitments require new loans that are unobtainable or hard to obtain, there will then be a financial panic in which the short interest rate may very readily *advance* relative to the long rate, even though liquidity desires are increasing. Long before this period arrives, the short rate may have advanced relative to the long, but this is as it should be. A business expansion is typically accompanied by lessened liquidity desires, and this is what the greater-than-proportional increase in the short rate reports, except in the above situation.

the absence of full utilization of the banking system's legal lending power, that is, so long as the banking system may conveniently expand its loans, then the spread between short and long rates serves as a convenient indicator of the state of liquidity desires.

Of the objective manifestations of changed liquidity desires, i. e., money hoarding—changes in the corpus of aggregate debt, and changes in relative demands for assets along the scale of their liquidity characteristics—the latter is the most easily ascertainable. Prices of more money-like short loans and less money-like long loans are quoted daily and, subject to the above qualification, reflect the third of these manifestations of a change in liquidity desires. This comparison of long and short rates must be made of loans of similar quality, that is, of comparable risks so far as the obliger's ability to service the loan is concerned. It must not be confused with the comparison of yields of prime and second-grade loans of similar maturities used by Col. C. E. Ayers of the Cleveland Trust Company as an "index of confidence." [17] We shall return to this question of interest rates and their relation to liquidity. A full treatment must be reserved until we have dealt with the subjects of debt and the banking system.

A shift in the type of assets desired by the community as a result of changed liquidity desires may result in a number of things. It may result in a propensity to hoard money if the liquidity desires are strong. In the next chapter we shall examine another phase of this shift in demand along the scale of assets, i. e., the desire of the owners of debt to exchange their debts for money by calling the debts for payment. But if the shift in liquidity desires is a moderate one and takes place slowly, the shift *could* be satisfied completely by a bidding up of the prices of more money-like assets relative to the less money-like. It does not *necessarily* follow that a retardation would take place in final buying. For instance, we have seen

[17] The Cleveland Trust Company, *Business Bulletin,* Vol. XIX, No. 2, Feb. 15, 1938.

above that the length of the journey of money to final buying through short-dated loans typically is no longer than through long-dated loans. But the desires for more or less liquidity appear to be volatile and strong. Moreover, they usually express themselves in all of three ways: a propensity to hoard money, a disposition to call debt for payment, and a change in the price relationships of all assets in favor of the more liquid. On balance, these phenomena are almost certain to cause a decline in the amount of final buying.

In the present chapter we have assumed that the amount of all debt, including money, is constant. A description of the full impact of changing liquidity desires must await a discussion of the significance to final buying of a changing corpus of debt other than money on the one hand and of a changing supply of money on the other. But hoarding may take place under the present assumptions. If the number of money units is unchanged, a change in their velocity reports an increase or decrease in hoarding. This increase or decrease in the use of money will take place in all parts of the economy, thus tending to boost or depress general prices. Part of the change in the rapidity of money use will be in final buying, where it will most effectively influence the production and distribution of new wealth.

Under our assumed conditions, as liquidity desires increase, hoarding in the form of a decreased velocity of money takes place, general prices sag, and the amount of final buying diminishes, possibly in physical volume as well as money volume. Aggregate money profits decline, and liquidity desires increase, thus completing the circle. Again we find a potential set of cumulative forces. Once a disturbance is initiated, increased liquidity desires may result in hoarding, a decrease in final buying, a decline in the price level, a drop in the aggregate of money profits, a further increase in liquidity desires, and so forth. As we shall see, the behavior of debt and the banking system accelerates rather than mitigates these cumulative pressures.

These forces act and react upon one another in a cumulative manner. Hence they cannot be placed in any unchanging ordered sequence of their development. To analogize, we cannot say that price determines demand and demand then fixes supply, or that supply sets price and price then fixes demand. So it is with fluctuations in liquidity desires, hoarding, final buying, the price level, money profits, and the corpus of debt. Fluctuations in these phenomena cumulatively act and react upon one another, not in an ordered sequence, but concomitantly. Moreover, they provide no self-correcting mechanism within themselves. The thought suggests itself that the means of the reversal perhaps may be found in connection with the initial source of disturbance. This is a subject to which we shall return.

OTHER INDUCEMENTS TO ACQUIRE MONEY TITLES

Money may be hoarded if there is a sharp rise in the community's desire for liquidity. But this is not the only reason for acquiring title to money, even though it appears to be a very significant one. For instance, it is an understandable custom for individuals possessed of titles to non-money wealth, which they are holding as a store of value divorced from personal use, to test from time to time their ability to get back to money by calling loans for payment, checking price lists, and so forth. If the use of the particular bundle of property in which they have vested their claim on future goods has been misdirected, it will be found to have a lessened money price, and perhaps a longer time will be required to get back to the reduced amount of money which now measures their claim. At the later period the degree of liquidity may have become less than had been anticipated when the title was acquired. Certainly the original value judgment would have been bad. The psychological effect of a number of such publicized experiences on the community's urge to hold more liquid titles, or even to hoard, is self-evident. On the other hand, if this liquidity and value-testing is successful, it is likely to be followed by the repurchase of non-money titles, without any impairment of economic activity.

Another reason for acquiring title to money, not of great interest to a discussion of hoarding, is that intermediary acquisition of money is the normal business means of shifting from one ownership position to another. In short, money is the medium of exchange. The obtaining of money for *use* or for the successful *testing* of non-money assets is likely to be followed by a compensating reëxchange of money for wealth. In a society of many persons, the process tends to become continuous. But a return to money because of greater uncertainty, or of general expectations of a declining price level, or because of previous unsuccessful liquidity testing is not accompanied by subsequent reëxchange of money within the average income-expenditure period. It is chiefly these latter phenomena that give rise to hoarding.

SUMMARY

The substance of the concept of hoarding under conditions of a constant number of money units is found in the direction and rate of change in the average time interval elapsing between one exchange of money against non-money assets and the next. This is to say that under similar conditions a change in the velocity of money reports an increase or decrease of hoarding.

We have applied the term hoarding exclusively to the holding of money. But this does not imply that an increase of hoarding is accompanied by an increase in cash balances and vice versa. As we shall see, when liquidity desires increase and there is a greater demand to hoard money, the actual number of money units available for holding is likely to *decline*.

Hoarding is chiefly important because of its influence on final buying. Money which is not hoarded but which is used in the interstitial and secondary circulations, that is for purposes other than final buying, may be a source of difficulty in much the same manner as hoarded money. The nature of the flow of money payments to final buying is determined in part by the organization of business and business firms and by the habit of trading in previously existing titles to wealth. Changes in the amount of the interstitial and secondary circulations, if they are uncompensated and are at the expense of final buying, are much like changes in hoarding in their end result. There will be an interference with the production and distribution of new wealth output.

The flow of money payments to final buying is influenced in still another manner. The acquisition of some types of assets involves a longer time-lag to final buying than others. For instance, the direct buying of real wealth involves a shorter time-period than indirect buying of real wealth through tokens. Changing desires for liquidity may change the amount of final buying because assets that involve different time-periods have different liquidity characteristics. There are different channels of the flow of money to final buying, and shifts in liquidity desires affect the selection of the typical channels used. Lastly, final buying may be changed because tokens are actively traded in markets without perfect knowledge, and sometimes their money prices significantly depart from basic values. The corrections of these dispersions may set in motion psychological forces which will change the amount of final buying.

With the exception of money and short debt, which fluctuate perversely in amount, the supply of wealth titles is comparatively inelastic in periods of weeks or months. But changes in liquidity desires are important in these intervals. Consequently, with an increase in liquidity desires, demand for particular kinds of assets shifts, relative to the supply, and the more money-like assets increase in price relative to the less money-like. Except in abnormal circumstances, the yield on short paper falls, relative to that obtainable on long paper, and the spread between the two provides a rough measure of liquidity desires. The active markets for debts of comparable quality and different maturities make this a more easily ascertainable and sensitive measure of liquidity desires than the unreliable data regarding money hoarding and changes in the corpus of debt.

Although changes in relative prices of more and less money-like assets of comparable quality seem to provide a suitable means of measure, they must not be taken as the sole result of a change in liquidity desires. A change in the corpus of debt and hoarding are concomitants. In the succeeding chapter we shall study the consequences of a changing corpus of debt. In the present chapter the significance of hoarding is found in its effect upon changing the amount of money exchanged for final new output. An increase in liquidity desires, if sufficiently strong, will be accompanied by hoarding, a decrease in final buying, a falling price level, a decline in the aggregate of money profits, and a further increase in liquidity desires. Again, we find a set of cumulative forces associated with shifts in liquidity preferences.

VIII

THE CORPUS OF DEBT

MONEY HAS BEEN DESCRIBED as a form of debt, namely, general claim debt. Other tokens evidencing debt are more or less like money, depending on their characteristics. Short-term debts are not greatly unlike money in their liquidity characteristics. Also, since they are payable in money in the near future, their value tends to remain close to the value of money. Changes in the total amount of debt, including money, are of importance to our problem. We shall first examine the significance of changes in the amount of debt other than money. To simplify this endeavor we shall continue the assumption, carried through the last chapter, of a constant number of money units.

THE RESPONSE OF OWNERS AND OWERS OF NON-MONEY DEBTS TO ALTERED LIQUIDITY DESIRES

When liquidity desires on the part of the public increase, individuals attempt to exchange their less money-like titles for ones which are more money-like. Among such transactions are those by which the owners of specific debt attempt to exchange it for the ownership of general debt, or money. This may be accomplished either by selling the title to the specific debt or by calling the debt for payment in money, if its provisions will permit. In substance, this behavior on the part of *owners* of debt is nothing more than a phase of a general movement in the community toward more liquid titles. But it has a peculiar significance of its own. It results in contraction of the sum-total of debt. Unlike other titles to wealth, the aggregate supply of debt titles does respond in short periods to changes in liquidity desires. It makes no difference whether the owner of the debt is a bank or an individual. This is the conclusion when the matter is looked at from the standpoint of creditors, the owners of specific debts. What are the conclusions when the matter is viewed from the standpoint of the *owers* of debts, or debtors?

The ownership of a title to wealth is the ownership of an asset. Debts owned, including money, are a part of such assets. But for every debt owned there must be a debt owed; for every individual or participating creditor, an individual or participating debtor. The liquidity status of an individual or a legal personality is determined in the first instance by the liquidity characteristics of assets owned, including debts. In the second instance, it is determined by the *liquidity characteristics* and *money amount* of assets owned, relative to the *maturity schedule* and *money amount* of debts owed. A change in an individual's liquidity status may be brought about either through a change in the nature of his assets per se, or through a change in the nature and amount of assets and liabilities relative to each other.[1]

The several processes concerned with the changing of the nature and amount of assets and liabilities, respectively, may be independent of one another, or they may be coördinated as reciprocal phases of the same general phenomenon. In three instances, in which these processes are independent of one another, they need not involve a net change in the amount of debt which an individual or legal personality owes.

1. Suppose an industrial concern succeeds in disposing of a part of its plant for money. If the money price realized for the plant is the same as the price at which it was carried in the concern's accounts, and if we assume that this was a true value, then there is no change in the money amount of assets. Nor will a change result in the amount or nature of liabilities. Only a change in the nature of assets will result. But the liquidity status of the concern will be improved.

2. Again, the concern may receive unencumbered money in-

[1] *Supra*, p. 16 *et seq.*

come in excess of unrecoverable money outgo. In this event it may add to its assets without substantially disturbing its liabilities or the nature of previously held assets. Conversely, negative money income may cause a deduction from assets, independent of changes in the amount or nature of previous liabilities. The liquidity status of the concern will be altered in each instance, even though no change may have taken place in the amount or nature of liabilities.

3. Lastly, the nature of liabilities will be altered without changing their amount and without disturbing the nature or amount of assets, if the due dates or interest rates of the concern's debts are altered by agreement or by law.

Three other means of altering the asset-liability relationship are available. All of these, in contrast to those previously noted, involve a change in the absolute amount of liabilities, or debts owed.

1. If our business concern uses the funds from its accrued net money profits to pay a part of its debt instead of adding to assets, a change in the asset-liability relationship, with somewhat different implications, will result. A reduction takes place in the amount of liabilities, independent of the amount and nature of previously held assets and without disturbing the nature of the remaining liabilities. An improved liquidity status for the concern is the result.

The other cases in which the asset-liability relation may be altered involve contemporaneous and dependent movements in the amounts of both assets and liabilities.

2. Suppose that instead of using the proceeds from the sale of a part of its plant for the purchase of raw materials, the concern uses them to pay a part of its debt. The nature of the remaining assets and liabilities need not be affected, but the amount of both will have changed, and in equal measure. In this instance there is a payment of a debt through a corresponding reduction of assets. In the earlier instance the debt payment was accomplished through the use of profits, without decreasing the amount of assets. Both operations involve the

payment of a debt and both result in an improved liquidity status for the firm.

3. Of equal interest is the case in which the asset-liability relationship is altered through increased borrowing. When additional liabilities are incurred through increased money borrowing, there must be a concomitant change in the amount of both assets and liabilities. Debt creation results, instead of debt payment, and the concern becomes less liquid.

This reasoning, illustrated by the case of an industrial firm, is applicable in appraising the liquidity status of any person, legal or natural, who owes debts. From it we may conclude that the means available to *debtors* to improve their liquidity status, with an increase in liquidity desires, are highly likely to involve a payment of debt on balance. We have previously seen that an increased desire for liquidity on the part of *creditors* does result in the reduction of debt. Thus it follows with a high degree of certainty that debt will be paid on balance, with an increase in liquidity desires. For converse reasons, debt will expand on balance, with a decrease in liquidity desires.

THE PAYMENT AND ESTABLISHMENT OF DEBT

Most debts are evidenced by marketable token-instruments, in which it is stipulated that the debt shall be discharged by the payment of money at a definite time. The amount of such money to be paid is fixed, and the place of payment determined. But all debt instruments are not so written. Conspicuous exceptions to this general rule will readily suggest themselves. British Consols and French Rentes have no maturity date and are presumably intended to remain debts in perpetuity. Loans to brokers on stock-exchange securities in New York are made payable at any time on the lender's demand. Many real-estate mortgage loans, such as some of those in Connecticut, are written without a maturity and are redeemable at the lender's option. Instruments such as shares with a fixed dividend payment guaranteed in perpetuity occupy a marginal position between debts and equities. The most significant form of debt not possessing a fixed maturity is money. We have previously described money as the debt of the issuer in the first instance, and in the second instance as the measure of the debt of the community, in terms of real wealth, to all the holders of money. Debt other than money is dischargeable in money. Money as debt is dischargeable in real wealth.

Although there are these sundry types of debt that lack a fixed maturity date, it may be observed that, even among these forms, most are payable at the creditor's demand. This, together with the fact that the greater part of debt has a definite maturity, no doubt has contributed to the ready acceptance by business men and economists of the axiom, "debt must be paid." A tacit corollary to this is that insolvency will follow if debts are not discharged at the time and in the manner provided in the instrument or by law. There can be no question of the verity of this proposition when we apply it to the case of an individual or legal personality. It is when we attempt to apply it to the community at large that a new set of complications arises.

R. G. Hawtrey put the point very well in stating that "Every day new debts are created and old ones are discharged, but these changes only modify and do not destroy the identity of the corpus of debts, which continues in being from day to day." [2] It is with the net changes in the size of the corpus of debts that we are ultimately concerned when studying the question of debt from the standpoint of the cumulative aspects of liquidity theory. We have seen that a greater desire for liquidity on the part of a creditor may result in the calling of his loan for payment in money if its provisions will permit; or, if it matures, he may decline to relend his money. A greater desire or need for liquidity on the part of a debtor may or may not result in a reduction of debt, depending on the means that are available to him for adjusting the relationship of his assets to his liabilities, in nature and amount. But, for the reasons previously stated, it is so highly probable as to be a practical certainty that the sum-total of all debt, that is, the corpus of debt, will con-

[2] Hawtrey, *Currency and Credit*, p. 212.

tract when the liquidity desires of the community are increased and will expand when they are lessened.

As debt payment is the reciprocal of debt establishment, it may be studied in terms of the latter. The establishment of debt takes place in three principal ways.

1. Even though gifts are excluded, title to real wealth or services may be passed without a contemporaneous and reverse passage of title to money. The receiver of the real goods and services then becomes the debtor until title to a prearranged amount of money has been paid, probably at a preappointed time.

2. Or title to money may be passed without a contemporaneous and reverse passage of title to real wealth. In this case the receiver of the money is the debtor until title to a prearranged amount of money has been passed at a preappointed time or times.

3. Finally, there is interest debt, which accrues by contract on previously existing debt of the first two descriptions.

To limit the case, for the present, to debts between individuals, we assume the absence of a banking system. This is consistent with our previous assumption of a constant supply of money. Debts between individuals can be established in all three of the above manners. The passage of title to real wealth without the payment of money may take the form of rendering a service, such as a wage earner performs, or perhaps of credit sales. The rendering of services, and credit sales, are in most cases associated directly or indirectly with the production and distribution of real wealth. The point has been made by Mr. Hawtrey:

> In the process of production, a service rendered creates a debt from the person to whom the product belongs to the person who renders the service.[3]
>
> The process of production . . . gives rise to a chain of debts. The manufacturer or contractor becomes indebted day by day to his employees, the merchant becomes indebted to the manufacturer.[4]

---

[3] *Currency and Credit*, p. 3.

[4] *Ibid.*, p. 453.

Mr. Hawtrey goes so far as to make a sale for metallic money a source of what might be called "instantaneous" debt:

> . . . a sale for metallic money is in all cases analysable into the creation and extinction of a debt, i. e., into two credit transactions. From the opposite point of view a sale for credit might perhaps be regarded as the uncompleted portion of a sale for money.[5]

The second of our three methods of debt creation involves a payment of money from the creditor to the debtor at the time of the establishment of the debt. Any loan of money is a case in point. The third method of debt creation results in interest debt, and does not involve a unilateral payment of either money or real wealth at the time of its establishment. Rather, interest debt automatically accrues by previous arrangement.

Debt arising from the passage of title to wealth without a reverse flow of money will be called *wealth debt. Fiat debt* will be the term applied to that which arises from the passage of title to money without a reverse flow of wealth, and *interest debt,* that which accrues on previously existing debt. It will be seen later that money, when viewed as debt, or *money debt,* is essentially a part of the second of these classifications, namely, fiat debt. Since nearly all debt is payable in money and is stated in terms of money, it might all be called money debt. It appears more fruitful, however, to base our terms on differences in the process of debt establishment.

Substantially all debts involve a payment of money at the time the debt matures, unless the due date is extended by agreement or by law.[6] This is not to deny that some debts are paid in wealth rather than in money. All forms of prepayment for services, or other types of intangible or corporeal wealth, are examples of debt that is established by a unilateral passage of title to money and subsequently discharged by a unilateral pas-

[5] *Currency and Credit,* p. 214.

[6] Through clearance, some debts may be set off against other debts. When this is done through the banking system, the banks first exchange their own debts for those of others. This is analogous to a money transaction, in the sense in which we have used the term money. Outside of the banking system, only debts of like provisions could be so cleared, and this is not likely to be an important phenomenon.

sage of title to real wealth. Conspicuous illustrations are found in prepaid contracts and in drawing accounts with retail establishments. In the aggregate, this type of debt appears to be of negligible importance, relative to the three kinds of debt previously described.

For the purpose of developing the argument, we shall assume that there is no debt payment in kind, and shall consider money, as we are using the term, to be the sole means of discharging all debts. This implies the further assumption of an absence of gifts. Under these limiting assumptions, all debts are dischargeable only in money. But not all are contracted as a result of an initial loan of money—for example, some debts are contracted by the unilateral passage of title to wealth. For the most part, these are the debts which are described by Mr. Hawtrey as accompanying the production and distribution of new wealth, of which credit sales are an important part.[7] But since by assumption all debts are repayable in money, and since no money passes at the time of contraction of this particular type of debt, a problem arises over the manner of obtaining money for repayment.

Although no money passes at the time of contraction of such debts, debts arising directly out of the production-distribution process involve, at the time they are incurred, the passage of title to real wealth from the creditor to the debtor. Such wealth may be in corporeal form or in the form of services or other intangibles. The money later required to discharge such debts may or may not be available, depending in part on the use made of the service or good received by the debtor. If the received service or good is used in successfully establishing new wealth of equal or greater value, the new wealth may be exchanged for money with which to pay the debt. If the service or good is used unsuccessfully in attempting to establish new wealth, or if the service or good is extinguished in use without

[7] Changes in debt of this description result in part from changes in money-payment habits. Professor Angell has many interesting comments on the significance of changes in money-payment habits in his article, "The Components of the Circular Velocity of Money," *Quarterly Journal of Economics,* LI (Feb., 1937), 224 *et seq.*

attempting to reproduce values, money will not be forthcoming from that particular operation for satisfying debt. The deficiency must be made up, if at all, out of money surpluses realized in other and successful productive activity. The contraction and discharge of wage debts and debts arising from credit purchases of raw materials are examples of debt for which repayment money is likely to be made available later from the production process itself. Installment buying of radios is an example of the contraction of debt for which repayment money must be obtained from other sources.

THE EFFECT OF A CHANGING CORPUS OF DEBT

With these several propositions in mind regarding the establishment and payment of debt, we may now attempt to ascertain the effect of an expansion or contraction of the corpus of debt which results, in part, from changed liquidity desires. Various phases of the question cause trouble. If prices are constant, is there a functional relationship between changes in the debt corpus and changes in the amount of wealth distributed? If so, is it the existence of a greater *quantity* of debt that makes possible the greater exchange of wealth, or is it the *increase* in debt that makes possible the greater exchange? Does our problem concern itself with several types of debt, or merely with that debt resulting from the passage of real wealth without money? Where does debt that results from the passage of title to money, without the concomitant passage of wealth, fit into the composition? What is the economic significance of interest debt, that is, debt which is constantly being established without immediate reference to the unilateral passage of either real wealth or money?

These are questions which we must of necessity approach with diffidence. In writing of periods of depression, Alfred Marshall concluded:

> It is true that . . . the disorganization of consumption is a contributory cause of the continuance of the disorganization of credit [debt] and of production. But a remedy is not to be got by a study of

consumption . . . the main study needed is that of the organization of production and of credit [debt]. And, though economists have not yet succeeded in bringing that study to a successful issue, the cause of their failure lies in the profound obscurity and ever changing form of the problem; it does not lie in any indifference on their part to its supreme importance.[8]

Professor Marshall did not use the term debt, which we have inserted in brackets in this quotation. Dr. Lauchlin Currie, in an extensive perusal of the pertinent literature, has found a large number of different uses of the term credit, both specific and general.[9] On the other hand, credit, says Mr. Hawtrey, "is a term which for some people assumes an almost mystical significance. . . . But in ordinary parlance it is simply another name for debt." [10] In this study we shall mean by the term credit the reciprocal of debt and nothing else. That which is a debt to a debtor is a credit to a creditor.

Even though Professor Marshall may have been using the term credit in this simple sense, and it is hard to see how the connotation could have been entirely excluded, the complexity of the problem he describes remains. It is not with the sanguine expectation of resolving these difficulties in a definitive manner that we approach these questions, but it is not too much to hope that a contribution toward their solution may be made.

We shall now add another assumption to those previously made, namely, that all business is transacted with currency. (It will be recalled that the number of money units is assumed to be constant.) Exchanges of title to real wealth, including services, are made only against money.[11] Credit as the reciprocal of non-money debt is not used in transactions. The corpus of debt is thus fixed, being measured by what Soddy has called the virtual wealth value [12] of all the money units outstanding.

8 Marshall, Alfred, *Principles of Economics* (8th ed.; London, 1920), p. 712 n.

9 Currie, Lauchlin, "Treatment of Credit in Contemporary Monetary Theory," *Journal of Political Economy,* XLI (Feb., 1933), pp. 58 *et seq.*

10 Hawtrey, *Capital and Employment,* p. 312.

11 Money is currency in this instance, since we eliminated bank debt when we eliminated the banking system by assumption.

12 *Supra,* pp. 43–44.

Money is paid for services at the time the service is rendered. Likewise, titles to corporeal wealth are transferred only on receipt of money.

What are the broad limitations on economic activity prescribed by these circumstances? Only those who have title to money will be able to acquire new wealth, in addition to the wealth which accrues to them from their own productive activities. In the first instance, the real wealth accruing to individuals from the ownership of assets placed in the production process is of a specialized nature. Its forms and amounts are in excess of personal requirements. The essence of capitalistic economics is the exchange of these excesses of specialized privately owned wealth for other forms of wealth personally desired. Within the limitations of our assumptions, including the absence of barter and gifts, this exchange must be accomplished through the medium of money. If we assume the virtual wealth as constant in amount, the quantity of specialized wealth that may be exchanged for money in a given period of time is determined by the number of units of money, multiplied by the number of times each unit of money exchanges against real wealth.[13] If interstitial and secondary payments are also constant, the exchange of money for the final output of new wealth, or what we have termed final buying, is determined in the same manner. We may abstract from such payments, to simplify our problem further.

Thus, granting a constant virtual wealth value of the money stock, a constant number of money units, and no use of debt other than money, the upper limit of the possible exchange of specialized wealth for money is set by the exchange velocity of money. This is substantially the same as saying that the upper limit of production of real wealth surpluses under a capitalistic

[13] By assumption, the number of units of money are constant. Also, the virtual wealth, or the real wealth value of the money stock is constant. Under these circumstances, each unit of money has an unchanging real wealth value. Thus the price level is constant. We have set up these assumptions to study the influence of a changing corpus of non-money debt. In the next chapter we remove the assumptions and study the influence of changing monetary phenomena. Unless the assumptions are kept clearly in mind, the present discussion may be confusing.

organization of society is likewise determined within the same hypothetical limitations. Specialized wealth in excess of personal requirements will not be produced for long unless it can be exchanged for other forms of wealth that are desired. Changes in the amount of surplus specialized wealth produced are roughly correlated (with some time lag perhaps) with changes in the amount exchanged.

WEALTH DEBT

Let us continue our assumption of an absence of fiat debt other than money. The type of debt we shall now admit to our problem is wealth debt—that which is incurred by the passage of title to real wealth and services without the passage of money. Under these conditions wages may be paid at periodic intervals, rather than at the time the service is rendered. Titles to corporeal real wealth may be delivered before payment of money is received. The corpus of debt in our earlier situation was equal to the virtual wealth value of money. We assumed the number of money units to be constant. The debt corpus in the present situation is equal to the virtual wealth value of money, plus debt incurred by the unilateral passage of title to real wealth. The appearance of the latter type of debt thus entails an increase in the aggregate debt corpus. What is the effect of this increase on the possible exchange of real wealth, which we have deemed to be substantially synonymous with the production of real wealth in a capitalistic economy?

We have seen that with a constant number of money units, a constant virtual wealth, and no debt other than money, the upper limit on the distribution and hence on the production of specialized wealth is set by the exchange velocity of money against final new output. But when we introduce debt, the establishment of which is incurred by the passage of real wealth and services without a contemporaneous reverse flow of money, we must raise the upper limit of the possible exchange of real wealth-titles in a given period, and hence raise the upper limit of productive activity. If we retain the same limiting assumptions, the upper limit of possible productive activity is now set by the exchange velocity of money against final new output, plus something more made possible by the passage of title to real wealth without a concomitant passage of money.

Suppose that 1,000 newly created units of real wealth are exchanged in a given period of time for $1,000, or for $1 each. Suppose further that there are 500 currency units. An exchange velocity of 2 will then be required to distribute the 1,000 wealth units at $1 each in the given period. In a second period, let us assume that the same conditions prevail, except that title to an additional 100 units of newly created wealth is exchanged without the payment of currency. It follows that in this period, titles to 1,100 units of the new wealth are exchanged. But the velocity of currency against new wealth is still 2. In a third period all of these conditions may continue to prevail, including the continued existence of the $100 debt. But if the number of units of currency and their velocity against new wealth remain constant, only 1,000 units of new titles will have passed. Hence it appears that it is the *increase* of debt, and not its existence, that makes possible the increase in exchanges of wealth and thus facilitates an increase in wealth production.

In a fourth period, suppose that the $100 debt is repaid, but that other conditions remain the same. By hypothesis we have made currency the only means of paying debt. Let us suppose that in this fourth period title to each unit of currency changes twice, as before. The velocity of currency is still 2, but we must now include the passage of currency for the payment of debt, as well as against new wealth. Hence the payment of money in discharge of debt appears to be an alternative use of money, comparable in significance to its increased use for trading or for interstitial payments. In this period 100 units of currency will pass once for the payment of the debt. Since each of the 500 units of currency changes hands only twice, there remain 900 such exchanges to be made against new wealth. The effect of a decrease in debt on the exchange of wealth, and hence on its production, is evident. Wealth distribution, and hence production, must be diminished under our assumption of a constant exchange velocity of money.

What is the situation when there is an increase and a decrease in debt which take place at the same time and in equal amounts? Here we have the case which must necessarily complement the several cases above, before we can make the argument analogous to the conditions of actual economic life. As Hawtrey has explained, the corpus or total size of debt does not in fact change through first the establishment and then the complete payment of all debts, but changes merely through differences between the flows of additions to and retirements of separate debts.[14] This case we may assign to a fifth hypothetical period, while retaining the same limiting assumptions as before.

Suppose that during the period a debt of $100 is incurred by the passage of title to wealth, without a reverse flow of money. At the same time, suppose that there is a $100 reduction of a debt previously incurred. The exchange velocity of money, we will say, remains at 2. The increase in debt does not enter this figure, since the debt is incurred by the passage of title to wealth without a money payment. Hence in the absence of the debt payment, 1,100 units of wealth could be exchanged during the period. But the payment of debt by the passage of currency is a part of the exchange velocity figure, making it possible to exchange titles to but 900 units of wealth if the figure is constant at 2. It matters not whether we add to this figure the additional 100 units of wealth, the transfer of which is made possible by the increase of wealth debt, or deduct from 1,100 units the 100 units which now cannot be transferred because currency is being used for debt payment. In both instances we find that only 1,000 titles to units of wealth may be exchanged.

We may summarize. If the amount of money, its virtual wealth value, and its exchange velocity are constant, the daily creation of new *wealth debts* and the payment of old debts will not influence the amount of new wealth exchanged unless these

[14] *Supra,* p. 154.

operations result in a net change in the corpus of debt. In this conclusion, it is clear that we have eliminated for the moment the influence of non-money fiat debt and of interest debt. An *increase* in the corpus of wealth debt makes possible a greater exchange of wealth, the increase in the money amount exchanged being measured by the money amount of increase in wealth debt. A *decrease* in the corpus of wealth debt reduces the money amount of wealth that may be exchanged by the money amount of the reduction when the exchange velocity of money is constant.[15] The mere *existence* of debt, apart from its interest feature, exercises no essential functional influence on the exchange of new wealth and hence none on the production of wealth. It is rather the net increase or net decrease of wealth debt that is the important matter.

We have here been talking about only one phase of the debt problem, namely, the expansion and contraction of all debt incurred by the passage of title to real wealth, without the reverse passage of money. Nothing has been said of the part played by debts arising out of the passage of title to money without a reverse flow of wealth, of the place of compound interest in this complex problem, or of bank debt, which not only represents an addition to fiat debt but also to the money stock. We shall now attempt to discover the modifications in the argument that follow the introduction of debt entailing the passage of title to money without the passage of wealth—what we have previously called fiat debt. The assumption of a constant amount of money will be retained; hence our attention will be directed to non-money fiat debt.

FIAT DEBT

Within the limitations of our earlier assumptions, real saving is a prerequisite to the establishment of wealth debt. Such saving

[15] It will be recalled that we have assumed constant prices. Of course, if prices are falling, a decrease in wealth debt may reflect no change in the *quantity* of wealth exchanged. But we have seen that falling prices, if they lead to an expectation of further decline, will reduce the amount of buying. The expectation of a falling price level may also induce a contraction of debt, including wealth debt, by making potential borrowers less willing to borrow. For further discussion of this point, *vide infra*, pp. 175–76.

may take the form of direct saving of newly established real wealth, the title to which is subsequently transferred from the saver-creditor to the debtor, without money payment. Or it may take place in a more complicated but more usual manner. The prospective creditor accumulates a money balance. With this he purchases real wealth from one who has previously abstained from its use. He then conveys title to the real wealth to a third party, thus creating wealth debt. Such would be the case if an individual accumulated a cash balance, bought a stock of merchandise and sold his wares on "credit." [16]

Those accumulators of cash balances who wish to become specific creditors have two broad means of accomplishing their purpose. One is described above: the use of the money to purchase real wealth and the subsequent conveyance of title to such wealth to a third party without money payment. This we have called the creation of wealth debt. But such a procedure, for one not appropriately placed in economic society, for instance a merchant, would be cumbersome. The second means of converting money balances to other forms of debt ownership is the obvious one of passing title to the money without concomitantly receiving title to real wealth, that is, granting a money loan. The debt resulting from this operation we have called fiat debt. If the title to money is passed, let us say, to a manufacturer, he may then use it for the production of real wealth, which wealth may be made the basis for the establishment of wealth debt. We have seen that an *increase* in wealth debt facilitates the exchange of real wealth in distributive channels and that this is tantamount to increased production. Hence one of the effects of an expansion of fiat debt is to make possible a greater productive activity by facilitating an increase in wealth debt.

The expansion of fiat debt facilitates the exchange of real wealth in another manner. It may result in placing money in the hands of those who are disposed to use it in exchange for real wealth, whereas the accumulator of the money balance may have

[16] Not all accumulators of money balances wish to become creditors. Some prefer to become direct or indirect owners of real wealth instead. Others may wish to retain their accumulations indefinitely in the form of a general claim on society of uncertain productivity—namely, in the form of money.

no personal or production use in immediate prospect. In this respect the expansion of fiat debt stimulates production by providing otherwise absent buyers for real wealth. At the same time, it facilitates the association for new production purposes of store and natural resources that may not have been brought together previously. This function of an expansion of fiat debt, namely, the placing of money in hands that will use it more quickly and possibly more productively, manifests itself through changes in the exchange velocity of money. A given number of money units is enabled to do more work. It will be recalled that, under our limiting assumptions, we found the exchange of final new output, and hence wealth production, to be a function of the exchange velocity of money, plus a correction factor to reflect the net increase or decrease of the corpus of wealth debt. The logical consistency of this proposition seems to be unimpaired by the omission of fiat debt as a factor, since changes in fiat debt are reflected through changes in money velocity and in the quantity of wealth debt.

An attempt has been made to describe the significance of debts between individuals and their aggregate changes by dividing them broadly into two categories, which we have called wealth debt and fiat debt. (Interest debt has not as yet been discussed.) It has been found that the establishment of either of these types of debt requires prior saving. But there is one type of fiat debt, the establishment of which does not require a prior decision to save on the part of an individual or a group of individuals of the community. Such debt is money per se, of which bank debt is a part.

Debts between banks and individuals differ from debts between individuals in two respects. First, no prior saving is required to bring bank debts into existence. Second, when established, they serve as the basis of a general claim to the economic wealth of the community, and hence as money. Since bank debt is established by the passage of title to deposit money, without a concomitant passage of title to real wealth, it must be classed as a part of what we have called fiat debt.

Previously, on the assumption of a constant number of money units and a constant virtual wealth value of the money stock, we made changes in new wealth exchanged, and hence in new wealth produced, a function of two elements, the exchange velocity of money against new wealth and net changes in the corpus of wealth debt. Fiat debt is related to changes in wealth production and distribution, not directly, but rather through these two elements. But money is a part of the corpus of fiat debt. A change in the quantity of money may lead to an increase in wealth debt and it may increase the number of times units of money exchange against real wealth. The latter is equivalent to an increase in the exchange velocity of an unchanging amount of money. Thus we may say that changes in the amount of wealth exchanged, and hence of wealth produced, are a function of net changes in the product of that part of fiat debt which serves as a general claim, namely, money, times its velocity, plus or minus a correction factor to reflect net changes in the corpus of wealth debt. This is true within the limits of our assumptions, which involve constant prices.

It may help to clarify these phenomena if we set them in the framework of the familiar Fisher equation. Depending upon one's definition of M and M′, this equation may or may not be a tautology. To quote Lauchlin Currie, "most . . . writers on the equation of exchange have, like Fisher, identified M′ with demand deposits." M, of course, is identified with money in the older sense of coins and currency. Let us lump the two and say that the term money applies to all debt *instruments* that serve as a general claim to the community's wealth. Then money does not include what we have described as wealth debt, which in most cases is not evidenced by an instrument at all, and, if it is, not by an instrument that serves as a general claim to the community's wealth. With this definition of money and the foregoing analysis, the Fisher equation must be slightly recast. $PT = M'V' + MV$ becomes $PT = MV \pm \triangle D$ where $\triangle D$ represents changes in wealth debt. Absent from this equation but influencing the wealth debt and the velocity of the money stock is that part of fiat debt that does not serve as a general claim, namely, that part which is not money.

The Fisher equation has been described as a tautology. Unless we include in the term money connotations that typically are not included, we must question this proposition. If in a given period of time there is a net increase in wealth debt, the quantity PT must of necessity exceed the quantity MV. The converse is also true. Moreover, there is no essential reason to believe that the MV and PT quantities are ever in balance, irrespective of the length of the time-period involved. Suppose a net increase in wealth debt; then PT exceeds MV. Then suppose that a part of the wealth debt is subsequently defaulted. Prices and transactions will both have been modified, without corresponding changes in the amount of money or its exchange velocity in the present or in the future.

THE CONSEQUENCES OF REDUCING THE CORPUS OF DEBT DISCUSSED FURTHER

In addition to looking at these phenomena in terms of hypothetical situations, they may also be viewed in terms of the factual results of debt repayment. What does the recipient of debt repayment do with the proceeds? (1) If the proceeds are relent to a new debtor, no change in the net size of the debt corpus results. The particular debt will merely have been shifted, in the sense that a different debtor has been supplied. The payment and reëstablishment of the debt by money passage may increase the exchange velocity of money. This it is very likely to do in these circumstances. (2) The recipient of the money payment may use it to trade in previously existing titles such as land, shares, or even titles to previously existing debts such as bonds. In this event there may be a net reduction of the number of effective money units available to use in final buying. Both M and V are altered, so far as concerns the use of money in the distribution of new real wealth. Other possibilities are also available to the recipient of the proceeds of debt repayment. (3) He may hold the money in a hoard. (4) He may exchange it for new real wealth which he uses for personal enjoyment. (5) He may directly exchange it for new real wealth, which he places in association with other wealth for the purpose of producing still greater utilities.

Creditors generally look upon their ownership of debt as part of their "personal capital." It is only under duress that they voluntarily divest themselves of all or a portion of the claim thus owned. Accordingly, it is least likely that the recipient of debt-repayment money will exchange it for new real wealth to be used for personal enjoyment, unless this wealth is in a form calculated to maintain the claim reasonably well through time—a house, for example. More probably the money will be (1) reloaned, or (2) used for trading in previously existing titles, or (3) withdrawn from circulation, or (4) directly exchanged for wealth to be used in new production. Of these, the withdrawal of the received money from all circulation and its withdrawal from final buying, through diversion to the secondary circulation, are detrimental to economic stability. It will be noted that both involve a payment of debt without its reëstablishment, a reduction in the corpus of debt.

Direct investment of the money in wealth for personal or productive use will also result in a net reduction in the aggregate debt corpus, but in this instance without undesirable secondary effects. Here, then, is a manner in which the corpus of debt may be reduced without unfavorable repercussions, namely, by converting debt into equities. The only other probable use of the debt-repayment money is relending, but, as we have seen, this does not result in a change in debt corpus. Relending is more analogous to the shifting of individual debt ownership through sale in the open market. A further method of getting rid of debt is through default.

Still another method of debt payment is sometimes referred to: "payment [of claims] may consist in the presentation of similar or offsetting, claims of simultaneous maturity." [17]

If a man sells a ton of coal to another, this will create a debt from the buyer to the seller. But the buyer will have been himself a seller

[17] Willis, *Theory and Practice of Central Banking,* p. 32.

to someone else, and the seller will have been himself also a buyer. The dealers in the market can meet together and set off their debts and credits.[18]

This is quite true if the claims are of simultaneous maturity, if the maturity corresponds to the time that all are presented, and if they share other characteristics in common, such as the same interest rates, and so forth. The function of the banking system in facilitating such offsets has long been recognized. But the offset is not effected directly. Rather it is accomplished through the banks first assuming the several debts, and the clearance is then made by means of the banks' own demand liabilities. Since we have treated demand deposits of banks as a part of the money supply, no difficulty arises in regard to the earlier proposition that debt is discharged by the passage of money, and that the discharge is reflected in the exchange velocity of money through what may be called debt velocity.

It thus seems reasonable to conclude broadly that except for refunding into equity and except for default, there are no means available to the community to pay off, without depressive consequences, the corpus of its debt on balance, that is, its total debt both public and private. This does not preclude the shifting of private debt to public debt, or, conversely, of public to private debt, by a process of paying off the one at the same time that the other expands. Reflection shows that debt has enormously increased with the evolution of industrial capitalism, and in fact has never been paid off on balance in any large quantity except for short periods, usually described as depressions.

INTEREST DEBT

We are now beginning to obtain some perception of the possible consequences of changes in liquidity preferences that result in an expansion or a contraction of wealth debt and fiat debt. As the argument has been developed to this point, an increase in debt appears to be about as favorable a thing as could happen to a community. Then why should there be a somewhat intuitive

18 Hawtrey, *Currency and Credit*, p. 2.

yet enduring fear of debt, a fear shared by intelligent members of the business and academic worlds? That the fear is justified is amply demonstrated by the experiences of whole communities and nations, as well as by the experiences of individuals.

When an obligor incurs "too much" debt, a readjustment of his or its affairs will follow with reasonable certainty. Yet it is true that debt has increased greatly with the development of economic life, not constantly or even continuously, but nevertheless at rates believed impossible by those viewing the matter at successive periods. From this point of view, we might answer the familiar axiom, "Debt must be paid," with the proposition that "Debt has never been paid." It has grown to gigantic proportions. But why be afraid of debt when we have always had it and when, except for brief periods, it has always increased? Why be afraid of debt when a presumably logical case can be made for the beneficence of debt expansion to the community, in terms of the production and distribution of real wealth?

At least a part of the answer to these questions may be found in the nature of the compound interest paid on a large segment of total debt. This brings us to the third type of debt in our earlier classification, namely, that type which, instead of being established by the unilateral passage of title to either money or real wealth, is established without immediate reference to any such passage. Such debt is interest debt.[19]

We have seen that the creation of wealth debt and fiat debt facilitates the distribution and hence the production of real wealth. Once these two types of debt are in being, they are apparently neutral in their influence. Only when an attempt is made to pay them off, in the sense of reducing their total corpus, do they become a burden. This seems to be the significance of debt, apart from interest. On the other hand, the creation of interest debt does not facilitate in a similar manner the distribution and production of wealth. True, the expectation of receiving interest on debt may encourage abstinence, and may thus provide

[19] Comparable to interest debt in some respects is debt resulting from bets, prize winnings, and so forth, but these appear to be relatively unimportant in their amount and economic significance, and we omit them from the discussion.

real wealth or money from which wealth debt, fiat debt, or direct investment may be derived. This has been explicitly held to be the case since the days of Nassau Senior, and has only recently been qualified by J. M. Keynes.[20] But once wealth or fiat debt is established, the accrual of interest thereon is not a factor contributing to the total of productivity. Rather, the owners of the accruing interest debt become the initial beneficiaries of the production-distribution process.

Interest debt, like all other debt, is discharged in money for the most part. Money incomes available to pay interest are derived from the prior exchange of real wealth for money. Such exchanges are induced by the previous production of wealth, the appropriation of natural resources, and trading in old titles. Thus we find the production of store, the appropriation of natural resources, and trading within the secondary circulation to be the ultimate sources of money incomes available for interest payment. Mr. Bassett Jones, when studying this problem, concluded that ". . . in the end all fixed charges, including the debt accrual, must come out of the gain from the sale of the goods produced." [21] If the gain per unit of production is fixed, then "production must grow as debt grows." [22] Pointing out that debt has expanded according to the law of compound interest and that charges on the debt, if fixed, grow as the debt grows, because they constitute a fixed fraction of the total, Mr. Jones concludes that this is an unbearable proposition. First, "the law of compound interest . . . is the only time-quantity relation that shows a *constant growth factor,* and therefore implies ultimately impossible results." [23] Second, "since about 1910 nearly every form of production (in the United States) has been increasing at a progressively slower rate of growth." [24] The instructiveness of Mr. Jones's metrical comparisons is lessened by the fact that

20 In *The General Theory of Employment, Interest and Money,* Keynes holds that ". . . interest has been usually regarded as the reward of not-spending, whereas in fact it is the reward of not-hoarding" (p. 174). It would appear to be quite correct that the anticipation of interest is not the only motivation to abstaining. But it would appear to be equally incorrect that the anticipation of interest is not *one* of the inducements to abstaining.

21 Jones, *Debt and Production,* p. 62.

22 *Op. cit.,* p. 82.

23 *Op. cit.,* p. 79.

24 *Op. cit.,* p. 34.

he compares physical-quantity production series with money-quantity debt series. The influence of a changing price level in easing or aggravating the debt burden thus is overlooked. But the tendencies which he describes apparently have validity.

We have remarked above that the money income of the community is derived from the exchange of money against new wealth and services and trading in old assets. But there are two ultimate determinants of the flow of national money income: the physical quantity of new wealth coming forward, and the amount of money exchanged for each unit of such wealth. The second factor is the price factor. Thus the national money income may be increased either by a greater quantity of physical wealth production and its distribution at a constant price, or by the exchange of more money units for an unchanged aggregate quantity of new wealth production. The relation of the size of national money income to the size of fixed charges on existing debt may vary as the result of (1) a change in the size of either of these elements, or from (2) an independent change in the money total required to meet the fixed charges of debt service.

It has been generally taken for granted that the greater the size of fixed charges on existing debt relative to the size of national income, the more difficult will be the resulting situation. Hence the urge to "reflate" when prices have substantially declined. There seems to be an implicit assumption in some of the popular discussions of this problem that, in some way, the part of the national income going to the payment of interest is lost to the national income. This, of course, is not the case, if the recipients of interest payments exchange the money received for new wealth. In this event, the national income will be impaired only to the extent that the somewhat more circuitous route of the money to exchange against new wealth reduces the amount of money used in final buying.

The chief importance of the size of fixed charges on existing debt relative to national money income is more logically to be sought in the fact that a part of the national money income is forced through an inflexible channel by the necessity of meeting these charges. The greater the requirements for debt service relative to the national money income, the greater is the proportion of the money income that will be so directed. Since the distribution of the ownership of debt is very uneven, a change in the *distribution* of national money income must result from a change in the debt-service national-income relation.

It would be more than a coincidence if a change in the distribution of national money income did not result in a significant change in the *composition* of the aggregate demand for new wealth. Specific producers, most of whom are debtors, would find themselves unhappily situated in the new condition, and it would become necessary or expedient for some of them to default on their obligations. These appear to be the economic sequences that follow when debt service charges change relative to national income, whether as a result of cyclical price changes or as a result of an evolutionary increase of debt faster than that of the money value of production. In either event, a redistribution of money income and a change in the direction of effective demand will ensue, requiring a readjustment of productive resources which varying degrees of specificity of the factors of production make difficult.

Thus our theoretical analysis does not refute the a priori proposition that the larger the interest-bearing debt relative to a national income, the greater will be the difficulty of servicing the debt. It does indicate, however, that this is the case only to the extent that the changing relation between debt and national money income increases the stress caused by inflexible elements in the general economy. Further, while the relation of the growth of debt to the growth of production is highly significant, other factors of importance which cannot be omitted from a consideration of the problem are price, the distribution of ownership of debt and money income, and the changes in the nature of demand which arise from changes in these elements.

SUMMARY

We have now traced some of the more important economic consequences of that phase of the liquidity problem which is associated with the expansion and contraction of the aggregate of debt other than money. This we have done by studying certain of the theoretical implications of increases and decreases in the size of the corpus of various types of debt. One manifestation of a change in the liquidity desires of the community is an effort to increase or decrease debt. An increase or a decrease in the total debt corpus is the result. We have found that the expansion of certain kinds of debt, which we have called wealth debt and fiat debt, is beneficial to the expansion of distribution and production of real wealth. There is, nevertheless, a limitation to the community's ability to expand debt, because of the establishment of interest debt that accompanies most debt creation.

Debt, once established, cannot be paid off by the community on balance without seriously depressive consequences. The elimination of debt by default has somewhat different consequences, but it may be equally serious. The only way in which to reduce debt without economic distress is through its conversion into equities. But for practical purposes, this means is not available when the liquidity desires of the community are raised and a reduction in debt is in process.

We now find another of the forces which fit into the complex of cumulative pressures that are associated with changed liquidity desires. The interplay of liquidity desires with expectations of future money profits and movements of the price level has been traced in earlier passages of this study. Throughout the present chapter we have assumed a constant price level. Within the limits of this hypothetical situation, it has been found that a change in liquidity desires, by affecting an expansion or contraction of non-money debt, will accelerate or retard business activity.

If the number of money units and prices are constant, business activity will expand and contract with changes in the velocity of money and with changes in the corpus of wealth debt. But we have associated an increase in liquidity desires with a fall in prices, as well as with a decrease in the debt corpus. The assumption of constant prices must be removed. Is it not true that a decrease in the corpus of debt, instead of reducing the "physical" volume of business, might be compensated by a decrease in prices, leaving business activity unabated? A partial answer to this question may be given at this point.

There are four elements to be considered: (1) the "physical" volume of business, (2) fluctuations in the aggregate of non-money debt, (3) price movements, and (4) the so-called effective supply of money, MV. Theoretically any one of the four could be held constant if fluctuations in any one of the other three were compensated by changes in the two remaining. For instance, business activity might be constant if a decrease in the corpus of non-money debt is offset by either an increase in MV, or by lower prices, or by both.

Lower prices may be counted on to compensate the other elements only if they are expected to stabilize or return to former levels. If prices are expected to decline further, money profit expectations will be low and liquidity desires will discourage final buying. Moreover, liquidity desires will induce hoarding, even though the number of money units may remain constant, thus reducing MV. That the number of money units will not remain constant with a rise in liquidity desires, but will *decrease,* is the subject of the succeeding chapter.

Only casual mention has been given to the motivation for and the significance of increases and decreases in that part of fiat debt which was defined as money. To this highly important phase of the theory of liquidity we are now ready to turn. We may do so by removing the assumption, carried for the past several chapters, of a constant quantity of money and an absence of any banking system.

IX

THE ORGANIZATION OF THE BANKING SYSTEM AND THE SUPPLY OF MONEY[1]

LIQUIDITY DESIRES, although an important source of change in the supply of money, are not the only source of such change. In order to judge the relative importance of liquidity desires in this respect, it is necessary for us to review briefly the various sources of money supply. We can then see why changes in liquidity desires are a source of change in the supply of money and the relation of this to the interest rate.

THE SUPPLY OF MONEY

We have previously defined money as anything that is, as a class, a general claim to future wealth.[2] The time element in which the claim is exercised may be extremely short or indefinitely long. In addition, money may, but need not be, a specific title to present wealth such as gold. But a general claim to wealth in the future it must be. The amount of future wealth claimable is not fixed, but there must exist an expectation of being able to claim it without question on demand, and by direct exchange, without first changing the form of the money. Thus the term money refers to nothing more than a prevailing social habit of thought and action—the psychologist might call it a behavior pattern.

[1] The subject of liquidity, as it relates to the exchange velocity of money, was discussed in the chapter on "Hoarding." This was done under the assumption of a constant number of money units. We are now ready to examine the influence of changing liquidity desires upon the number of money units.

[2] *Supra*, pp. 40–44 ff.

Gold has been considered money for millennia merely because there has existed a widely held belief that it would be acceptable in exchange for other forms of wealth at any time and under any but the most fantastic circumstances. Currency, partly because of its earlier convertibility into gold and partly because of the obvious convenience of its existence and use for clearances in a complex community, has come to share similar expectations. In the United States and England the medium in which much the greatest part of transactions are now settled, it is well known, is bank deposits. Like the currency of a decade or so past, which in certain instances was a specific claim against precious metals, bank deposits are in the first instance a claim against the specific assets of a particular bank. As currency, through need, use, and habit, became a general claim against future wealth, so demand deposits of banks have assumed for practical purposes this monetary function. Now publicly recognized as a general claim against future wealth in the sense that, except in abnormal circumstances, they will be acceptable in exchange without question at any time, both currency and demand deposits now qualify under most definitions of money.[3] Subsidiary coin should be mentioned as another form of money, but one which is unimportant to this study.

A significant change in the total amount of money may thus arise from a change in the amount of any one of its three principal forms. These forms are related to one another in banking legislation. Effective changes in the monetary gold stock may result from mining activity, international gold movements, variations

[3] The exceptional cases in which the owners of demand deposits cannot use them as money are recognized. A traveler may be unknown in a new community. Such instances appear to be unimportant in the aggregate. If a bank has been closed by the authorities, deposits are of course no longer demandable at will. If for any reason a deposit is not acceptable in exchange without question at any time, it ceases to qualify under the above definition of money.

Professor Angell defines "circulating money" as "outside currency plus deposits subject to check, after deduction of duplications." (Vide, *The Behavior of Money*, p. 10.) Adjusted demand deposits of member banks, as reported by the Federal Reserve Board, consist of demand deposits, plus certified checks, plus travelers' checks, plus government deposits, minus all items in the course of collection.

in public hoarding or industrial use of gold (if not prohibited by law), and modifications in the statutory value placed on a given weight of gold. Changes in the amount of currency, if represented by government notes, may result from arbitrary decisions or from variations in the government's acquisition of precious metals. If represented by bank notes, variations in the amount of currency may arise from a change in the stock of gold, in the amount of deposits, or in the relative desire or need of the public for currency as against deposits.

But the greatest variations in the number of money units arise from the changing amount of demand deposits. Bank deposits come into being in three principal ways. Originally they represented receipts, redeemable on demand, for gold or silver placed with a bank for safe keeping. As these receipts gained general acceptance in the evolution of banking, they took on the form of what is currently called bank notes. The placement of one of these receipts, or bank notes, with a bank could also give rise to a deposit. In the course of time more efficient techniques developed to effect the transfer of these credits, held by the public with banks, by using drafts. Thus one way of establishing deposits is by placing at the disposal of a bank precious metals, bank or government notes, or drafts—in more conventional terms, gold, currency, or checks.

The other two means of bringing bank deposits into being give rise to what are called "derivative" deposits. A bank may buy assets in the open market. Its own demand liabilities or those of others, with which it pays for the purchase, must find lodgment somewhere in the banking system unless hoarded in the form of currency. If the banking system is organized on the basis of fractional reserve requirements, there is no limitation to the possible expansion of deposits in this manner except that established by the physical limitations of the reserve itself—for instance, the quantity of gold or the legislated relationship of gold to currency.

A third method of deposit creation is analogous to the second. When banks make loans, the operation involves, in substance, the establishment of two debts and their subsequent exchange: "the debt of the customer to the bank payable at a specified future date and the debt of the bank to the customer payable on demand." [4] This latter debt takes the form of a deposit and, being readily acceptable as a general claim on future wealth, represents an increment to the supply of money. It may be held that this is not necessarily so. The bank may have previously received a draft on another bank or in other ways become possessed of the equivalent of money sufficient to pay the customer's debt. This is quite true. In this event no increment to the supply of money results. But great variations in the total of "derivative" deposits are a matter of reasonable inference, and this is the phase of the problem with which we are concerned, since it plays an important part in the theory of liquidity.

For a number of reasons significant changes in demand deposits, and hence in the supply of money, may not be exactly correlated with changes in the asset side of the bank's balance sheets. For instance, a bank which is suspended on a given day will report the same assets the following day, but all of its deposits will have been removed from the supply of money. Time deposits do not qualify as money under the definition we are using. Shifts between time and demand deposits may occur without direct reference to changes in the amount of assets, even though reserve requirements for the two classes of deposits differ. Other significant sources of differences in the movements of bank deposits and earning assets have been described by Dr. Lauchlin Currie:

> . . . banks, without increasing their deposits, may increase their earning assets simply by increasing their liabilities in the form of capital, surplus, and undivided profits, or by decreasing the proportion of their assets which they keep in the form of cash reserves. Moreover, member banks which lose cash through adverse clearing-house balances and customers' demands for cash can, by borrowing from the reserve banks, maintain their earning assets unchanged while their deposits are shrinking. . . . Again, a change can occur in loans and investments unaccompanied by a corresponding move-

[4] Hawtrey, *Currency and Credit*, p. 10.

ment in individual deposits simply through a change in inter-bank and foreign bank deposits in the system's balance sheet.[5] In an accompanying footnote he adds: If the Federal Reserve System included all banks in the country, the "due to" and "due from" other banks item would be equal. As it is, the former exceeded the latter in 1930 by over 2 billion dollars.

Even though total deposits may vary relative to total earning assets as a result of changes in the capital item, the cash reserve item (which reflects gold movements or fiat currency issues), and the amount of borrowing at the central bank, a rough correspondence does exist between total deposits and the expansion and contraction of bank loans and investments. Chart I clearly demonstrates the fact that *total* deposits and total loans and investments, for both member and non-member banks, tend to move in the same direction.

Though the relationship between demand and time deposits may vary without affecting assets, this variation typically is not great in periods in which shifts in liquidity desires are important.[6] This may be a matter of a few weeks or a few months. We may conclude that the earning asset of banks and the supply of bank money in the form of demand deposits tend to move in the same direction. It is not essential to our thesis that there be a close positive correlation. That loans and investments and demand deposits tend to move in the same direction is sufficient.

THE EFFECT OF CHANGES IN LIQUIDITY DESIRES ON THE AMOUNT OF DEPOSIT MONEY

If it is true that the supply of deposit money tends to fluctuate with the earning assets of banks, then factors which influence an expansion or contraction of earning assets will affect the supply of bank money, not *pari passu* but in the same direction. The

[5] Currie, "Treatment of Credit in Contemporary Monetary Theory," *Journal of Political Economy*, XLI (Feb., 1933), 62.

[6] Studies of the relative size of time and demand deposits as percentages of total deposits have been made by Dr. Lauchlin Currie. *The Supply and Control of Money in the United States*, Table 4, p. 70, and by Professor Angell, *The Behavior of Money*, Chart XXV, p. 169. These show the gradual shift to time deposits, but no significant variation around this trend.

CHART I

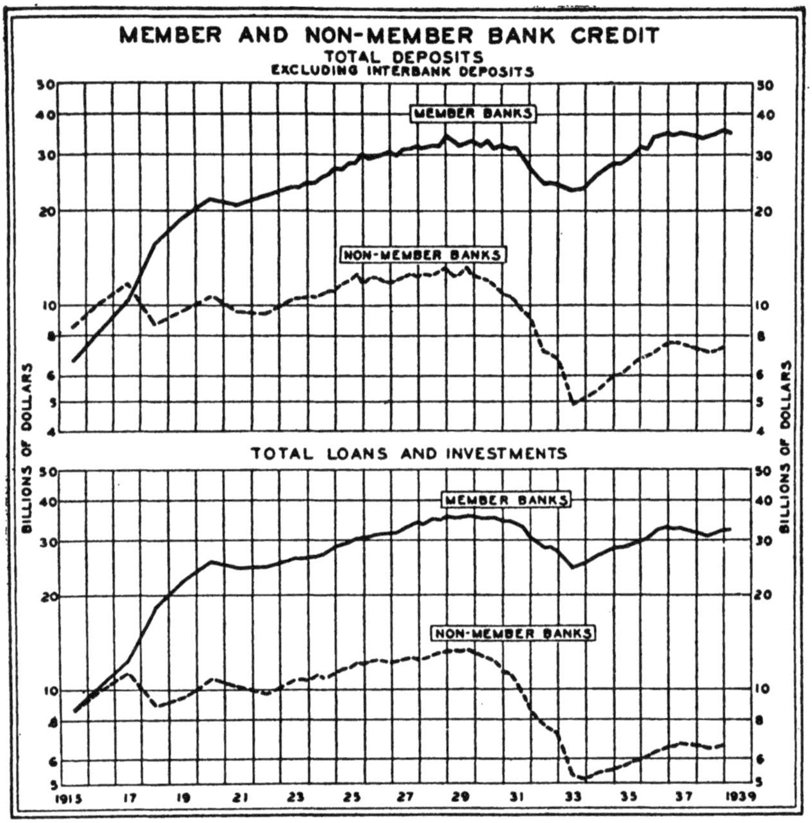

Source: reproduced with permission of the *Annalist.*

management of an individual bank has two principal obligations: to remain solvent and to earn a return on the bank's invested capital commensurate with "prudent" conduct of its affairs. The nature of the bank's earning assets and their extension and contraction are arranged by banking officers with these objectives always in mind. Depending on the prevailing psychology of the moment, first expansion and then contraction will occupy a position of primary importance.

A highly significant characteristic of banking is that the successful operation of an individual bank requires conformity to broad movements of expansion or contraction in the banking system of which it is a part. To the extent that a single bank can induce deposits away from, or loses deposits to its competitors, it may depart from this conformity. Otherwise, the penalty of departure is a greater amount of collections presented than it can meet without impairment of its reserves, or a failure to earn an optimum return on its capital by an inefficient use of its reserves. When the banking system is contracting, the individual banker must of necessity contract, to protect his bank's solvency. When the system of which he is a part is expanding, he would be deemed incompetent by his board of directors if he did not emphasize the other principal objective of bank management, i. e., profits, by expanding his earning assets. But, in conforming to the broad trends of the system, the individual banker is inadvertently contributing to the strength of the movement toward expansion or contraction. We have seen that within limits there is a positive correlation of the supply of money, as represented by demand deposits, with the earning assets of the banking system. This peculiar operating characteristic of the banking system, in reducing the supply of money at a time of contraction and increasing it at a time of expansion, plays an important part in liquidity theory.

The necessity that an individual bank conform to the broad contraction movements of the system of which it is a part, and the tendency of an individual bank to conform to the broad expansion movements, are matters of empirical generalization. The reasons underlying the phenomena may be better understood in the light of a description of banking operations written by Professor C. A. Phillips some years ago. Since central bank deposits are now readily convertible into currency, we have attempted to simplify the following passages by parenthetically complementing the term cash with the term reserves, where this connotation is appropriate:

> Now as loans increase, in the case of an individual bank, cash [reserve] tends to diminish. This is true partly because a few borrowers take all or part of the proceeds of their loans in cash. An attempt on the part of an individual bank to expand its loans is normally met by an immediate and positive reduction of its cash

[reserves]. The *immediate* contraction of cash [reserves] is, however, almost negligibly small and is not the only restraining force affecting the execution of a liberal loan policy.

A second check on the loan expansion of an individual bank consists in the fact that loans result in an increase in deposits, and as deposits increase a given reserve becomes less and less adequate to sustain their growing volume. Moreover, when the proceeds of loans are left on deposit with the bank, the balances created are soon reduced—funds are borrowed to be used—through checks drawn by the borrowers in connection with the payment of current obligations. Such checks are in most cases remitted to creditors who are not depositor-customers of the drawer's bank, which stands to lose cash [reserves] when the checks are presented, directly or indirectly, for payment. As the deposit structure, i. e., liabilities payable in cash on demand or at short notice, rises as a result of rising loans, the cash [reserve] base on which it rests becomes smaller and smaller. The liberal loan policy of an individual bank is opposed, then, in the process of its execution, by a double check: as loans are extended (a) cash [reserves] tends to diminish; and (b) deposit liabilities arising from loans tend to swell,—the prelude to a further loss of cash [reserves].

A bank . . . will continue to expand its loans until through a slight increase of deposits arising from loans and the decrease of cash [reserves] resulting from loans, the ratio of reserve to deposit liabilities becomes what the bank management regards as normal or desirable.[7]

If all the banks in a system are increasing their loans and investments at the same rate, the cash [reserves] of any one bank will tend to remain constant. . . . For the banking system as a whole, the only check on expanding loans is that represented by swelling deposit liabilities.[8]

In these passages the discussion concerns only the expansion phase of banking operations. But if an individual bank, because of the reasons cited, will lose reserves from a disproportionate expansion of its loans and investments, it will likewise lose reserves from a disproportionate *maintenance* of loans and investments if the banking system is contracting. The only means by which an individual bank can depart significantly from this con-

[7] Phillips, *Bank Credit,* pp. 20–21.
[8] *Ibid.,* pp. 77–78.

formity is to attract a larger *percentage* of the total extant deposits of the system.

The earning assets of banks consist almost exclusively of debts. In the previous chapter we studied the expansion and contraction of non-money debts in response to changed liquidity desires. The debts owned by banks are no exception to the general rule. A highly important secondary effect of the response of the debts making up bank assets to changed liquidity desires is the change of the supply of deposit money in the same direction.

A period of contraction on the part of the banking community is empirically and logically concomitant with a surge toward liquidity on the part of the public, a retardation in the rate of final buying, a falling price level, a declining aggregate of money profits, increased hoarding, and a decrease in the corpus of non-money debt. In other words, at the same time that the desires of the public to hold claims to future wealth in more liquid titles strengthen, the most liquid of all titles, or money, is declining in absolute amount. Instead of providing a curative mechanism, the organization of banking here acts as a contributing and accelerating force. Conversely, a period of expansion on the part of the banking community is concomitant with a public surge toward illiquidity. There results an increased supply of money, when it is in less demand as a store of value but in greater demand for use in production. Each unit of money also tends to be exchanged more rapidly against real wealth, with the consequence that both the exchange velocity of money and its supply increase. Again we find the banking organization acting as an aggravating rather than as a smoothing factor.

THE "PUBLIC'S" CONTROL OF THE MONEY SUPPLY

Mr. Keynes, it will be recalled, has held that the supply of money is unresponsive to changes in liquidity desires: ". . . the quantity of money is not determined by the public." On the contrary, it would appear that the supply of money is not only responsive to public behavior, but responsive in a highly sensitive though irrational fashion. A more careful survey of the public's control of the supply of money has been made by Mr. Durbin:

> To begin from the beginning—it is very generally recognized that the public can do nothing to *increase* the quantity of money or the total liabilities of the Banks without the consent of the Banks themselves. Entrepreneurs and the consuming public can reduce the volume of deposits very easily by paying off their overdrafts or loan obligations to the Banks at an accelerated rate. Moreover, they can increase the total volume of monetary expenditure by turning over their stocks of money more rapidly, but they can do nothing to increase the size of those stocks if the Banks are not willing to lend. The stocks of credit money in the system are controlled by the volume of advances made by the Banks to their customers and it is plainly impossible for the public to force the hands of the Banks in any conceivable way if they (the banks) will not increase their credit accommodation.
>
> But it is not so obvious and yet it is equally true, that the Banks cannot increase the volume of effective money without the consent of the public. The Banks can always increase the quantity of money stocks. . . . But this does not involve any necessary increase in the effective quantity of money (MV). An increase in the quantity of money it holds does not force the public to spend any greater total sum and if there is no inducement for it to increase its monetary *expenditure* the increase in the volume of money will be offset by an exactly proportional reduction in the average velocity of circulation and the quantity of effective money will remain constant.[9]

Thus, says Mr. Durbin, the public may not increase but it may decrease the aggregate of bank deposits without the consent of the banks themselves. Further, the public alone may increase or decrease the velocity of the available money. Let us first look at the question of the public's ability to increase the amount of the money stock.

It is obvious that a prospective borrower cannot obtain a bank loan without the consent of the bank. Since a bank loan is the reciprocal of the bank's debt, and since the bank's debt is money if it is a demand debt, it follows that an individual acting alone cannot increase the supply of money without the consent of the banks. But "the public" is a term applied to a group of individ-

[9] Durbin, *The Problem of Credit Policy*, pp. 78–79.

uals, and the behavior of bankers is highly sensitive to the *dominant* desires of the public. If the public psychology is such that liquidity desires are decreased, it is still literally true that the bankers' consent must be obtained to an increase in the money stock. But it is also true that the consent becomes substantially easier to obtain. When "the public" wants more money *for use* in production-distribution activities, as a practical matter it will be forthcoming within the limits of the ability of the banking system to provide it. Those desiring it are willing to assume obligations to obtain it.

A different conclusion pertains when the public wants more money to hold as a *store* of value. The demand for money as a store of value is derived from a belief that money prices will decline, or from a desire for liquidity resting on uncertainty. A holder of money owing an obligation which is equal in amount to the money he holds and written in terms of money, does not stand to gain either of these objectives. The demand for money as a store of value is a demand for money *alone*. The demand for money to use in production is a demand for money, accompanied by a willingness to assume corresponding loan obligations.

If liquidity desires are high, not only is the public reluctant to assume new loan obligations, it is in a mood to pay off old ones. There is a lower level of final buying, an expectation of falling prices and money profits, and, as we have seen, a reduction of the aggregate of debt. Bank debt is no exception to the rule. It follows that an increase in the demand for money as a store of value, which is a typical accompaniment of increased liquidity desires, will not be met by an increase in the supply of money. On the contrary, *there will be an actual decline in its amount.*

A somewhat similar treatment of this matter of the demand for money and loans is provided by Dr. Currie, who remarks that ". . . the demand for loans and the demand for means of payment vary inversely." [10] When business is expanding, he holds that there is less demand for idle balances and more demand for loans. When business is contracting, there is more demand for

[10] Currie, "Treatment of Credit in Contemporary Monetary Theory," *Journal of Political Economy,* XLI (Feb., 1937), p. 68.

idle balances, and less demand for loans. But Dr. Currie appears to impair the usefulness of his proposition by treating the demand for loans as a demand for loans per se. No one wants to incur an obligation merely for the sake of doing so.[11] The demand for loans is derived from the demand for money to exchange against real wealth. Dr. Currie's proposition might be rephrased: the demand for money to use in exchange against real wealth and the demand for money to withhold from such exchange vary inversely. Of course they vary inversely: they are antithetical in nature. The important point is that the demand for money to use in exchange will be substantially satisfied, whereas the demand for money to hoard will not be satisfied. In the first case the supply of money will be positively elastic; in the second case it will be negatively elastic.

These are the conclusions which appear defensible with respect to the public's ability to *increase* the supply of money. Mr. Durbin has said that the public may *decrease* the supply of money without the consent of the banks "by paying off their overdrafts or loan obligations to the Banks at an accelerated rate." Subject only to the theoretical possibility (which is not a probability) of the banks buying securities at a compensating "accelerated rate," this proposition is not debatable. If financially able, an individual may pay off his loan with the banking system when it matures and not renew it. Since every day a large number of such loans mature, a substantial contraction in the aggregate of all bank loans may be effected if the public so desires. But this is an academic question, not a practical one. We have seen that when the public is in a mood to pay loans, the dominant psychology also entails a lessened expectation of money profits, a declining rate of final buying, and a general contraction in economic activity. The banks as a group are quick to sense the situation. As a group, they adopt a policy of contraction. An individual bank cannot operate in opposition to the group behavior. Hence, in all probability, the banker is even more anxious to have a loan paid under these circumstances than the borrower is to repay it.

11 Unless there is a tax aspect of the action.

The public, if by the public we mean the personification of a dominant psychology motivating a dominant course of action, cannot for long decrease the supply of money *without* changing the psychology of the banks and thus causing them to consent.

It will be recalled that Mr. Durbin has held that the public possesses the final decision in the matter of the velocity of money. On this view, the public thus exercises a highly important influence over the *effective* supply of money, irrespective of the question of its control over the absolute amount. But even this seemingly obvious statement cannot stand without some modification. The banking system also exercises a circumscribed control over the use and hence over the velocity of money. We shall briefly examine the nature of this control.

The use of the proceeds of each new loan is approved by the banks before the loan is granted. This means that the *initial* use of those additions to the aggregate deposit-money supply arising out of new loans is approved by the banks. Even though the aggregate supply of money is constant or decreasing, the banks control the initial use of that segment which is continually coming into being to replace, in whole or in part, that which is canceled by loan repayments. Thus the banks may direct the use of one segment of the flow of money.

A significant part of the total money stock circulates as currency outside the banking system and is *never* deposited. It is obvious that the banker has no control over the use of this segment. Again, the banker exercises no appreciable control over the use of that part of his deposits which is represented on the asset side of his balance sheet by his "till-money" currency and by his own redeposits. In a sense he exercises a negative control, however, if he accumulates currency and makes redeposits in excess of his normal requirements relative to his own deposit liabilities. Such bank hoarding is quite as significant as individual hoarding.

The banker does exercise some control over the use of that part of the money stock which is represented by deposits that are not expected to be withdrawn on balance under normal circumstances. These deposits come to be looked upon by the banker as a more or less permanent though fluctuating fund, and as such available to him to place in less liquid titles as a means of covering the expenses of his business and obtaining a profit therefrom. He buys debts and pays for these less liquid titles with money, including drafts on himself. Thus the sellers of the less liquid titles to the banks are now possessed of money which, in the first instance, presumably had been deposited by someone else and not withdrawn. There appear to be two owners for the same unit of money, each owning it entirely.

This may or may not be the case, depending upon the use of the money received, which is made by the seller of the less liquid title to the bank. If the seller happens to be another bank, from which the money was withdrawn in the first instance, the money may be used to pay a temporary loan or to replenish a balance with the central bank. Here the money is canceled. But if the seller of the less liquid title is an individual, two units of money now appear where one existed before. The original depositor holds title to one of them. The seller of the less liquid title holds title to the other.

Without adequate reserves, this duplication could not be accomplished. With adequate reserves, it is a common phenomenon in periods of expansion. When the bank exchanges deposits for less liquid titles, it receives titles either to loans or to investments. If the former, it no doubt first gave its approval to the use of the proceeds of the loan. In other words, to the extent that bank assets consist of *new* loans, the control by banks over the initial use of money and the influence of their operations on the supply of money are two phases of the same general phenomenon.

An exception to this statement should be noted. If the sum of additions to loans and investments is exactly offset by deductions from loans and investments, the activity will cause no change in the aggregate supply of money. Since the control by banks of the use of money is a function of the number and size of their new loaning and investing operations, and since with a constant supply of money the number and size of new loaning and investing operations is a function of the number and size of deductions from loans and investments, it is evident that banker control of the use of money is in part measured by the frequency of the maturity or sale of the banks' assets.

The point should be made that while the ability to determine to whom loans shall be made, and the purpose to which the proceeds of new security purchases will be applied, gives the banks a considerable influence over the use of money, it does not constitute even an approach to tight control. In the interval between the making and paying of a loan or the purchase and sale of a security, the particular money emitted by the banks may circulate many times (against corporeal and intangible wealth or other tokens put to a great variety of uses), without necessarily affecting the earning assets of banks. As there is always a large though fluctuating total of such banking assets, there must always be a large supply of deposits which the owners are free to use without banking restraint.

Something more than casual mention has been made of this matter of the control of the use of money, since it occupies a significant place in the general problem of liquidity. It will be recalled that an initiating cause of an increased desire for liquidity is a misdirection of economic resources relative to public wants. Public wants are expressed only in exchanges of money against final goods. Decisions which result in the application of economic resources are expressed in exchanges of money against primary and intermediate goods as well as against final goods, and give rise to what we have called interstitial payments and final buying. The economic desirability of these money exchanges in the earlier stages of production cannot be determined until final public desire has expressed itself.

It is frequently assumed that the banker, since he has contact with various phases of the business system, is better situated than the industrial or commercial enterpriser to judge the desirability of using money for given purposes. This, of course, depends entirely on the capacity of the individual banker. There is no empirical reason to conclude that bankers as a class are better able than other intelligent members of the community to direct the use of economic resources within the productive system. In practice, the banker's opinion is usually derived from contemplation of the specific problem in question, viewed more or less independently of its setting in the larger economic composition. But this is also the manner in which the bank's customer usually approaches his decision. All that can be said is that the banker usually is less anxious to assume risks and hence probably prevents many mistakes from being made in the use of resources. Conversely, he probably prevents many uses of resources that would not have been ill-advised. Which influence predominates one will never know.

THE BEHAVIOR OF "THE" INTEREST RATE IN SHORT PERIODS

Now that we have examined the influence of changed liquidity desires on the effective supply of deposit money, we may consider again their influence on the interest rate in short periods, a topic introduced in the latter part of the chapter on hoarding.[12] There we found that an increase in liquidity desires results in an increase in the demand for more liquid assets relative to less liquid assets. One phase of this shift is a relatively greater demand for short-dated debt instruments than for long-dated ones. An increase in the spread between long and short interest rates results. But we have still to examine the question of the influence of changed liquidity desires on movements of "the" interest rate, as contrasted with the spread of interest rates. After we have done this, we shall reconsider the question of the spread of interest rates, to see whether our present conclusions are confirmed or should be modified.

Perhaps the best way to approach this task is by a comparison with the familiar Keynesian treatment of liquidity and the interest rate. Mr. Keynes places much emphasis on the rate of interest as the inducement not to hoard, ". . . a rise in the rate of interest is a means *alternative* to an increase of hoards for satis-

[12] *Supra*, pp. 141–46.

fying an increased liquidity preference." Interest is held to be the premium which we require to make us part with money:

> . . . the rate of interest is the reward for parting with liquidity for a specified period. . . . It is the "price" which equilibrates the desire to hold wealth in the form of cash with the available quantity of cash;—which implies that if the rate of interest were lower, i. e., if the reward for parting with cash were diminished, the aggregate amount of cash which the public would wish to hold would exceed the available supply, and that if the rate of interest were raised, there would be a surplus of cash which no one would be willing to hold.[13]

Although it is not certain, presumably Mr. Keynes is referring to currency plus demand deposits when he uses the term cash in this passage. It is held that the amount of money does not increase in response to greater liquidity desires.

> Moreover, it is impossible for the actual amount of hoarding to change as a result of decisions on the part of the public, so long as we mean by "hoarding" the actual holding of cash. For the amount of hoarding must be equal to the quantity of money . . . and the quantity of money is not determined by the public.[14]

Or again:

> When . . . liquidity preferences are sharply raised, this shows itself not so much in increased hoards—for there is little, if any, more cash which is hoardable than there was before.[15]

Without specifying the interest rate to which he refers, Mr. Keynes seems to hold that since the supply of money is unresponsive, there is a positive correlation between the level of a composite of interest rates and the level of liquidity desires. "The rate of interest is the factor which adjusts at the margin the demand for hoards to the supply of hoards." [16]

From these propositions we might expect the interest rate to rise with an increase in liquidity desires and to fall when they

[13] Keynes, *The General Theory of Employment, Interest and Money*, p. 167.
[14] *Op. cit.*, p. 174.
[15] "The General Theory of Employment," *Quarterly Journal of Economics*, LI (Feb., 1937), 211.
[16] *Ibid.*, p. 217.

fall. Moreover, the rate would rise until it was sufficiently high to induce a cessation of hoarding or fall until it induced an amount of hoarding compatible with the quantity of money and the existing state of liquidity desires. These, as we shall see, are debatable propositions.[17]

Contrary to Keynes's view, the supply of money is responsive to changes in public desires, of which liquidity desires are one. It is responsive in peculiar ways. An increased demand for money to use in exchange will be accompanied by an increased supply. An increased demand for money to hold as a store of value will be accompanied by a *decreased* supply. There is no adequate basis on which to judge the aggregate demand for money in both of its functions. If we may assume this aggregate demand to be constant—that is, assume that the real wealth value of the money stock at any moment in time is constant [18]—then an increase in the demand to use money in exchange must be accompanied by an equal decrease in the demand for hoarding. The aggregate supply of money units would thus fluctuate, relative to a fixed

17 There is one sense in which Keynes appears to be correct in holding that "interest rates" will rise with an increase in liquidity desires. In this situation, there is a disposition to dispose of assets poorly protected by earnings, as well as of less liquid assets, and the concomitant fall in asset prices may be taken as the equivalent of a rise in the interest rate. The important point here is that asset prices fall because there exists an expectation of smaller money profits *accompanied by greater risks.* Interest, so far as we are aware, has not been used in the past typically to describe compensation for assuming risk. It is more nearly correct, but not wholly correct, to say that interest describes the compensation received for not assuming risks. Still more properly we might say that interest is the compensation received for parting with money, *after* the compensation for the accompanying risk has been deducted.

The suggestion has been made by Bissell, "The Rate of Interest," *American Economic Review,* Suppl. XXVIII (March, 1938), 23–40, that the rate of interest be defined broadly as an index of the availability of capital. We assume he means the availability of loanable money. This seems to be closely akin to the concept that Keynes *implicitly* uses in his liquidity preference theory of interest. If so, it is unfortunate that he has not been more explicit. It has not been the general practice so closely to identify interest and money profits in the past. By so doing, distinctions of value are lost.

18 This is an assumption which is not tenable in fact, but it is still sufficiently true to illustrate the point under discussion. See Edwin Cannan's "The Application of the Theoretical Apparatus of Supply and Demand to Units of Currency," *The Economic Journal,* XXXI (1921), 453 ff.

aggregate demand. The price of money, measured by the price level, would then behave as one would expect, falling when the supply increases, and rising when the supply decreases. But interest rates behave differently. We shall see that they tend to rise with an increased supply of money, while they may or may not fall with a decreased supply. Mr. Keynes may have confused the interest rate as the price of money with the price level as the price of money, in holding that "Changes in the propensity to hoard . . . primarily affect, not prices, but the rate of interest; any effect on prices being produced by repercussion as an ultimate consequence of a change in the rate of interest." [19]

The proposition that a change in the propensity to hoard will not affect prices directly apparently rests on Mr. Keynes's rejection of velocity as a useful analytical tool and on the questionable postulate that a change in the propensity to hoard will leave unaffected the number of money units available for hoarding. We have concluded that the supply of money does respond to changed public desires, including liquidity desires, and that this change in the supply of money is synchronous with price-level changes. This variation in the supply of money will affect interest rates, but not in a manner automatically stimulating or retarding the propensity to hoard. Moreover, there appears to be no fixed correlation, positive or negative, between the propensity to hoard and changes in a composite of interest rates. We may elaborate these propositions as follows.

The holder of a certain amount of money, who owes a debt of equal amount payable in money, does not stand to gain from a fall in the price level, nor will he improve his liquidity status by such a fall. The demand for money to hoard is not a demand for loans, and in consequence it is not felt in the money markets as a positive determinant of the interest rate.

The demand for money to use in exchange, on the other hand, is reflected in the money markets through a demand for loans. This demand for money to use in exchange declines when li-

[19] "The General Theory of Employment," *Quarterly Journal of Economics,* LI (Feb., 1937), 216–17.

quidity desires are raised. At the same time, the supply of money, as measured by demand deposits plus currency outside the banks, will decline. But unless the reserves of the banks have changed, the *potential* supply of money will remain unchanged. It therefore appears that changes in the interest rate in short periods are a result of changes in the demand for money to use in exchange, this demand being gauged not relative to the *actual* supply of money as defined, but relative to the *potential* supply. The latter is a function of the reserve position of the member banks. Any factors that change the relationship of reserves to deposits thus become of outstanding importance.

A decrease in the supply of money is an accompaniment of a general desire for increased hoarding. Suppose that this desire to hoard takes the form of deposit hoarding. It then follows that this decreased supply of money will be in the form of smaller deposits on the books of commercial banks. The ease or tightness of the money market is chiefly a matter of the relation between the liabilities of the commercial banks and their deposits with the central bank. But their deposits with the central bank (their reserves) are not influenced either by the decline in their own customer-deposits or by the slower turnover of their remaining customer-deposits.

The amount of reserves of commercial banks is affected by gold movements into and out of the banking system, changes in the amount of outside circulation, changes in the volume of earning assets of the central banks, and shifts of government deposits from commercial banks to central banks. These are factors which are not directly responsive to a general desire for more or less deposit hoarding. If we assume them to be constant, the *absolute* amount of reserves of member banks will be unchanged. The increased desire for deposit hoarding, however, will be accompanied by a decrease in deposits of commercial banks. A *relative* increase of reserves of the commercial banks will result. This is tantamount to an easing of the money market. At the same time, the demand for money to use, which is the demand for loans, is lessened. Both result in a lowering of the interest rate.

But hoarding is discouraged by rising interest rates and encouraged by falling interest rates, according to Mr. Keynes. "The rate of interest is the factor which adjusts at the margin the demand for hoards to the supply of hoards." [20] ". . . The rate of interest is the reward for parting with liquidity for a specific period." [21] If the interest rate rises, the *inducement not to hoard* is alleged to increase to a point at which the supply and demand for hoards is equal at the margin. If the interest rate falls, the *inducement to hoard* is alleged to increase to a similar equilibrating point. But, *ceteris paribus,* we have seen that an increased desire to hoard deposits will result in a falling interest rate. According to Mr. Keynes, the inducement to hoard will thus become still greater. If this were completely true, the logical outcome would be the hoarding of all deposits and a complete cessation of all related economic activity—which, of course, is unthinkable.

On the other hand, the increase of hoarding may take the form of *currency* hoarding. Both in the case of deposit hoarding and currency hoarding, a decrease of the commercial banks' earning assets will result. The psychological factors motivating currency hoarding are perhaps even more effective in reducing the earning assets of banks than those motivating deposit hoarding. If this were all that we needed to consider, currency hoarding would be even more effective than deposit hoarding in reducing interest rates.

But in the case of currency hoarding another and technical factor enters, and one which works in the opposite direction. Currency hoarding results in an exchange of deposits for currency. In the United States, so long as the Federal Reserve banks have the legislated requirements of gold certificates and government bonds or commercial paper to place behind their currency issue, all deposits of the member banks with the Reserve banks are readily convertible into currency. The size of member bank balances with the central banks, that is, the size of their reserves, determines their ability to get cash within these limits. However,

[20] *Supra,* p. 193.

[21] *Supra,* p. 192.

for every dollar in currency received by the member bank from the central bank, the member bank loses a dollar of reserves. But each dollar of reserves supports a multiple sum of customer-deposits of the member bank. It follows that in a banking system organized on the basis of fractional reserves, for every unit of currency withdrawn to outside circulation there must be a multiple contraction of customer-deposits. A ratio of about five to one is suggested by the reserve requirements now prevailing in the Federal Reserve System.[22]

We have seen how deposit hoarding results in a lower interest rate, since the liabilities of member banks are decreased through the sale of securities and the repayment of loans, without changing the absolute amount of their reserves. The liabilities of member banks are decreased for the same reasons in the case of currency hoarding. They are also decreased in this event by the conversion of deposits into currency and the withdrawal of such currency from the banking system. Unlike the sale of securities and the repayment of customers' loans, however, both operations which do not affect the absolute amount of their reserves, the withdrawal of currency from the banking system depletes the banks' cash on hand, that is, their reserves.

Short-period changes in money-market interest rates result from changes in the relation of member bank reserves to their customer-deposits, and from changes in the amounts of their own borrowing, if any, necessary to acquire reserves. From the table shown in footnote 22, it may be seen that in the United States $1 of reserves will legally support about $5 of customer-deposits in member banks.[23]

Hypothetically, the relation of member banks' customer-deposits to currency and reserves will be unchanged, if the decrease in deposits from the repayment of loans, the sale of securities, and the withdrawal of currency are five times as great as the

22

Reserves against time deposits:	5 percent
Reserves against demand deposits:	22.75 percent in central Reserve cities
	17.5 percent in Reserve cities
	12 percent in other localities

23 The actual amount of deposits would, of course, depend upon the distribution of the Reserves.

decrease in deposits from the withdrawal of currency alone. In this event, a change in the general level of interest rates need not result.

In practice, such an outcome is improbable. A period of currency hoarding is a period of hysteria. According to the estimates of Professor Angell, outside currency in circulation increased about 2 billion dollars, or from about 3.75 billion dollars at the end of February, 1931, to about 5.78 billion dollars by the end of February, 1933. In the same two-year period, he estimates that corrected circulating deposits (excluding time deposits) declined from 20.97 billion dollars to 15.36 billion dollars, or by 5.61 billion dollars.[24] His estimate of total deposits shows a decline of 11.08 billion dollars between the June call dates of 1930 and 1932.

Interest rates, which on this showing should have exhibited an upward tendency during the period, were prevented from doing so by the purchase of large amounts of government bonds by the central banks in the latter part of 1932. If the earning assets of the central banks had been constant during the period, it would have been theoretically necessary to have had a reduction of about 20 billions in total deposits to maintain stable interest rates on the basis of the then existing reserve requirements. If for no other reason, the sheer sluggishness of the mechanics of banking seems likely to prevent any such catastrophic decline of deposits. Thus a *rise* of interest rates is the logical result to be expected from currency hoarding.

Even though a rise in "the" interest rate is probable in the special circumstance of currency hoarding, it does not necessarily follow that this rise is the factor accounting for a reversal of the public attitude toward hoarding. A priori, it seems more probable that an event or series of events not proximately associated with the interest rate, but which have the effect of more directly modifying profit expectations, will be more potent in diminishing the desire to hoard.

To accept the proposition that a rise in interest rates is what

[24] Angell, *The Behavior of Money*, Appendix B, Table I, p. 175, and Table II, p. 179.

induces a reduction of hoarding thus seems to involve a dubious assumption, namely, that short-term movements of interest rates are substantially synchronous with changes in money profits and in money-profit expectations. Without entering the controversy of what determines the rate of interest through long periods, we may say that it is doubtful if the trend of money profits in periods extending over several years is the determining factor. Witness the large increase of money profits and national money income in the United States from the middle of 1932 through 1936, while interest rates steadily declined. Certainly there was a diminution of liquidity desires during this four and one-half year period; and interest rates were not rising—they were falling.

The point may be raised that though interest rates declined during the period, they did not decline as much as they would have done if money profits had not expanded. It is true that a case can be made for the view that an expansion of money profits will be accompanied by an expansion of business activity and by greater demands for bank loans. If all other factors are unchanged, this will also entail an increase of interest rates. But all other factors do not remain unchanged. The aggregate influence of variations in *central-bank* earning assets, of gold and currency movements into and out of the banking system, and of changing reserve requirements, are of overshadowing importance in the determination of interest rates in short periods. It might even be said that synchronization in the movements of aggregate money profits and of a composite of interest rates would be more of a fortuitous coincidence, in short periods, than a development naturally to be expected under existing banking organizations and techniques.

In the absence of currency hoarding, higher interest rates appear more likely to follow than to precede a lessening of liquidity desires. An increased supply of money, we have seen, is an accompaniment of lessened liquidity desires. The demand for this increased supply of money will be a demand for money to use in exchange, rather than for money to hoard. This increase in the supply of money is likely to result in a higher level of interest rates. It will do so in fact, unless it is offset by other factors which increase the reserves of the member banks.

In the absence of movements of gold and currency into and out of the banking system, and of changes in the earning assets of the central banks, the increase in the demand for money to use will work to raise interest rates, as the member banks approach the limits of their customary or legislated reserve. If they resort to borrowing at the central bank, thus increasing the latter's earning assets, the rates quoted to customers may or may not reflect the increment added to the member banks' expense by the central-bank borrowing. Lastly, orthodox theory also expects a loss of gold by the banking system, as a result of higher prices accompanying the increased money supply. But in recent years international gold movements have not conformed well to this expectation.

The less the desire for liquid titles, the greater may be the supply of money and the higher the interest rate may go. Yet, according to Keynes, the higher interest rate reports greater liquidity desires, since it is the price exacted for parting with liquidity. In short, the higher the interest, the less will be the desire for liquid titles. Again we seem to have encountered a self-stimulating spiral, the logical outcome of which is an indefinite and incredible expansion of bank debt. The supply of money, whether increasing or decreasing, is found to be a cantankerous quantity, not suited at all to the molding of a neat theory in which the interest rate is treated as an adjusting mechanism. Only on the seemingly false assumptions that changes in public desires leave the supply of money unchanged and that the interest rate is the reverse side of the price of assets has Mr. Keynes been able to construct his theory that liquidity desires are adjusted by the interest rate.

We may now return briefly to examine the difference between long and short interest rates for prime quality paper, as an index of changing liquidity desires, and compare this index with the movement of the interest rate. *Ceteris paribus,* a decrease in liquidity desires will result in an increase in the interest rate. It

CHART II

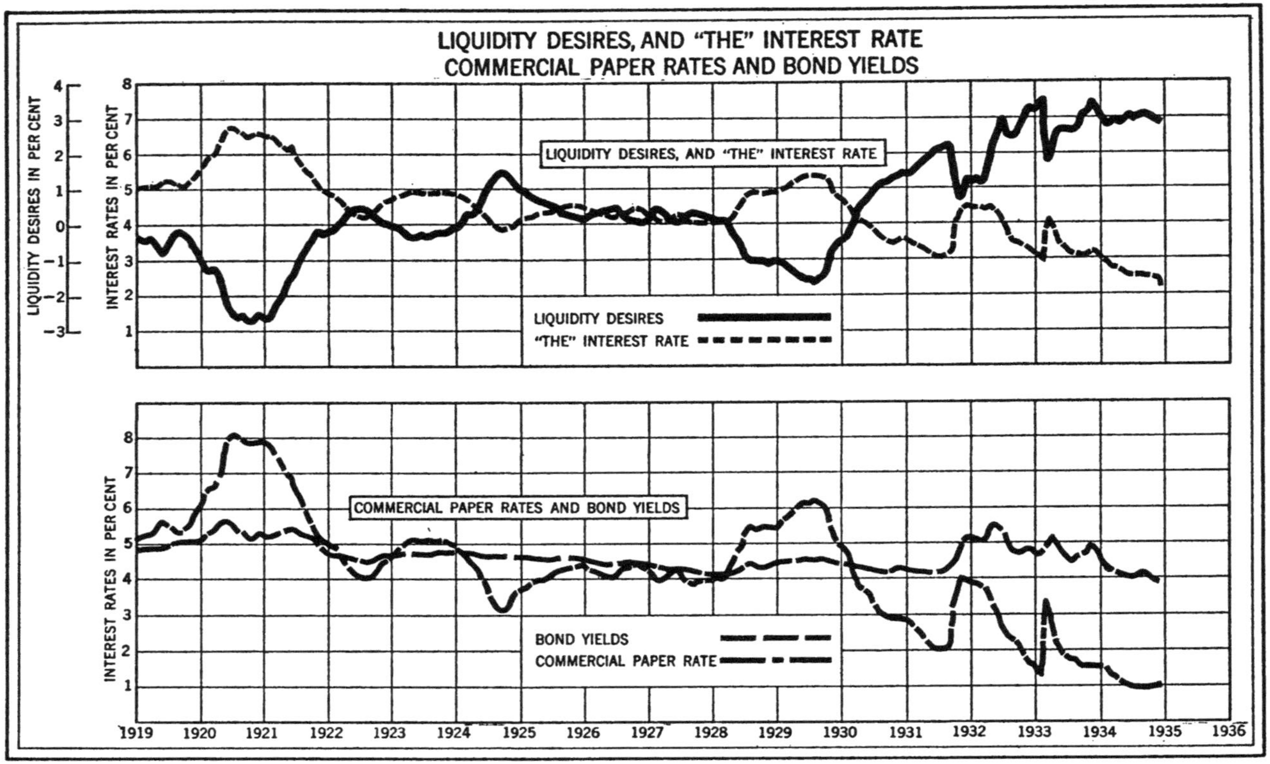

Source: Commercial paper rates and bond yields as published by the *Annalist,* July 13, 1939, p. 62.

The curve describing changes in the direction of change of liquidity desires is derived by deducting commercial paper rates from bond yields; the curve describing "the" interest rate is simply commercial paper rates and bond yields added together and divided by 2.

will be recalled that it will also reduce the *relative* desirability of short- over long-dated paper of comparable quality. The short rate deducted from the long rate will leave a smaller remainder. There are periods when the remainder becomes a negative quantity, the short rate advancing above the long.[25] Again, *ceteris paribus,* an increase in liquidity desires will result in a decrease in the interest rate. But if currency hoarding reduces member bank balances at the central bank, it may not do so. An increase in liquidity desires will also increase the *relative* desirability of short- over long-dated paper of comparable quality. The short rate deducted from the long rate will leave a larger remainder, and the spread between the two will be wider. According to this reasoning, the interest rate should rise as the spread between the long and the short rate diminishes and should fall as the spread widens. But a decrease in the spread reports a lessening of liquidity desires with a rising interest rate, and an increase in the spread reports a strengthening of liquidity desires with a falling interest rate.

To test these propositions, we have used a sixteen-year sample of short and long interest rates published by *The Annalist.*[26] The short rate is the open-market rate for prime two-name commercial paper of thirty to sixty days' duration. The long rate is computed from a list of high-grade non-callable railroad bonds. Changes in this list of bonds were necessary during the period under observation, when the factor of risk began significantly to influence prices. These changes are as follows:

From 1919 to end of February, 1931:

Atchison Topeka & Santa Fe general mortgage 4s, 1995
Chicago Burlington & Quincy general mortgage 4s, 1958
*Chicago & Northwestern general mortgage 4s, 1987
*Chicago Rock Island & Pacific gen. mortgage 4s, 1988
*Illinois Central first and ref. mortgage 4s, 1955
Norfolk & Western first cons. mortgage 4s, 1996

[25] This is contrary to Mr. Hicks, who has held that ". . . the long rate must be a sort of average of the probable short rates over its duration and . . . this average must lie above the current short rate." *Vide* "Mr. Keynes and the 'Classics'; A Suggested Interpretation," *Econometrica,* V (1937), 154–55.

[26] July 13, 1939, p. 62.

Northern Pacific gen. lien & land grant 4s, 1997
*St. Louis & Southwestern first mortgage 4s, 1989
Southern Pacific first cons. & refunding 4s, 1955
Union Pacific Railroad railroad & land grant 4s, 1947

Those bonds marked with an asterisk were eliminated in a revision of March 7, 1931, and replaced by:

Chesapeake & Ohio gen. mortgage 4½s, 1992
N. Y. Central & Hudson River mortgage 3½s, 1997
Pennsylvania R. R. cons. mortgage 4½s, 1960
Reading Company gen. & ref. mortgage A 4½s, 1997.

In Chart II the index of liquidity desires represents the *difference* between the yields to maturity of prime commercial paper and these high-grade corporate bonds for each month of the sixteen-year sample.

The curve representing "the" interest rate is drawn from a simple arithmetical average of the same short and long yields. More complicated procedures have been considered and discarded. Weighting, in this instance, is meaningless, since loanable funds, unlike carrots and tomatoes, are homogeneous and flow readily from one market to another. A simple arithmetic average seems quite as satisfactory as more complicated averages, since the size of neither rate completely dominates the other in the period under review. Moreover, we have implicitly assumed that a series of interest rates of different maturities, but of similar quality, when plotted form a straight line and not a curve. There are an infinite number of interest rates corresponding to an infinite number of maturity dates. The average level on the y axis of a straight line made up of an infinite number of points all of equal value (unweighted) may be obtained by adding the polar or extreme points and dividing by 2. The *direction of change* in the *level* of the line on the y axis may be safely estimated by similarly averaging the position of points near the polar points, so long as they are the same points. This we have done with long and short interest rates, to estimate the direction of change in "the" interest rate.

A rather close inverse relationship is disclosed. As the index of liquidity desires rises, "the" interest rate falls. As the index of liquidity desires falls, "the" interest rate rises. This, of course, is antithetical to the liquidity theory of interest as developed by Mr. Keynes. On the other hand, if our preceding reasoning in regard to movements of "the" interest rate is valid, it confirms the logical consistency of using the difference between long and short rates of prime debt instruments as an index of changes in liquidity desires.

Objection has been raised increasingly in recent years to the use of the phrase "the interest rate." Its limitations, not unlike those of the similar phrase, "the price level," are recognized. However, broad changes in the cost of borrowing money are matters of common knowledge, in the same way as knowledge of changes in the price level. In Chart II we have plotted also the short and long rates from which the curves of liquidity preference and the interest rate are derived. The short and long rates typically move in the same direction; hence they both move with their average. As would be expected, the long rate is fairly stable, while the short rate fluctuates within wide ranges.[27]

SOME AGGRAVATING AND AMELIORATIVE EFFECTS OF A CHANGING SUPPLY OF MONEY

Insofar as increased liquidity desires give rise to a decreased money supply, the two phenomena interact and feed upon each other in accelerating the contraction phase of the business cycle. Likewise, insofar as decreased liquidity desires give rise to an in-

[27] Each of these four curves might have been corrected for changes in the reserve balances of member banks. Rates in the money markets change, because of changes in the reserve position of commercial banks. Reserve ratios may change, because of absolute changes in member banks' liabilities, without proportional changes in members' reserves. This is the source of change we have identified with liquidity desires. Again, interest rates in the money market may change, because of absolute changes in members' reserves without proportional changes in their liabilities. This is a factor that operates independently of liquidity desires. Experiments to eliminate this independent influence show no significant change from the raw curves until 1933. If adjustment is made for the large absolute increase in member-bank reserves in 1933 and 1934, liquidity desires will be reported as declining and the interest rate as rising in this period. The treatment of these two years will recur in connection with Chart III, *infra*, p. 234.

creased supply of money, the phenomena feed upon each other in accelerating the expansion phase of the business cycle. In both instances the result is a cumulative increment to the forces making for cyclical disturbance. This is a severe condemnation of the extant organization of banking. Were this the only effect of an expansion and contraction of deposit money, it would be difficult indeed to make a case for continuing the present organization. But there are other and more salutary results from the flexible nature of our extant money supply.

Earlier in this study it was held that an acceleration or retardation of the exchange of money against final new output, which we called final buying, is the ultimate determinant of economic well-being under the conditions prescribed by specialization of activity. But these exchanges of money against final new output constitute but a small part of the total of money exchanges. Suppose, hypothetically, that total exchanges of money in a given period are 100, made up as follows: 10 exchanges against final new output, 10 against debt payment, 30 against previously existing wealth-titles (the secondary circulation), and 50 against wealth coming forward in the production-distribution process (the interstitial circulation).

With these imaginary ratios we can see how a small percentage change in the requirements of the financial or interstitial circulation can materially affect the exchanges against final new output. Suppose, for purposes of illustration, that total exchanges of money remain constant and that changes in the secondary or interstitial circulation are reflected exclusively in the final output circulation (which of course in actuality they are not). A 10-percent increase in the secondary circulation would reduce the final output circulation by 33⅓ percent; a 10-percent increase in the interstitial circulation would reduce the final output circulation by 50 percent. Of course no such rigid shifts among the several circulations have realistic meaning. One reason is that the quantity, MV, is not constant. Greater or smaller requirements for money in any particular segment of economic activity are met in part by an increased velocity of money in that segment.

But increased requirements in one segment of activity also tend to attract money units from other segments. Here is a potential source of disturbance which the banking system is now equipped to counteract.

The undertaking of new business ventures of a productive or speculative nature, or the adoption of new forms of business organization, without the approval of the banks, may result in a change in the total quantity of money needed without a change in the supply. A resulting shift in the use of the available (constant) money supply would then constitute a source of disturbance. But if the acts leading to the change in money requirements have had the approval of the banks, and if the banks have manifested their approval by granting new loans, the additional money will be supplied. The close contact of individual bankers with business men, coupled with the bankers' ability to create deposit-money, makes the banking system highly sensitive to these more or less independent changes in segmentary needs for money.

Within these limits, we find a fluctuating supply of money to be an ameliorative influence. It is a phase of the problem of banking organization which those studying the possibilities of various so-called 100-percent reserve plans may not have adequately treated.[28] But the point remains that the larger changes in the aggregate money stock are of an aggravating and not of an ameliorative nature. There exists no mechanism or precedent whereby the commercial banking fraternity may effectively recognize and supply the social need for more money at a time when the public prefers more liquid titles. Rather, each individual commercial bank must either become a participant in the surge to liquidity or pay the price of insolvency. In the opposite situation, it must either become a participant in the surge to illiquidity or pay the price of lost earnings opportunities.

[28] See, however, Professor Angell's treatment of this point in *The Lessons of Monetary Experience, Essays in Honor of Irving Fisher,* edited by A. D. Gayer (New York, 1937), pp. 83 ff.

SUMMARY

In the preceding chapter we found that the supply of non-money debt expands when people are less liquidity-conscious and contracts when they are more so. This expansion and contraction of non-money debt has a highly significant effect on the distribution of new real wealth, and hence on its production in a society with division of labor. These conclusions are equally applicable to that form of current debt which is money.

When there is an increase in liquidity desires, the supply of money will contract in two senses of the term. The effective supply of money will contract because each unit of money will be used less frequently. Second, there will be fewer units of money. This follows as a consequence of the nature of the banking system. Each individual bank must be managed in a manner to conform roughly to the broad movements of expansion and contraction of the banking system, if it is to maximize earnings on the one hand and remain solvent on the other. As banks vary their earning assets, there is likely to be expansion or contraction in the same direction as that of their deposit liabilities payable on demand. This is the chief source of change in the number of money units outstanding.

To the extent that public attitudes influence the direction of change of the earning assets of banks, these attitudes, within the limits that have been described, will also effect a change in the number of money units outstanding. As the liquidity desires of the public increase, earning assets decline and the number of money units diminishes. As liquidity desires decrease, earning assets expand and the number of money units increases.

This is contrary to Mr. Keynes's position, which holds that the public has no control over the quantity of money. If the public collectively wants more money to use in production-distribution activities, it will be forthcoming within the limits of the banking system to provide it through loans. On the other hand, the demand for money as a store of value is a demand for money alone, rather than for money from a loan. In this case, instead of increasing the earning assets of banks, there will be a decrease in all kinds of debts, including earning assets, for reasons we have previously discussed.

The public exercises these influences over changes in the number of money units. It exercises even more influence over the effective supply of money, through its control of the use of money. However, we have seen that it does not exclusively control the use of money, the banks exercising an imperfect and partial control.

Without attempting to discuss the factors setting "the" rate of interest over long periods, we have taken the position that changes in the interest rate in short periods result from money-market factors, including technical banking conditions. These factors may be catalogued under two headings: the demand and the supply of money. But we have considerably qualified the content of both demand and supply when applied to the determination of the interest rate.

The aggregate demand for money includes its demand for use in exchange, and its demand for use as a store of value through time—that is, to hoard. Both of these demands enter into the determination of the value of money as the reciprocal of the price level. But only one of them appears to be applicable in determining interest rates. The demand for money to use in exchange may be accompanied by a demand for loans. It obviously enters as an interest-rate determinant. But the demand for money to hoard is not a demand for loans. One who owes a debt payable in money of an amount equal to his hoard, does not stand to gain in any way. The demand for money to use in exchange is a demand for loans *and* money. The demand for money to hoard is the demand for money alone. The demand for money to use in exchange decreases, with an increase in liquidity desires. Thus, judging the matter from the demand side, we might expect the interest rate to fall when liquidity desires increase.

We must also qualify the meaning of the supply of money as an interest-rate determinant. We have defined money as anything that will serve as a general claim against the economic wealth of the community. This includes currency outside the banking system and the demand deposits of commercial banks. The supply of money thus defined will decrease, with an increase of liquidity desires. But this is not the only supply of money that enters as a determinant of the interest rate. Of great importance in short periods is the *potential* supply of money, as reflected in the reserve position of the commercial banks. Instead of decreasing, the potential supply of money will probably remain unchanged, if raised liquidity desires take the form of deposit hoarding. This follows from the proposition that the deposit liabilities of commercial banks in these circumstances may decrease, without any effect on their own reserves. A lowering of the interest rate will result, since the demand for loans has declined, relative to an unchanged supply. But if the hoarding takes the form of currency hoarding, the result is likely to be reversed. In this event there will be a reduction of the necessary reserves of commercial banks that is more rapid than the decline of their own deposit liabilities. The potential supply of money is thus reduced, and an increase in the interest rate may result, in spite of the decreased demand for loans.

The flexibility of the banking system in increasing or decreasing the amount of money may be ameliorative or aggravative in its influence on business stability. It is the latter when the change in the amount of money has resulted from a change in the dominant liquidity desires of the community. In this circumstance, the phenomena of expanding and contracting bank money must be added to the complex of cumulative forces of business change, related to liquidity desires. It will be recalled that, in addition to changes in the amount of bank money, these forces include *changes* in hoarding, the amount of final buying, the price level, aggregate money profits, and the corpus of non-money debt.

X

THE NATURE OF BANKING ASSETS AND THE SUPPLY OF MONEY

IN AN EARLIER SECTION of this study we reviewed briefly the accounting practice of industrial corporations as it relates to current assets and current liabilities.[1] This practice of showing current assets and current liabilities, as a convenient means of demonstrating the degree of solvency or liquidity possessed by a given enterprise, is highly useful in the case of substantially all firms operating in non-banking fields. No such practice has developed in the case of banking houses, however, for the very good reason that it would have no significant meaning. Examination of why it would have no significant meaning will serve to illustrate certain important characteristics of banking of interest to our discussion.

SOLVENCY IN BANKING

Although banks are usually engaged in sundry activities, their principal function, and that in which we are interested, is the receiving of deposits and the making of loans and investments. The deposits appear as liabilities and the loans and investments as assets. If we relate these assets and liabilities as we did in the case of the industrial and commercial concerns, a striking point of difference stands out immediately. Unlike those of other concerns, the liabilities of banks are not determinable with precision from the standpoint of time. The greater part of deposits

[1] *Supra*, pp. 16–22.

(demand deposits) may be called for at any time—in other words, their time factor *may* be zero. From the legal standpoint, the time factor of the remainder of deposits (time deposits) is known, but in practice competition has forced banks to relinquish even this safeguard in many instances.

If the accountant were to draw up a balance sheet for a bank in the same manner as that of an industrial corporation, practically all liabilities (except those to owners) would have to be shown as current. Hence all assets, including a part of those represented by ownership, would have to be current in order to show a positive working-capital item. Such a condition is seldom to be found. Thus if the assets and liabilities of a representative bank are related on the severe time and price basis applied to the industrial corporation, they will be found to show a highly dangerous position at all times. But when judged on a more liberal time basis, the representative bank will be found to be solvent except under unusual circumstances. Such judgment normally is reached by a bank's creditors, its depositors. Their confidence underlies the solvency of any particular bank and, even more, the solvency of the banking system as a whole. This is a precarious position and it is recognized as such, tacitly or explicitly, in practically all literature on banking.

Predicated on the nature of the banking process itself, there is another manner in which the solvency of a banking house is made less secure than that of the commercial firm. As Professor Kester puts it, it is to certain assets, "or rather to the cash realized from them, that current creditors must look for the liquidation of their claims." [2] In the case of non-banking firms, this cash is usually realized from the "cash" sale of assets, borrowings, and the collection of outstanding trade credits, or receivables. In the case of banking firms, this cash can be realized from the sale of security investments, borrowings, and the collection of outstanding loans. The operations of industrials and banks do not seem greatly different. But in their secondary repercussions they may be strikingly different.

[2] *Supra*. p. 21.

If the non-banking firm sells its assets to, or collects its bills or borrows from other non-banking parties, there need be no secondary repercussions. Likewise, if the banking house sells its investments to, or collects its loans or borrows from other banking parties, there need be no secondary repercussions. But when these transactions take place directly or indirectly between banking and non-banking firms or persons, as they so frequently do, they are automatically followed by repercussions of a secondary nature.

First, take the case of a non-banking firm selling assets to, or borrowing from a banking firm. We have seen that when a bank buys an asset or grants a loan, an increase of like amount in deposit money may result. Assuming no decrease in the average velocity of all money, this addition to its supply acts as a fillip to the economic activity of the community. Liquidity desires tend to be lessened, and the difficulty and necessity of disposing of additional assets by the non-banking firm is thereby diminished.

But if a banking firm sells investments to, or collects loans from a non-banking firm, the process is reversed. There may be a decrease of like amount in deposit money. If this is not compensated by an increase in the average velocity of the remaining money supply, a contraction in the economic activity of the community may result. Liquidity desires tend to be raised, and the difficulty and necessity of disposing of additional assets by the banking firm is enhanced.

Thus the exchange of non-money assets for money by a bank either may not change the amount of money in the community, or it may lead to its contraction and further demands for liquidity. The exchange of non-money assets for money by non-banking interests either may not change the amount of money in the community, or it may lead to its expansion and to lessened liquidity desires. To the extent that the realization of money for a bank's less liquid assets is accompanied by contraction in the money supply, the sale of additional assets is made the more difficult. The contraction may manifest itself both in lower money incomes of its remaining debtors and in the price of its remaining securities.

The significance of this phenomenon is not so clear when the matter is viewed from the standpoint of an individual bank's transaction with a non-banking party. It becomes more apparent if it is recalled that when the banking system is contracting, all banks must join in the movement. The penalty placed on an individual bank which attempts to stem the tide either by purchasing assets from, or by increasing its loans to the public, at a time when the banking system is contracting, will be a loss of reserves through adverse clearings. Hence during a period of contraction, banks, individually as well as collectively, must reduce their assets. Paradoxically enough, the more such assets are reduced, the more difficult is the conversion of the remaining assets to money.

These secondary cumulative influences of banking operations, together with the demand nature of a large part of bank liabilities, makes solvency for the banking system rest largely on public psychology. In a strict sense, the banking system is not and never has been solvent. We may now examine a phase of banking theory that is derived from a recognition of the inherently insecure solvency of individual banks and of the banking system as a whole.

THE NATURE OF BANKING ASSETS

An enterprise in precarious financial condition might be strengthened either by an alteration of its liabilities relative to assets, or by an alteration of assets relative to liabilities. Recently some attention has been given to making liabilities of banks more precise from the standpoint of maturity and perhaps lengthening the period of the maturity.[3] But for many

[3] See *Banking Developments in New York State, 1923–1934* (New York, 1935), p. 69, in which the question is posed as to whether a bank's liabilities should be adjusted "to the nature and maturities of its assets by the issue of debentures or certificates of deposit with maturities of one year or more rather than passbook credits, which in practice are payable on demand." The booklet was prepared by a commission of the New York State Bankers Association.

years the emphasis has been placed by students of the subject on the nature of banking assets. Recommendations have been made to bring assets closer to conformity with liabilities as constituted.

It has been observed that the time factor of converting a bank's liabilities into money may be zero. So that assets may conform to liabilities as closely as possible, writers have long recommended that they be restricted to assets that can be exchanged quickly for money. This has been the position taken, regardless of whether the emphasis is placed on obtaining money through the payment of loans or through the sale of assets.

A bank's liabilities, while possessed in the main of an extremely short time factor, also are fixed in terms of money. Hence in recommending banking assets that most closely conform to banking liabilities, writers have uniformly rejected those assets which are not correspondingly fixed in terms of money, or as nearly fixed as human foresight can make them. Our study of wealth and wealth-titles pointed out that debts are fixed at maturity in terms of money. Furthermore, titles to debts, evidenced by possession of negotiable tokens, are among the assets most quickly exchangeable for money.

Though debts as a class provide the most suitable form of property-title for banks' assets, there are many types of debts of varying graduations of liquidity, and of which the money price may fluctuate little or much. Several criteria may be used to judge the liquidity and the possible change in money price of a debt, and hence its suitability for banking assets:

1. The nature of the debt-token per se;
2. The nature of its association with other property-titles, either directly through a secured lien or indirectly through ownership of titles by the debtor;
3. The characteristics of the associated property;
4. The place and relationship of the associated property in economic life in general.

A token per se, evidencing a debt, may take the form of a bearer instrument in which the debtor agrees to pay a stated amount at a stated place at a stated time. If so, the instrument may possess all of the intrinsic liquidity characteristics inherent in tokens—impersonality, mobility, and probably divisibility. Its transferability is expedited by the law of negotiable instruments and may be increased through the aid of organized markets.

This is the nature of most long-dated debts. But in spite of these impressive liquidity characteristics, the token evidencing a long debt is not so suitable for a banking asset as it might seem. Money is lent and debts are created in order to earn interest. The rate of interest to be paid is stipulated for the life of the loan. The money prices of a token may be influenced through time not only by the changing nature of the associated real wealth, but also by autonomous changes in open money-market interest rates, relative to the fixed rate stipulated in the loan. The longer the debt, the more subject will its capitalized value be to the latter influence.

This is not a matter of the liquidity status of the debt-token. The ability of an owner to exchange it for money in general, but not for a specific amount of money, is the measure of the degree of its liquidity. If the money price declines because of autonomous changes in interest rates, it does not mean that the debt-token per se has necessarily lost liquidity. This is a matter of relative values, rather than of changing liquidity status of the asset. But the liquidity or solvency status of the bank owning the instrument is determined by factors additional to the liquidity status of the instrument. The money amount of its assets declines without a corresponding reduction of liabilities, and it is the liquidity or solvency of the bank that, in part, guides bank managers in their decisions.

Other debt-tokens are written so as to be payable to a specific party. They are substantially comparable to bearer instruments, however, in that they may be made such by endorsement. They may be short or long as regards maturity, but are usually short, and it is not uncommon to find that organized markets are available for their transfer. The acceptance and the commercial-paper markets serve as examples.

Debt-tokens may be directly associated with particular corporeal and intangible wealth by stipulation in the instrument or indirectly through the ownership of unpledged property by the obligor. The money price of the instrument may be related to that of the underlying property through both of these associations, which supplement each other. A strongly secured mortgage bond may not lose its money value, even though the obligor becomes insolvent. The obligation of a financially strong debtor may maintain its money value, even though the property specifically securing the debt becomes worthless.

In the establishment of debts, an allowance usually is made for a differential, or margin of safety, between the money amount of the debt and the appraised money value of its associated property. If in the course of time this differential tends to disappear, the liquidity of the debt need not change, but fluctuations in its money price may take on the characteristics of those of a share in equity. In this circumstance the debt-token will become more closely associated with the value of the underlying property, at a money price less than the face amount of the debt. One of the ways in which this may transpire is through failure to provide for periodic repayment of the debt, on a basis comparable to extinguishment of the economic usefulness of its associated property.

A measure of the suitability of real wealth as security for debt-tokens has long been found in the place and relationship of the wealth in economic life in general. The sale of goods to consumers is a continuous process. The movement of goods through production to final sale is less regular, but is nevertheless continuous. If industry and commerce consisted of nothing but vertically integrated business units, goods would not exchange against money in the process of production and distribution. To the extent that production units are not so integrated, a frequent purchase and resale of uncompleted and unplaced production must result. This gives rise to what we have previously described as interstitial transactions.

For long it has been believed that this particular type of business transaction provides the best means of establishing "liquid" debts. This conviction rests essentially on two factors. First, the time between the purchase and the resale of the underlying property is usually short. Second, the underlying property occupies a relationship to economic life that is unlikely to be changed during the period of the loan. Both factors point strongly to the probability that the price and time factors of the real wealth are unlikely to change materially from those expected at the time the loan is made.

There is a further aspect of interest to the lender. Not only does he have every reason to believe that the property *can* be sold at an expected price in a given period of time, but he believes that it *will* be sold, thus providing the money to pay the loan. The frequent maturity and repayment of loans provides the banker with an opportunity to make short-period judgments, which generally are subject to less error than those of a long nature. The characteristics and use of the underlying property serving directly or indirectly to secure a debt may thus materially influence the money price of the debt-token. But this is a matter of value and not of liquidity. A ninety-year bond may be exchanged for money more readily than a prime two-name ninety-day note can be collected. But one is more certain of receiving the exact face value of the note than of the bond.

One, and only one, conclusion can be drawn from this brief discussion of banking assets. When judged solely from the standpoint of the banking system or of an individual bank, without considering the position of either in the general economy, a policy of restricting assets to short-term marketable industrial and commercial paper (whether notes or bills) seems to be the most advisable. Certainly this is the policy best calculated to strengthen an inherently vulnerable solvency. To the extent that business organization and public policy are consistent with this type of banking operation, but only to this extent, it is the policy which should be recommended and the one most likely to be pursued in the long run.

For many years banking literature has been filled with recommendations to confine banks' assets to short-dated commercial and industrial loans. Examination of the composition of banking assets, on the other hand, shows a marked tendency toward increases of long-dated paper, without *proportional* increases of the short variety. We have always had a liberal quantity of long-dated paper in the American banking system. But, in spite of many bank failures and the announced policy of bankers themselves, as reflected through their convention resolutions, no tendency to place a greater part of assets in short-dated paper is discernible through time. In fact, the tendency has been in the opposite direction.[4]

Various reasons have been advanced for this phenomenon. In recent years industrial and commercial firms have been able to operate with lower inventory requirements, as a result of improved transportation facilities. Bank loans for working capital purposes have correspondingly decreased. The growth of finance companies, which "carry" goods for the final consumer, relieves the seller from so doing. The access of large enterprises to the bond and stock markets has been facilitated by frequent easy-money policies of the banking authorities. Dr. Currie suggests that perhaps it is also due to the fact that borrowers have come to realize "the dangers inherent in loans of any description and particularly bank loans." [5] Perhaps each of these causes has been a contributing factor. No ready means are available for measuring the relative importance of any one of them.

That the nature of banking assets is closely identified with the nature of the businesses which the banks serve is indicated by a highly suggestive article by Mr. Bray Hammond, in which he describes the banking system of New Orleans in the two decades before the east and west railroads and the Civil War cut the Mississippi River traffic.[6] Extremely rigid conditions were prescribed for the banks of this important trading port

[4] Currie, "The Decline of the Commercial Loan," *Quarterly Journal of Economics,* XLV (Aug., 1931), 698 ff.

[5] *Op. cit.,* p. 708.

[6] Hammond, "Long and Short-Term Credit in Early American Banking," *Quarterly Journal of Economics,* XLIX (Nov., 1934), 79 ff.

during this period. All loans in excess of capital funds were limited to ninety days, though loans of paid-in capital might be made for a longer period. Other stipulations prohibited renewals and dealt with the specie reserve and similar matters. The system worked wondrously well, but Mr. Hammond does not find it used elsewhere.

Although the banks of New Orleans were well known throughout the country for their strength and dependability, nevertheless they were not generally emulated. Perhaps an adequate reason for this was that most American banks, situated where they were, found both the specie and short-term paper requirements of the New Orleans banks utterly out of their reach. As a legislation committee report . . . had said in 1837, the commercial paper of the New Orleans banks was sustained "by the annual receipt of the produce of the valley of the Mississippi, amounting now to at least $75,000,000, and increasing annually with the population. . . . The position of New Orleans is unique: there is no place on the globe possessing so many elements and sounder materials for banking." [7]

During the Reconstruction period the New Orleans banking system was superseded by free banking, partly through the organization of national banks and partly through the organization of new state banks under a local free banking law. Mr. Hammond does not state why he believes the older system did not last. Perhaps a partial explanation may be found in the following passages pertaining to the trade of New Orleans:

The value of the receipts of produce from the interior at New Orleans in 1830 amounted to $22,065,518. In 1840 the total value was $49,763,825. In 1850 it was $96,897,873, and in 1860 it reached the large figure of $185,211,254. The largest part of this great increase resulted from the growth of cotton receipts, which in 1860 constituted 60 per cent of the value of all commodities entering the city. . . . Charleston and Savannah captured some of the cotton trade when their railroads were extended into Alabama and Tennessee, but, notwithstanding this, New Orleans easily maintained the lead.[8] . . .

However, evidence was not lacking that railroads would ultimately

---

[7] *Op. cit.*, pp. 100–101.

[8] Johnson, E. R., *et al.*, *History of the Domestic and Foreign Commerce of the United States* (Washington, 1915), I, 243.

> gain the ascendancy over the river, even in the transportation of cotton and other southern products. One notable proof of the superiority of the railroad was the rise of the so-called "overland movement" of cotton, which in 1859 began to take on large proportions. . . . None of the cotton sent north by rail passed through New Orleans. . . . It represented a definite loss to the commerce of New Orleans.[9]

Cotton received at New Orleans declined from 2,139,000 bales in 1860 to 1,142,000 in 1870.[10] It would thus appear that the nature of New Orleans's commerce, reflected through its business institutions, may have had a determining influence on the kind of assets its banks possessed. Perhaps it is more than a coincidence that the nature of the assets of the English banks also exhibited a tendency to change after that nation's foreign trade began to reflect the unfavorable post World War conditions.

Regardless of the reasons for the presence of large quantities of long-dated paper in the portfolios of the banking system, the fact of the matter is that the paper is there. Moreover, it exhibits an undesirable tendency through time to increase, relative to total assets, rather than to diminish. It remains an unsettled question among serious students of banking why this divergence has developed between the conclusions of theory, which prescribe short-dated assets, and practice, which has resulted in increasing amounts of long-dated assets. Especially does this seem to have been the case in recent years. The purchase of bonds and the making of non-commercial loans is one way in which bank assets have tended to become longer dated. We may quote Mr. W. A. Morton.

> The holdings of securities of all active banks in the United States as a percentage of total assets have increased from 20 per cent in 1914 to 39.56 per cent in 1937. . . . Loans and discounts of all active banks declined from 56 per cent of total resources in 1914 to 49 per cent in 1932 and 33 per cent in 1937.
>
> While total loans held up well until 1930, it should not be inferred that this was due to true commercial borrowing. On the con-

[9] *Ibid.*, p. 247.

[10] *Ibid.*, Table 29, p. 281.

trary, as has long been known, there has been since 1914 a constant downward tendency in holdings of true commercial paper.[11]

Perhaps the reasons for this situation are so firmly embedded in the institutional organization of American business that a remedy for the situation would involve prohibitive costs in the terms of change. We strongly suspect that the nature of banking assets is chiefly dependent upon the particular methods and organization of the business life of the community.

If the emphasis of bank investment could be shifted from long-dated to short-dated paper without adversely impinging on the general business life of the community, the result would be beneficial to the degree of solvency possessed by individual banks and the banking system as a whole. To know whether such a shift is feasible through time, it is first necessary to know something of the real forces that have resulted in the present condition. This is a subject too broad to be attempted in the present study. For our purposes here, it will suffice to note the existing status of banking portfolios and to consider the significance of this condition for the cumulative aspects of economic change.

THE INFLUENCE OF THE NATURE OF BANKING ASSETS ON THE SUPPLY OF MONEY

Changes in liquidity desires create pressures that induce business change. These forces feed upon themselves in a cumulative manner and contain within themselves no self-reversing correctives. Our study has traced these forces as they operate through the exchange of money for real wealth, the fluctuations in the aggregate of money profits, hoarding, and the expansion and contraction of debt, including money. The potency of changing liquidity desires in modifying economic activity through these elements is related to the institutional organization of wealth-titles. One phase of this organization is the banking system and the characteristics of the assets which it owns.

[11] Morton, "Liquidity and Solvency," *American Economic Review,* XXIX (June, 1939), 273.

In our sense of the term, there is no valid reason to believe that bank assets per se have become less liquid as they have become longer dated. But the liquidity status of the banks themselves will be impaired if, for one reason or another, the money price of their assets declines in relation to the amount of their liabilities. We have previously seen how the problem of value maintenance through time enters into the determination of the liquidity status of individual and corporate persons, even though it has no place in determining the liquidity status of things.

Long-dated assets are more likely to change in money price than short-dated assets in a given period of time. A given change in the market rate of interest will change the capitalized market price of a thirty-year bond by many times the amount of the change in the capitalized price of a six-month note.

There is another factor of even greater importance in making the long-dated loans more subject to change in market price, through time, if not in a given period of time. All loans, regardless of the use to which the funds may have been put, may be regarded as "capital" assets of the lender. The current value of loans will depend in part upon the prospects of receiving the principal when it is due, plus regular interest payments in the interim. This prospect is largely conditioned by the realization of current money profits on the part of the obligor and his prospects of future money profits. It follows that the value of capital assets of all kinds, including that of loans, is sensitive to changes in the aggregate of money profits.

This is true of both long-dated and short-dated loans. But the difficulty of foreseeing significant changes in aggregate profits over long periods exceeds the difficulty over short periods. To this extent the banks have increased the risk of their own illiquidity through their relatively greater acquisition of long-dated loans.

It will be recalled that bank managers have two principal responsibilities: (1) to remain solvent so far as public confidence is concerned, and (2) to earn a profit commensurate with prudent handling of the bank's affairs. Since the business community has not provided a sufficient amount of short-dated paper to fill the banks' need for earnings, the second of these responsibilities has encouraged the disproportionate increase in long-dated paper.

The presence of the long-dated paper in the banks' portfolios, in turn, has a very real significance for the first of the responsibilities, i. e., to remain solvent. For the reasons stated above, the money price of long-dated assets is apt to fluctuate more, relative to the amount of liabilities, than is the money price of short-dated assets. Bankers as a class, recognizing the dangers inherent in this situation, are thus more sensitive to changes in liquidity desires. In these circumstances, they may be quick to attempt the disposal of assets with a change of attitude. This is not to say that bank holdings of long paper fluctuate more than the holdings of short paper. The short may fluctuate the more, *because* of the holding of the long. Rather, it is to say that, *ceteris paribus,* the aggregate of bank earning assets fluctuate more because of the proportional increase of long paper. But the nature of banking assets is not the only factor influencing their expansion and contraction.

The importance of the liquidity status of banks exceeds that of other legal personalities for one and only one reason. The banks provide the community with the greater part of its stock of money. When they contract their earning assets or close their doors to business, a decrease in the money supply is an almost inevitable corollary. All of the deflationary forces which we previously have examined are brought into operation, including the repayment of debt, a declining price level, and a reduction of the aggregate of money profits.

This is also the nature of events when individuals reduce debts with one another. But in this case someone must actually hoard (unless debt is refunded into equity), and the pressure of unused money is then apt to be great. In the case of debt contraction by banks, the hoarding takes the form of an obliteration of money. It thus seems that the prevalence of long-term paper in the portfolios of the banking system is chiefly important because it supplies additional pressure to the forces of cumulative business change. Again we find the institutional organization of economic life developing in a way to increase the importance of changes in liquidity desires.

PRESENT ATTITUDES TOWARD BANK LIQUIDITY

If it were not for the effect on the money supply of shifts in liquidity desires of bankers, there would be no more reason to provide them with liquidity than any other group in the community. But in view of the unique significance of the liquidity status of banks to the economic life of the community, it is not surprising to find that special attention has been given to the question.

There was a time when it was hoped that banks might be restricted to short-term commercial paper and that this would provide against fluctuations in the market price of assets relative to liabilities, without further concern by the community. This, we have seen, has been a frustrated hope. Society now must provide some institutional mechanism to supply the lost liquidity or suffer the consequences of frequent and rapid changes in the supply of money.

Liquidity for banks might be provided simply by guaranteeing the money prices of their assets. But there is no certainty that an effort to freeze particular prices, such as those of bank assets, would succeed in the long run. Much would depend on the appropriateness of the prices guaranteed, and this, in turn, would rest upon the goodness of the underlying security. The quantitative size of the guarantee is an additionally significant factor. Moreover, there is apparently no necessity for society to single out a favored group and protect them against mistakes of judgment. Present legislation and official attitudes in regard to the liquidity of banks seem to rest largely upon these premises.[12]

The Banking Act of 1935 has made it possible for a Reserve bank to loan to member banks on notes "which are secured to the satisfaction of such federal reserve banks." This provision,

[12] The next several paragraphs borrow liberally from Morton's "Liquidity and Solvency," *American Economic Review*, XXIX (June, 1939), 272–85.

together with the joint ruling relative to asset valuations for bank examinations, issued on June 27, 1938, by the Board of Governors of the Federal Reserve System, the Secretary of the Treasury, the director of the Federal Deposit Insurance Corporation, and the Comptroller of the Currency, provides the essential machinery for dealing with this problem.

By this ruling loans are no longer catalogued as "good, slow, doubtful and loss." Instead, they are judged on the prospects of repayment, regardless of maturity, and appraised accordingly. Bonds are graded according to quality. If of good quality according to recognized ratings, they are carried at cost. Bonds of poorer quality, if selling below cost, are written down by a part or the full amount of the depreciation, depending upon their status. Since the Board of Governors of the Federal Reserve System has given its sanction to these valuations, it is assumed that it will be willing to loan on assets at the value listed in the bank statement.

It should be observed that while these arrangements provide a measure of protection to the banks against intermediate fluctuations in the prices of bonds and against the inability to dispose of long-dated loan paper, should depositors want their funds, the arrangements do not provide a guarantee of bank assets. Nor do they protect the banker against losses arising out of mistakes of judgment. Losses on bad paper accrue initially to the bank which made the original loan or bought the bond. They accrue to the Reserve bank (the member banks as a whole, in the first instance, and society at large in the second) only if the original lending bank becomes legally insolvent. The provisions should help to mitigate the effect of shifts in liquidity desires upon the supply of money. But they cannot be expected to eliminate the effect. Moreover, the provisions are new and comparatively untested. It is impossible to say how efficacious they may be in a depression of the proportions of that of the early thirties. The member bank still carries the initial risk.[13]

[13] Mr. Morton seems to think these provisions so significant that "The distinction between liquidity and solvency disappears. Any bank which the examiners now say is solvent is also liquid. Immediate liquidity is simply 'rediscountability'

There are at least two ways of looking at the question of the liquidity of the banking system. One, followed in the above described provisions, attempts to fortify the banking system against the impact of expected economic change. The procedure is thoroughly desirable and necessary, but it seems to be somewhat analogous to building a fort, rather than trying to stop a war. Both are necessary. In the same sense, it is necessary to think of the question of the security of banks in terms of their relationship to business change and the prospects, if any, of reducing its amplitude.

We have seen that the phenomenon of liquidity is inextricably tied into the problem of business change. The nature of banking assets and the liquidity of the banking system thus may be looked upon as but one phase of an extremely difficult problem, and not soluble *in vacuo*. Rather, it seems to fit into the larger composition of liquidity and cumulative change, and its ultimate solution, if there is a solution, can be accomplished only as a phase of the treatment of the related phenomena. This is not to say that inducements should not be offered to encourage bankers to restrict their assets to short-dated paper. These inducements are unlikely to be very effective, however, since the developing organization of business life does not provide an abundance of this type of obligation. Nor is it to say that provision should not be made to fortify the banking system against price fluctuation and

and long run liquidity is identical with solvency." True, the liquidity of long-dated unmarketable loans has been increased. It is not so certain that the liquidity of bonds has been increased. The amount of money which can be obtained for bonds has been fixed, subject to certain stipulations, but this is a matter of money value through time rather than of the liquidity of the asset per se. Even in this instance, any losses are chargeable initially against the member bank. The liquidity of the bank has been increased, in the sense that money may be obtained for certain of its assets more expeditiously. But unless the Federal Reserve banks intend to absorb eventual losses, the money amount of bank assets has not been increased relative to liabilities. It still seems to be true that although any bank which the examiners say is solvent is also liquid, a bank's assets may be liquid and yet the bank may be insolvent. It is well to keep in mind the distinction between the liquidity of assets and of legal persons. The degree of solvency or liquidity of banks has been improved, but not to the same extent as the liquidity of bank assets. The distinction between liquidity and solvency has not disappeared except in the limited sense of the degree of solvency being synonymous with the liquidity of persons.

lack of liquidity of its long-dated loan paper. But these measures are more like palliatives than cures.

SUMMARY

The inherent solvency of banks and the banking system is very much less secure than that of many other forms of enterprise. In the severe business or common-law sense of the term, our banking system is not and never has been solvent. This precarious position results from two characteristics of banking. First, a bank's debts—that is, its customer-deposits—are payable on demand. Second, when a bank sells assets or calls a loan it may become more difficult to sell other assets or to call other loans because of the secondary repercussions which have been noted.

To strengthen this inherently vulnerable position, banks should hold assets that possess a high degree of liquidity *and* enjoy stable money prices. Such assets are short-term, well secured debt-tokens. But this conclusion, deduced from a consideration of the banking system taken alone, is not necessarily valid when we consider the universe of economic activity. It may be that the changing arrangements of economic life fail to provide the type of assets which the banks most need. At the same time, the business community may want and need the demand liabilities of banks in an undiminished or even an increased amount. The question naturally occurs as to whether business shall adjust itself to the requirements of banking, or whether banking shall adjust itself to the requirements of business. The record points strongly to the latter answer.

In spite of all that has been written and said about the desirability of short-term commercial loans as banking assets, the banking system has been characterized increasingly by the possession of long-dated paper of one form or another. Furthermore, there appears to be no change in the tendencies that have resulted in the present situation. Those concerned with such matters are thus presented with a state of fact.

The nature of banking assets is a given condition which must be included as one of a number of factors that bear on the larger problem of liquidity and its implication. It is a factor which adds to the strength of the forces of cumulative business change, since the possession of long-dated assets makes bankers, already sensitive to their precarious solvency, more responsive to increases in the public's liquidity desires. As bankers dispose of assets (they may be short-paper, since the long may have depreciated previously), there will be a tendency for the money supply to decrease correspondingly. Another factor is thus added to the forces making for contraction in business activity. In this way the presence of long-dated assets in the banking system intensifies cyclical fluctuations, although, of course, it is not the only or even the most important factor making for cyclical fluctuations. In turn, cyclical fluctuations may impair the liquidity of individual banks and the banking system.

XI

LIQUIDITY AND PRICES

LIQUIDITY is a term that means different things to different people. We have tried to sharpen its meaning. When applied to assets, it is synonymous with exchangeability for money in various periods of time. Exchange may be made through sale, by pledge of the asset as security for a negotiated loan, or through institutional arrangements making loans more or less routine, such as the present relations between member banks and Reserve banks. In the absence of subsidy, loan value must depend ultimately on sale value. Since loans in the final analysis rest on prospective sale, the liquidity of assets has been defined in terms of marketability. An asset is more or less liquid, according to the period of time required to sell it at a price within an expected range of prices. This definition of the liquidity of assets per se *excludes* the factor of the fluctuation of their money price through time.

In several respects the definition of the liquidity of legal persons, corporate and natural, stands in contrast to the definition of the liquidity of assets. Persons are more or less liquid according to the relationship of the assets they own to the debts they owe. Two considerations are important in the case of both assets and liabilities. The assets themselves may be more or less liquid *and* they may vary in money amounts through time. The money amounts of liabilities may change, *as well as* their maturity schedules. In judging the liquidity status of a person, we must consider the money amount of assets relative to the money amount of liabilities, as well as the liquidity status of the assets per se relative to the maturity schedule of liabilities. The liquidity status of persons is thus analogous to their degree of solvency.

When we speak of a shift of liquidity preferences, or, better, of liquidity desires, we speak of the wants of persons. In contrast to the concept of liquidity as applied to things, liquidity as applied to persons *includes* the question of the money value of assets through time. Thus the phrase "a shift in liquidity desires" means more than a disposition of the public to acquire assets that are more liquid per se. It means this, but in addition it means that there has been a shift in value judgments. Still more, it means there has been a change in public attitudes toward owning and owing debts.

Changes in liquidity desires thus mean more than the desire for more or less liquid assets. At times this seems to be the meaning of liquidity preferences, as that term is used in the Keynesian analysis. At other times the concept appears to be even further narrowed, to mean a desire to hoard more or less money. In this connection liquidity preference is described as the instantaneous desire to hold money as a function of the interest rate. It is a more exact description of economic life to say that shifts in liquidity desires refer to a desire for a different average degree of liquidity in the assets owned. But this is still not enough. Because individuals think of liquidity in terms of their over-all affairs and not exclusively in terms of their assets, it is proper to include shifts in their attitudes toward the debts they owe as a part of their liquidity consciousness. Thus a change in liquidity desires in our sense of the term will result in changes in three factors: (1) a change in money hoarding, (2) a change in the scale of prices for assets of different degrees of liquidity, and (3) a change in the corpus of debt.

The *importance* of shifts in liquidity desires lies in their influence upon the production and distribution of real wealth and services. The *strength* of this influence is related to the institutional organization of wealth and wealth-titles within which liquidity desires operate. The growth of highly organized markets, the practice of financing with debt instruments, the development of the corporate form of business organization, and even the institution of money itself have developed *in part* to supply the community's want for more liquidity. The corporation has divorced the liquidity of ownership from the liquidity of the associated real wealth. In turn, these institutional phenomena provide a means of making shifts in liquidity desires effective in influencing the level of economic activity.

All wealth or titles to wealth provide a store of value, that is a claim to other wealth, within the limits of liquidity. This store of value is maintained within these limits until the wealth has been extinguished in the sense that it is no longer economically useful. Individuals in the community arrange their assets according to their personal wants, their value judgments, and their desires for more or less liquidity in their assets. Among such assets is money, which serves as a general claim to all wealth. Variations in personal wants, relative value judgments, and desires for more or less liquid assets all influence the amount of money exchanged for new wealth production. Under conditions of specialization of production, this can mean only a diminution or acceleration of new wealth production and a lower or higher level of material welfare.

Obviously, shifts in desires for more or less liquidity in assets owned are not the only factors leading to economic changes. They are not even among the most important factors. Shifts in the desire for personal liquidity, which may include a change in relative value judgments, are much more important, but still do not include all of the forces of economic change. Changes in personal wants remain as the underlying source of change. Shifts in personal wants, value judgments, and liquidity desires affect differently the demand for various kinds of wealth. But the demand for wealth that is indispensable to economic stability is the demand for *all* new wealth production of *all* descriptions. The exchange of money for new wealth production we have called final buying.

An increase in liquidity desires may retard the amount of final buying. In turn, diminished final buying will result in increased liquidity desires through revised value judgments and an intensification of the feeling of uncertainty about the future. These are cumulative forces that seemingly might continue in a given direction of change indefinitely. We know that they do not do so. The circle is broken by the other important determinant of economic change, i. e., personal wants.

The wants of the community are expressed through relative prices. Again, limited supplies of various kinds of economic wealth are related to effective wants through prices. As prices reflect a more (or less) perfect balance between effective demands and limited supplies, in detail as well as in gross, an increase (or decrease) in final buying will result. This will result in greater (or lesser) liquidity desires. In turn, there will be more (or less) final buying.

So far as liquidity desires and final buying are concerned, the relationships are cumulative. A change in the direction of change in economic activity must come from another source. A plausible initiating source of change is the degree of correspondence (or lack of correspondence) of effective demand and limited supplies of economic wealth through the price *system or structure.* Thus we describe the degree of balance in the price structure as the *initiative or generative* source of change in economic life. A workable balance is made more significant to well-being, in view of the accompanying *cumulative* sources of change related to liquidity desires.

The focus of our analysis has been these sources of cumulative change. Various aspects of the matter have been considered: fluctuations in the aggregate of money profits, hoarding, changes in the corpus of debt, and variations in the supply of money as these variations relate to the organization and assets of the banking system. All of these phenomena act and react cumulatively with changes in liquidity desires. The manner of this action and reaction has been discussed in preceding chapters and need not be repeated here at length.

It is sufficient to recall that movements of the price level and expectations of price-level movements play an important role in this complex of forces. What we have called a lack of balance in the price structure may result in a fall of the price level and the expectation of a further fall. There is a revision of value judgments in favor of money and other liquid assets, an increase in hoarding, a retardation of final buying, an attempt to reduce the corpus of debt, and a decline in the money stock. If there is no expectation of a further fall in the price level or if there is an expectation of a rise in the price level, then the reverse of this situation exists. Lessened liquidity desires are accompanied by dishoarding, an acceleration of final buying, an increase in the corpus of non-money debt, and an increase in the money stock. "We have an expansion of credit."

These phenomena act and react upon one another concomitantly and not in any ordered or unchanging sequence. They afford an explanation of business change in a given direction, once the change has been started. They provide no explanation of the turning points of business activity. These are explainable by the appearance of a greater or less degree of balance in the price structure in its relation to productive arrangements and effective wants of the community. Liquidity desires and their associated phenomena intensify but do not start business change.

A PARTIAL TEST OF THE THEORY

It is difficult to test these conclusions with the available data. There are no figures to describe fluctuations in the aggregate of money profits, in the sense in which we have used that term. The data relating to non-money debt are improving, but they are still too rough to make them adaptable to our use here. Figures for the supply of money are more complete. A partial test of our conclusions may be made by comparing our curve of changes in liquidity desires (itself an approximate index) with indices of prices, production, and money supply. It will be recalled that changes in aggregate money profits are closely related to the amount of new wealth distributed, times its price. Moreover, production tends to be closely geared to sales. If prices and production tend to change in the same direction at about the same time, we may reasonably conclude that the aggregate of money profits is likewise changing. Thus Chart III serves roughly to compare the direction of change of liquidity desires with that of aggregate money profits and the supply of money. The comparative rates of change do not interest us. The precise time of change in direction does not bear upon the analysis. We are interested only in discovering whether there is a tendency of the quantities to change inversely to changes in liquidity desires.

The curve of liquidity desires is a reproduction of that appearing in Chart II. In connection with its presentation there, it was explained that the curve was not corrected to eliminate the independent influence of changes in the absolute amount of member bank reserve balances.[1] Experiments to eliminate this influence demonstrate that changes in reserves had no material effect on *the direction of change* of the liquidity curve until 1933. The uncorrected curve reports liquidity desires more or less stable during 1933 and 1934. The corrected curve reports falling liquidity desires.[2] In our reading of Chart III we shall use the corrected curve from July, 1932.

Especially since September, 1924, does there appear to have been an inverse relationship between the directions of change in liquidity desires on the one hand and money supply, prices, and production on the other. This is what our theory leads us to expect and suggests that shifts in liquidity desires may be increasing in importance.

It is instructive to break the chart into several periods, in which changes in liquidity desires appear to be fairly well marked. This will enable us to study it in greater detail and to discover how frequently this inverse correspondence occurs. The follow-

[1] *Supra*, p. 204.

[2] This correction is made in the following manner:

Let a = long rate
b = short rate
r = reserves of member banks
c = reserves as of any fixed base date

$$\frac{r}{c} = x$$

Since r increases as x *increases* and r increases relative to members' deposits as liquidity desires *increase*, the influence of an absolute change in r on the liquidity desires curve may be eliminated by $\frac{a - b}{x}$.

CHART III

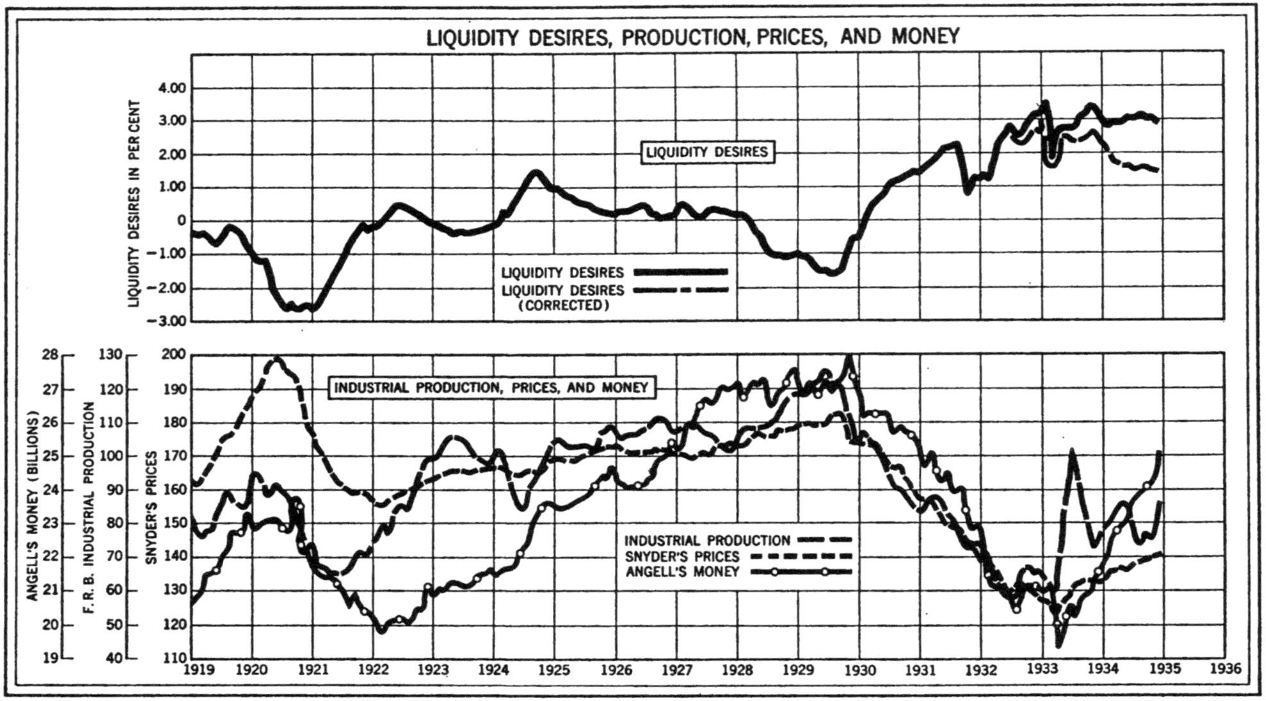

Sources:

Angell's money: Angell, *Behavior of Money,* Table II (outside currency plus circulating deposits), pp. 178–79.

Industrial production (adjusted): Federal Reserve System, *Board of Governors, Annual Report, 1937,* Table 81, pp. 173–78.

Snyder's index of the general price level: F. R. Macaulay, *The Movements of Interest Rates, Bond Yields and Stock Prices in the United States since 1856,* New York, 1938, Table 27, pp. A266–A269.

ing table, read from Chart III, describes the principal direction of change of the subject quantities in the several periods. To attempt a more detailed reading of minor changes in the directions of change would be specious. Changes in liquidity desires clearly are not the only force making for changes in the other quantities, even though they are a significant one.

DIRECTION OF CHANGE OF SUBJECT QUANTITIES

	Time Elapsed in Months	*Liquidity Desires*	*Money Stock*	*Prices*	*Industrial Production*
Jan., 1919, to Aug., 1920	19	Down	Up	Down	Up
Aug., 1920, to Feb., 1921	6	Stable	Up and *down*	*Down*	*Down*
Feb., 1921, to June, 1922	16	Up	Down	Down	*Up*
June, 1922, to May, 1923	11	Down	Up	Up	Up
May, 1923, to Sept., 1924	16	Up	*Up*	*Stable*	Down
Sept., 1924, to Jan., 1926	16	Down	Up	Up	Up
Jan., 1926, to March, 1928	26	Stable	*Up*	Stable	Stable
March, 1928, to Aug., 1929	17	Down	*Stable*	Up	Up
Aug., 1929, to March, 1933	43	Up	Down	Down	Down
March, 1933, to Dec., 1934	22	Down	Up	Up	Up

Italicized in this table are those instances in which the amount of money, prices, or production move in directions opposite to that in which they might be expected to move in terms of our theoretical discussion. The curves behave as expected in about 80 percent of the instances. In terms of elapsed time, the experience is still better, since three of the seven contrary instances, i. e., the behavior of the price level, industrial production, and prices during the period of August, 1920, to February, 1921, occur for but six months. Explanations might be found for the cantankerous behavior of the curves in these and the several other instances noted. It is sufficient for our purpose, however, to note the extent and frequency of the inverse correspondence of the curve of liquidity preferences and those of the other series, which is what our theory leads us to expect.

The presence of a considerable amount of inverse correspondence in the series studied does not prove that the several forces we have related to liquidity desires act and react upon one another in a causal sense. On the other hand, it does not disprove the thesis, and both experience and theoretical reasoning suggest a causal relationship of the nature that has been described.

SOME CONSIDERATIONS LOOKING TOWARD A SOLUTION

Practical solutions to economic problems are always difficult. When the problem is as complex as that encompassing broad business change, proposals for a solution obviously must be offered tentatively. In that which follows, the reader is counseled that although a careful attempt has been made to describe realistically economic life as it has been observed, the argument of this work is largely deductive in nature. Accordingly, it is subject to all of the limitations and possibilities of error generally associated with this approach. The conclusions derived from the argument are offered with the caution that they are subject to further debate and empirical confirmation. But since for the most part these conclusions indicate a change in emphasis, rather than a redirection of public policy, it does not seem inappropriate to include them as a part of this study.

Our analysis leads us to believe that liquidity desires intensify but do not start business change. The price structure in its relation to production arrangements and effective demand, although not the only source of initial change, is a highly important source of change. We have suggested the phrase "degree of balance" as being descriptive of the behavior of the price structure in this respect. If the price structure is unbalanced, attempts to offset changes in liquidity desires by insuring or guaranteeing prices will be successful only so long as the guarantee continues. Upon its termination, the initial source of disturbance will remain. Moreover, an attempt to combat the unstabilizing effects of shifting liquidity desires would necessitate the securing of a wide range of prices, so great, in fact, that public confidence in the insurance fund (the value of government money) might be undermined.

If, in some manner, all prices were fixed or frozen at unchanging levels and relationships, the whole problem of liquidity as applied to *assets* would disappear. This would be true, at least, if the frozen prices were real prices and not nominal prices. But the problem of liquidity as applied to *persons* would remain. Its urgency would depend upon two conditions.

First, it would depend upon the relation existing between the money price of servicing non-money debt and the money price of a representative bundle of real wealth at the time prices were frozen. This is a question of the price level, related to the total money cost of servicing debt. It resolves itself into a phase of the degree of balance among closely related prices, the third of our sources of unbalance in the price structure. We have noted the tendency of debt to increase and the difficulty of its payment by society. It follows that if all prices are frozen, the real wealth cost of servicing the aggregate debt will increase as the debt increases, and the problems of liquidity as applied to *persons* may be aggravated through time.

Second, the urgency of the problem of the liquidity of persons under conditions of frozen prices would depend upon the ability of the fixed prices to equate present demand and supply and future demand and supply. These are the first and second of our sources of unbalance in the price structure. We have noted the interdependence of all prices and the necessity of change in their relationships as the result of changing techniques, tastes, and so forth. It follows that if prices are frozen, the degree of unbalance in the price structure is very likely to be increased through time. Specific debtors will find it increasingly difficult to service their debts. Their liquidity status will be impaired, relative to their desire for liquidity. They will take measures to increase their liquidity. Again, we find that under conditions of frozen prices the problem of the liquidity status of persons is aggravated through time.

It appears that an attempt to cope with the questions of liquidity by indiscriminate guaranteeing of prices does not promise success. The effort is likely to lead to unbalance in the price structure in all of its phases and to intensify the difficulties of liquidity, as that term is applied to persons.

More promising theoretically, and of much greater practical difficulty, is the attempt to bring greater balance into the price structure by the continuous study of all prices and their relationships. In earlier chapters we traced the effects of a changing price structure on the price level and, in turn, of a changing price level on the aggregate of money profits and, through money profits, on the desire for liquid titles, on hoarding, on the contraction and expansion of debt, and on the behavior of the banking system. All of these were found to influence positively the production and distribution of real wealth. Moreover, the influence of these combined quantities, directed uniformly toward expansion at one time and contraction at another, appears to be strong, too strong perhaps to be controlled—short of totalitarian measures—without getting at the root of the trouble. It thus becomes highly important that the source of the infection be found and corrected, so far as human knowledge will permit.

The problem of economic policy thus presented is indeed a difficult one. It is one thing to describe theoretically the implications of a lack of balance in the price structure. It is another to know in practice when such a condition exists. It is still another to know how to cope with a discovered condition, in a country whose traditions are strongly influenced by the philosophy of liberalism, but whose business practice has become increasingly non-competitive so far as prices are concerned. Yet, if our diagnosis is correct, this lack of balance in the price structure is the chief initiating source of the economic vicissitudes which increasingly threaten the very foundations of liberalistic society.

A discussion of the means that are available to discover the precise nature of this lack of balance *before* it has exhibited its effects is outside the scope of our present study.[3] The means of

[3] An illustration of such a study, made after the event, is Professor Paul Douglas's treatment of the price of "labor" per unit of output and the price of the units of output produced in the period 1922–29. See his *Controlling Depressions* (New York, 1935), pp. 53–60.

correcting a lack of balance that has been discovered is likewise a subject that does not bear directly on the question of liquidity and cumulative change. But we may look briefly at some of the problems presented.

The question of balance among closely related prices is likely to command first attention in a democratic society with non-competitive and quasi-competitive institutions. This close relationship of a price to other prices is a factor in determining the degree of balance in the price structure, in addition to the functions of prices equilibrating present demand and supply and future demand and supply.[4] It is the phase of the problem that primarily concerns group interests, and it is well known that democratic states are governed more and more by so-called pressure groups.

Furthermore, in a sense this phase is the only concrete phase of the problem. The point may properly be made that with our present knowledge of the price structure and its behavior, there are no precise means of determining contemporarily the existence of changes in the degree of over-all balance. On the one hand, there are no adequate means of measuring real values in order to compare them with prices; we know only after the event that prices have or have not equated demand and supply. Again, the present distribution of income is at best an approximate guide to future demand. If it is true that unbalance in the price structure is the initiating cause of our recurring economic distress, our controls will be highly imperfect until much more has been learned about these phenomena.

Professor F. C. Mills, who has done the most careful work in the statistical study of prices, price movements, and relations, has said: "If the price system could be fully explored, if all ties and connections could be traced and all fluctuations explained, then, perhaps, man could understand and control the economic system he has created." [5]

[4] *Supra*, p. 77.

[5] Mills, *Behavior of Prices*, p. 33.

CONTEMPORARY PUBLIC PRICE POLICIES

It is interesting briefly to review contemporary price policies in the light of the high significance they have been given in our preceding analysis. From the theoretical angle, the least complex of the possible attacks on this question of balance in the price structure is the effort to enforce competitive conditions. But our present policies designed to accomplish this have not been conspicuous for their effectiveness. For nearly fifty years, we in the United States have attempted to keep a balance in our price structure through laws intended to compel "fair" price competition.

Not being subject to human fallibility, competition is the best regulator of relative prices. Perfectly competitive conditions will compel relative prices that truly reflect relative desires for all forms of wealth. Although the factors of production are not mobile, they might be sufficiently mobile to adjust themselves to long-period changes in the nature of demand under competitive conditions. The difficulty arises from the fact that our attempts to compel competitive conditions by statute have failed badly. Professor Arthur R. Burns, after studying the matter for a number of years, concludes: "The anti-trust laws have been a notable failure as a means of maintaining competition." [6]

Moreover, he suggests that "the development of monopolistic behavior has been an inevitable consequence of the development of large-scale production involving the use of durable equipment and productive organization incapable of instantaneous creation or abandonment." [7]

It logically follows that "attempts to restore competitive behavior by law offer no prospect of dealing with the development of monopolistic control in industry." [8]

And that "striving after individual competition as a neat self-regulating device is fruitless because, by its nature, it cannot be established and maintained by law." [9]

[6] Burns, *The Decline of Competition*, p. 523.
[7] *Ibid.*, p. 524.
[8] *Ibid.*, p. 526.
[9] *Ibid.*, p. 529.

This is not to say that competition is nonexistent. But it takes many forms, and price competition is the last to be tried in many fields of activity. Price competition is highly imperfect at best.

Moreover, from the standpoint of production it is not clear that an organization of business is desirable that would permit perfectly competitive conditions. The units of production would have to be small relative to their markets, and in some cases the technical advantages of large-scale operations would be lost. The point may also be made that we have moved far from a condition of competition, owing to changes in business organization. These changes have come about in the course of the last century. The attempt to return to an earlier state of society in a shorter period of time might be accompanied by a prohibitive social cost in the transitional period.

In addition to the attempt to compel competitive price controls, more *direct* methods of price control have been used. Until a few decades ago, direct attempts by public bodies to control prices in the United States had been most conspicuous in the judicially defined public-utility field. The effort in these instances has been chiefly to prohibit price discrimination among purchasers and exploitation of consumers by charging prices that are presumed to be out of balance with other prices. More recently, direct control of the prices of human abilities has been extended in a limited way through minimum-wage and maximum-hour laws that apply to men as well as to women and children.

Another field in which direct control of prices has been attempted in recent years is provided by the Federal Reserve Board's control of the price of new loans through the more sensitive interest rates in the money markets—this by means of the discount rate and open-market operations. Direct control of interest rates on old debt contracts has been effected through such Federal government agencies as the Home Owners' Loan Corporation, the Federal Farm Mortgage Corporation, and many others.

Other attempts at direct price controls may be cited. Prices may be set directly by decree, as in totalitarian states, or they may be modified by entrance into the market on either the buying or the selling side. There has been a gradual broadening of the acceptance of the idea of the government entering markets to influence prices. Such an attempt was the Federal Farm Board's financially unprofitable support of the wheat market in the late 1920's and early 1930's.

More recently the Commodity Surplus Corporation has been purchasing a wide variety of surplus goods for the double purpose of influencing prices and of subsequently distributing the purchases to those needing relief. From our previous argument we might conclude that purchases of this nature will be most effective if care is taken to purchase only wealth-forms that have passed completely through the production process. The prices thus influenced appear to be the most important prices, and the withdrawal of wealth at this point will have a tendency to "pull" other wealth through the productive process.[10] In a very real sense the Works Progress Administration's activities have been similar in the field of human effort to those of the Commodity Surplus Corporation in corporeal wealth. Surplus labor has been purchased by the W.P.A., thus removing it from the labor market.

That there is much precedent for price control is further evidenced by the many instances of *indirect* attempts to modify prices, in addition to these attempts to control them directly. The oldest of our indirect price controls is the tariff. In recent years the field of indirect controls has been greatly broadened, both through the financial markets and without specific reference to the financial markets.

[10] In fact, when times of stress call for ameliorative action, something might be said for the proposal to have the government acquire antiquated dwellings, automobiles, railroad equipment, factories, and so forth, and demolish them. The materials recovered might be sold or retained. At best, the recovered materials would contribute but a fraction of their cost. The difference is a socialized loss. But this sort of scarcity policy seems to have two distinct advantages over scarcity policies applied to raw materials: (1) It may result in a deficiency of forms of wealth that will then be produced, making for a general improvement in activity. Government subsidy would take the form of a "pull" through the production process. (2) It would remove something of a dead weight of obsolete wealth from the back of technological progress.

In the second category, the so-called "scarcity" policies characterizing the Agricultural Adjustment Administration are designed to match similar production and price policies believed to exist in industry. It might be observed in passing that if our objectives are full employment and distribution, this type of policy, at best, can only establish a balance which may later lead to full utilization and enjoyment. It cannot contribute to this end, however, until it has done its work and been partially or wholly abandoned throughout the universe of economic activity.

Another experiment in indirect price control was provided by the National Industrial Recovery Act. Although specific price control was not generally approved, various arrangements through so-called codes were made among business men, which influenced prices in multifarious ways. These codes were approved and sanctioned by governmental agencies. In substance, they thus constituted an attempt by business men, under the supervision of a public authority, to control prices, the public authority indirectly controlling prices.

So far as the prices charged by private interests are concerned, the Tennessee Valley Authority represents a new departure in indirect price controls by public bodies in this country. The Authority by directly setting certain prices, for instance, those of labor, electric power, and fertilizer, is able indirectly to influence prices charged or paid for similar wealth-forms by private persons. The government in this instance has entered into price competition with otherwise quasi-monopolistic concerns.

The prices of some wealth-forms, commonly described as capital assets, are dominantly influenced by the money profits that accrue to their benefit. We have seen how a condition of unbalance in the price structure will ultimately impair the aggregate of money profits. Changes in the aggregate of money profits are sensitively reflected in the prices of capital assets. A number of attempts at indirect price controls have been chiefly concerned with capital prices. The Reconstruction Finance Corporation has concentrated its activities, since its inception, on the support of prices for capital assets. For the most part it has done this by granting new loans. The Federal Deposit Insurance Corporation now insures the capital values embodied in the great majority of the public's deposits in commercial and savings banks. It does not, however, insure the capital prices of the assets of banks. The R.F.C. has supported these bank-asset prices through its loan policy. Of greater interest, the Federal Reserve banks, by liberalizing their eligibility rules, which in substance means their lending relations with member banks, have thereby expressed a willingness to exchange their notes, which are currency, for capital assets, the money prices of which are less certain to be otherwise maintained.[11] The Securities Exchange Commission interests itself more in the capital prices registered in the security markets, and while it does not insure or guarantee such prices in any way, it does attempt to prevent their change by manipulative or fraudulent practice.

All of these attempts indirectly to control prices are concerned with specific prices or groups of prices. Other attempts indirectly to control prices are concerned with *the price level,* rather than with any particular price or group of prices. These efforts invariably are made through the financial markets. The increase in the dollar price of gold in 1933, as a means of raising the dollar prices of other forms of real wealth, is an example. We may add that it appears to have been a naïve maneuver, if it was expected to be effective in a short period of time. There has been no short-period correlation between the dollar price of gold and the dollar price of other wealth-forms.

Conducted through the Public Works Administration and partly through the Works Progress Administration, the public works program has been viewed by many as an indirect means of raising the price level. The basis for this view seems to rest chiefly on the expectation that a dollar spent on public works will increase the national income by a multiple amount and on the fact that the public works have been paid for largely by bank loans made to the government. The money supply has been increased thereby.

11 These provisions were reviewed above, pp. 224–25.

Public works come under the heading of investment, in the typical meaning of that term. A change in investment is expected to have a multiple effect on the national money income. A rising national money income may be accompanied by a higher price level. Previously, we have examined the alleged multiple effectiveness of so-called investment in raising the national income [12] and found it to depend largely on questions of definition. Actual experiment with public investment on a large scale has had no precisely correlated effect on the price level, even though it has been financed largely through increased bank deposits. It is true that from 1933 to 1937 there was a larger increase in the national income than in government expenditures. But when net government expenditures began to decline, the increase in national income was lost in part.

Although there is no basis for a definitive conclusion, the preceding arguments of this study lead us to suspect that the benefit per dollar of public expenditure can be greatly enhanced and have more enduring influence, if questions of investment versus consumption expenditures and of their relative effects on the price level are forgotten. In their place should be substituted a study of the influence of government fiscal operations, including both expenditures and taxes, in detail as well as in the aggregate, on the degree of balance in the price structure.

We suspect that if prices are unbalanced and remain unbalanced, a large net expenditure by the government can do no more than lift the economy to a higher level of activity *while the expenditure continues.* Whereas, if a much smaller net expenditure of the government had the result of creating a better balance in the price structure, it might accomplish the same salutary result, except that when the expenditure stopped, the greater activity of business might be expected logically to continue until other forces again unbalanced the price structure.

Other attempts at indirectly controlling the price level have been essayed through the banking system. The main implements, in these cases, are the discount rate, open-market operations, and

[12] *Supra*, pp. 56–62.

changes in reserve requirements of member banks. Ostensibly, changes in the discount rate transmitted to the money markets will vary the demand for investible funds. When the discount rate is lowered, traders or middlemen, finding the carrying charges lower, build up inventories (Hawtrey); or enterprises, able to finance long-period borrowing more advantageously, increase their fixed commitments (Keynes, in the *Treatise*). In both instances there is presumably an increase in what is called investment, and the price level is expected to rise.

In times that have been described as "sensitive," which seems to be another way of describing a period in which the price structure is in comparative balance, changes in the discount rate have resulted in an expansion or contraction of investment in this sense. But it has not followed necessarily that the price level subsequently has advanced or fallen. In "tough" periods, however, when the price structure is substantially out of balance, changes in the discount rate have had little influence.

To supplement changes in discount rates and to make them more effective, the technique of open-market operations of the central banks has developed. If the money markets are "tight," the sale of earning assets by the central banks is likely to be very effective in forcing a decline in the earning assets of member banks. The impact of this contraction in all probability will end in an increase of liquidity desires and a decline in the price level. The calling of loans and the decrease in the supply of deposit money both work toward this result. But if the money markets are "easy" and the member banks are possessed of excess balances with the central banks, then further purchases of earning assets by the central banks are unlikely to be effective in reducing liquidity desires and thus in raising the price level. This condition probably represents a situation in which a high degree of unbalance exists in the price structure.

The third and most recently developed technique of the central banks is to change the amount of reserves that member banks are required to keep against each dollar of various classifications of their customer-deposits. In ultimate results this is unlikely to differ materially from the results of increasing or decreasing central banks' earning assets, and what we have said about the latter seems applicable here also.

With these many instances of direct and indirect attempts to control specific prices, groups of prices, and the price level, it is idle to talk of the free play of the market as the determining agent. Add to them the many private attempts at price control and the rigidities that appear as the natural result of the extant organization of society—for example, long-period contracts of all kinds—and we find it a far cry indeed from the hypothetical assumptions of a perfectly competitive situation.

An inference of interest to be drawn from this brief summary of contemporary price policy is that the chief concern in price controls typically is focused on the effect of the control on the fortunes of buyers and sellers *at that price*. An exception to this is the control of the interest rate as a price, for the purpose of influencing general economic behavior. But there is no more reason or no less to expect singular control of the interest rate to be effective for this purpose than to expect singular control of other key prices, such as those for wages or for energy in various forms, and the like, to be effective. The effectiveness of the interest rate as an instrument of control has been increasingly questioned in recent years. The same skepticism may be entertained as to the effectiveness of any single price. Success in the effort to control economic behavior through the control of prices can be expected only if the control encompasses the universe of prices and their relations to one another.[13]

Price controls, even when administered by the Federal government, are not infrequently looked upon as the instruments of various pressure groups. These are self-seeking bodies (we do not use the term necessarily in a derogatory connotation) that view the problem of prices from a particular rather than from a broad standpoint encompassing the whole of society. There is little wonder that a high degree of unbalance in the price structure

[13] A start, however, might be made through attempting to control the direction of change of individual prices of a selected group of key prices. This might prove to be sufficient.

is becoming more chronic. It is easy to say that what is needed is a completely objective approach to the universe of prices. It is equally difficult to conceive of a group of impartial experts sufficiently objective to be entrusted with power to carry out the price adjustments that their studies may prescribe. Human values permeate the entire question, and, when human values enter, it is characteristic of objectivity to leave in spirit if not in form. But our study has indicated that until a degree of balance in the price structure can be attained and maintained, the absence of this condition will continue to generate forces that subsequently feed upon themselves in causing economic distress.

Since competitive price controls appear to be highly imperfect, it seems necessary that other price controls supplement them in the accomplishment of a greater degree of balance. Such controls, unlike many of those now current, must be exercised from the vantage point of the universe of prices. Moreover, they must be protected by the correlative control of successive additions to productive capacity. Otherwise, price controls would become progressively more difficult. In substance, this implies an interference with the distribution of money incomes. Money profits, as that term is now applied to returns on corporeal wealth and intangible wealth exclusive of human abilities, are also involved.

The fact must be emphasized that the needed price controls do not necessarily take the form of preventing price changes. The attainment of balance in the price structure may require the lowering of certain prices, the raising of others, while still others remain unchanged. The problem resolves itself into a continuous study of individual prices from the vantage point of the universe of economic activity. It is not necessary to stress the difficulties of the task.

This suggestion of an extension of price controls is made with the full knowledge that it represents a further modification of the concept of private property, as that term was used by the liberalistic philosophers of the eighteenth century. They stressed the right of private property as a natural right. "The social laws established by the Supreme Being prescribe only the preservation of the right of property, and of that liberty which is inseparable from it." [14] The right to own property implied the right to use property without encumbrance, so long as the property rights of others were not invaded. Conversely, it implied the right to prohibit others from using property. Private property thus became a metaphysical concept—a bundle of rights attached to various objects.

Competition was expected to prevent the abuse of these rights. But as competition has been lessened in the course of time, many of these rights have been withdrawn, thus modifying the status of private property. In many cases the right freely to fix prices has been among the rights that have been lost, for example, in the non-competitive public-utility fields. The suggestion that public price controls become more general is merely an extension of a tendency that for many years has been changing an essential element in the capitalistic organization of society.

CONCLUSION

We have found the economic forces related to liquidity to be important, not as factors initiating business change but as factors accelerating changes that have been initiated by other agents. The significance of liquidity considerations as an economic determinant depends chiefly upon the institutional organization of wealth-titles. Wealth-titles have assumed increasingly liquid forms through time. It follows that change in liquidity desires have become correspondingly more influential in modifying business activity. Since expectations of future changes in the price level influence liquidity desires, a relatively constant price level is highly desirable when the matter is viewed from the standpoint of liquidity theory.

Liquidity and the desire for more or less of it stand as potentially disturbing factors in the economy. They have become increasingly so in past years. But it does not seem feasible or especially desirable that this potential source of disturbance be

[14] Du Pont de Nemours, *Origines et progrès d'une science nouvelle,* quoted in Randall, J. H., *The Making of the Modern Mind* (New York, 1926), p. 324.

mitigated by a general modification of the institutional organization of wealth-titles.[15] A more reasonable means of coping with liquidity factors is through an attempt to prevent a high degree of unbalance from appearing in the price structure, thus smoothing out expectations of changes in the price level.

Contrary to Keynes, our study leads us to believe that attempts to influence the price level through interest rate changes are likely to succeed only when the price level has been relatively stable and is of limited importance in liquidity matters. A priori, the dynamic forces of expansion and contraction related to changes in liquidity desires appear to outweigh considerably the influence of changes in any single price. Changes in these desires are given effect by expectations of future changes in the aggregate of money profits, of which changes in the price level are an important determinant. It appears that expectations of future changes in money profits and in the price level are more conditioned by specialized knowledge of the degree of balance in particular sections of the price structure than by the theoretical implications of money-market changes.

Money-market techniques, such as changing the discount rate, open-market operations, and changing reserve requirements, seem to be of significant consequence only if the situation is one of comparative stability or if the techniques are used to induce a contraction by forcing the payment of debt. Apparently, they are of limited importance if the price structure is badly out of balance. Correspondingly, government fiscal operations are of less importance if the price structure is not balanced in degree. It follows that attempts to combat great changes in liquidity desires with available "financial" techniques do not promise enduring success unless they are operated in unison for their effect on price relations.

Again, the indiscriminate guaranteeing or insuring of prices by a central agency, in order to keep them from changing, is

[15] An exception to this, to which we subscribe, is the recommendation that much of existing debt financing be replaced with equity financing. Indeed, the suggestion has been made that all corporate reorganizations be effected through equity securities and no other kind.

fraught with peril and little promise. If prices are certain to remain fixed, the inducement to anticipate price change is eliminated. But experience has taught us that the cost of financially controlling prices is too heavy to be sustained indefinitely, short of totalitarian measures. So far as the strength of the forces we have examined can be appraised, it appears to be too great to be controlled directly in a liberalistic society. Fixed prices are likely to become unbalanced prices in the course of time, thereby making their control progressively more difficult. It follows that the insuring or guaranteeing of prices does not provide a permanent solution to the problems of liquidity. It can at best restrain forces which may be relieved by economic change in the course of time. It can at worst restrain forces which may exert themselves the more potently in the course of time. The latter is the more probable.

The solution, if a solution is to be found, seems to lie in a detailed study of the price structure, with a view to reducing the degree of unbalance, which seems to be the chief initiating cause of changes in the aggregate of money profits and in the price level. If a relatively stable price level is once attained, the problems of liquidity will take care of themselves, for the most part, through institutional development. It might even be that a protracted period of stability in the price level would be followed by a somewhat lessened desire for a highly liquid institutional organization of wealth-titles.

Once the exceedingly difficult task of attaining a greater degree of balance in the price structure is successfully performed, the problems of liquidity and the cumulative forces in business change will assume less importance. More direct means of successfully coping with the forces that we have identified with changed liquidity desires do not appear to be available in liberalistic societies.

APPENDIX

A NOTE CONCERNING INTANGIBLE WEALTH

THE INCLUSION of intangible or incorporeal wealth as a part of the total of all wealth has a long history. H. D. MacLeod quotes Aristotle and Socrates in defense of the concept of "immaterial wealth." [1] Adam Smith conceived to be the most sacred and inviolable form of property, "the property which every man has in his own labor, as it is the original foundation of all other property." [2] Here he seems to be using the term property as the equivalent of wealth. The distinction between property as "ownership" and wealth as the corporeal or incorporeal thing per se does not come into economic literature until about a century later. Still more specifically, Adam Smith refers to a part of what we call intangible wealth when he describes fixed capital as including:

> . . . the acquired and useful abilities of all the inhabitants or members of the society. The acquisition of such talents, by the maintenance of the acquirer during his education, study, or apprenticeship, always costs a real expense, which is a fixed capital and realized as it were, in his person. Those talents, as they make a part of his fortune, so do they likewise of that of the society to which he belongs. The improved dexterity of a workman may be considered in the same light and abridges labour, and which, though it costs a certain expense, repays that expense with a profit.[3]

Thus ability to labor, being a part of capital to Smith, becomes a part of wealth. Not being material or corporeal, it must by nature constitute a part of intangible wealth.

Nassau Senior continues the inclusion of personal abilities as a part of wealth. Subject to certain contingencies (not of great

1 MacLeod, H. D., *Principles of Economical Philosophy,* I (2d ed., London, 1879), 135–40.

2 Smith, Adam, *The Wealth of Nations,* I (Everyman's ed., New York, 1933), 110.

3 *Ibid.*, I, 247.

importance), "personal qualities are wealth and wealth of the most valuable kind." [4]

A more significant treatment of intangible wealth comes from H. D. MacLeod, who stresses the significance of the difference in meaning between material things, immaterial things, and abstract rights wholly separated from any material substance. The latter he calls incorporeal wealth. Immaterial wealth to him, seems to be made up chiefly of abilities. Incorporeal wealth includes bank notes, bills of exchange, public debts, shares, patents, copyrights, good will, etc. The true economic meaning of the word wealth is held to be an exchangeable right.[5] Thus all economic wealth became intangible in the sense that the attention of the economist is focused on a subjective thing rather than on a material object.

Alfred and Mary Marshall, writing before publication of the famous *Principles,* include in wealth personal or non-material wealth. Material wealth consists of the material sources of enjoyment which are capable of being exchanged. Personal or non-material wealth consists of "those human energies, faculties and habits, physical, mental and moral, which directly contribute to making men industrially efficient. . . ." [6] In this position, they follow Smith and others in including ability to labor as a part of wealth. A shift of opinion takes place a few years later. Writing alone, Marshall includes in an individual's wealth, "immaterial goods, which are external to him, and serve directly as the means to acquire material goods, such for instance as the good will of his business or his professional practice." However, in an accompanying footnote he adds: "But it excludes all his own personal qualities and faculties, even those which enable him to earn his living." [7] This was a broad distinction to which he held through the many revisions of the *Principles.*[8]

4 Senior, Nassau, *Four Introductory Lectures on Political Economy* (London, 1852), p. 70.

5 *Op. cit.,* pp. 135–61, *passim.*

6 Marshall, Alfred and Mary, *The Economics of Industry* (London, 1888), p. 6.

7 Marshall, Alfred, *Elements of the Economics of Industry* (London, 1892), p. 53.

8 Marshall, Alfred, *Principles of Economics* (8th ed., London, 1936), pp. 54–57.

Some years later, Irving Fisher used the term wealth to signify only those material objects owned by human beings. The existence of utility, an essential attribute, is implied by the appropriation of the objects to ownership. The right to use wealth is called property, or, more explicitly, a property right. Property and services are inseparable from wealth, and wealth from them, but they are not wealth. The enumeration of various attributes of wealth describes the wealth, and it is in this way that the attributes enter economics, but they do not enter separately as an immaterial sort of wealth. The skill of a mechanic is not wealth in addition to the man himself; it is the skilled mechanic who should be put in the category of wealth.[9] In this case the owner and the material thing owned coincide.

Here we have intangible wealth completely eliminated. Wealth is restricted to material things that are owned. In 1776, Smith recognized intangible wealth in describing a man's ability to labor as the most sacred of all wealth. By 1879, MacLeod had made exchangeable but abstract rights the sum and substance of economics. In 1906, Professor Fisher eliminated intangible wealth completely. But the Institutionalists brought the concept of intangible wealth back into economic science in no uncertain terms.

Richard T. Ely, writing in 1914, notes Marshall's earlier rejection of personal qualities as a part of wealth and held it to be somewhat artificial. "Man is the end, but personal qualities trained are some times trained not as an end but as a means, just as land is improved in order to secure greater yield." [10] The term intellectual property is introduced, by which was meant property in books, in inventions, patents and copyrights, property in the product of one's intellect.[11] By the term property is meant the exclusive right to control an economic good.[12] It includes every valuable right or interest, whether it be with reference to cor-

[9] Fisher, Irving, *The Nature of Capital and Income* (New York, 1906), Chaps. I, II, *passim*.

[10] Ely, R. T., *Property and Contract in Their Relations to the Distribution of Wealth* (New York, 1914), p. 128 n.

[11] *Ibid.*, p. 152.

[12] *Ibid.*, p. 101.

poreal or intangible things. In an appendix, compiled by Dr. Samuel P. Orth, court decisions are cited in support of this view.[13]

John R. Commons, after examining many of the same decisions, concludes that the judicial definition of property has been changed from physical things to the exchange-value of anything.[14] This exchange-value is not corporeal—it was behavioristic. There are only two kinds of property, both invisible and behavioristic: incorporeal property, consisting of debts or promises to pay, and intangible property, consisting of the exchange-value of anything, whether corporeal property or incorporeal property.[15] As with MacLeod, everything thus becomes intangible property. The concept of future expectancy enters conspicuously. All value is expectancy. Use-value is the expected behavior of

[13] *Ibid.*, p. 857. In Appendix IV Dr. Orth cites the following cases:

"*The term Property includes every valuable right or interest.*

Boston, etc., Ry. Co. *v.* Salem Ry. Co., 2 Gray (Mass.) 1 (1854); Stanton *v.* Lewis, 26 Conn. 444 (1857); Smith *v.* McCullough, 104 U. S. 27 (1881); Williston Seminary *v.* Hampshire Co., 147 Mass. 427 (1888); Wilson *v.* Beckwith, 140 Mo. 359, 41 S. W. 985 (1897); Scranton *v.* Wheeler, 179 U. S. 141 (1900); St. Louis *v.* Hill, 116 Mo. 527, 22 S. W. 861 (1893); Low *v.* Rees P. Co., 41 Neb. 127, 59 N. W. 362 (1894); Smith *v.* Furbish, 68 N. H. 123, 44 Atl. 398 (1894).

"*It embraces everything to which right of ownership can be attached.*

Stanton *v.* Lewis, 26 Conn. 444 (1857); Barker *v.* State, 109 Ind. 58 (1886); Carlton *v.* Carlton, 72 Me. 116, 39 Am. Rep. 307 (1881); Wilson *v.* Ward Lumber Co., 67 Fed. 674 (1895); Fears *v.* State, 102 Ga. 274, 29 S. E. 463 (1897); N. W. Mutual Life Ins. Co. *v.* Lewis etc., 28 Mont. 484, 72 Pac. 982 (1903).

"*Corporeal or incorporeal:*

King *v.* Gotz, 70 Cal. 236; 11 Pac. 656 (1886).

"*Tangible or intangible:*

Stahl *v.* Webster, 11 Ill. 511 (1850); National Tel. N. Co. *v.* Western Union Tel. Co., 119 Fed. 294 (1903).

"*Visible or invisible:*

N. W. Mutual Life Ins. Co. *v.* Lewis *et al.* 28 Mont. 484; 72 Pac. 982 (1903).

"*Real or personal:*

White *v.* Keller, 68 Fed. 796 (1895).

"*Property includes everything that has exchange value:*

Slaughter House Cases, 16 Wall. 36 (1872); Dixon *v.* People, 63 Ill. App. 590 (1895); Harbison *v.* Knoxville Iron Co., 103 Tenn. 421; 53 S. W. 955 (1899).

"*Including labour and the right to labour:*

In re Parrott, 1 Fed. 481 (1880); *In re* Marshall, 102 Fed. 323 (1900); Jones *v.* Leslie, 61 Wash. 107; 112 Pac. 81 (1910); but see Gleason *v.* Thaw, 185 Fed. 345 (1911)."

[14] Commons, John R., *Legal Foundations of Capitalism* (New York, 1924), p. 18.

[15] *Ibid.*, p. 19.

things in man's activity of production and consumption. Exchange-value is the expected behavior of people in buying and selling.[16]

From this welter of opinion we may distill certain conclusions. There appears to be no denial that wealth consists of all of those things which directly or indirectly contribute to the satisfaction of individual wants. Economic wealth is that which has been appropriated. Implied in the act of appropriation is scarcity. Although agreement has not been general on the point, it can be held tenably that economic wealth is embodied in either corporeal or intangible form. The ownership of wealth is made evident by a legal title. Legal title may or may not be represented by a legal instrument, or token. The specific nature of these titles may vary widely. The organization of titles to economic wealth has assumed different characteristics with the evolutionary development of economic life.

For some purposes it might be desirable to follow MacLeod and Commons in treating all wealth as the intangible property of ownership. In this event, one's study would be restricted to the organization, nature, and behavior of titles. The term token has been used as an inclusive term to describe the legal instruments evidencing wealth-titles. Hence one's study would then be concerned only with tokens and with those wealth-titles which, according to custom, require no legal evidence. Even were this the case, we would find that the nature and behavior of tokens are derived in large part from the nature and behavior of the associated real wealth.

Accordingly, when speaking of intangible wealth, one may, with profit, mean a different thing than what was meant by MacLeod or Commons. The sum total of real wealth may be conceived to consist on the one hand of corporeal, substantive, or material forms, and on the other of intangible or invisible subjects.[17] Overlying these categories of corporeal and intangible

[16] *Ibid.*, p. 25.

[17] The term tangible wealth, as the antithesis of intangible wealth, has purposely been avoided. In a sense, everything that can be converted to cash or that can be made to produce a result is tangible to the business man.

wealth, which together make up the sum total of all wealth, is ownership. Ely calls it property, MacLeod and Commons call it intangible wealth. It may be called title. Its legal evidence takes the form of tokens.

As the connotation of the term indicates, intangibles have no physical being. Some forms of intangible wealth are derived from the social or natural heritage and are, for practical purposes, generally accessible. Religion in relation to business ethics, climate, and the printed accumulations of knowledge of the arts and sciences afford examples.

More personal types of intangible wealth may be designated as good will and reputation, special abilities of all kinds, contracts, contacts, competitive advantages arising out of economic loyalties and lack of perfect knowledge of markets, trade secrets, franchises, business organization, and what Richard T. Ely calls "intellectual property"—inventions, patents, and copyrights. These are all subject to appropriation or development in the sense that economic advantage accompanies their possession. Although they have been described as personal types of intangible wealth, some of these wealth-forms may be divorced from their owners by transfer of title, as in the case of patents, royalty contracts, and the like. Others are inseparable from their owner, such as special abilities, contacts, and so forth.

The classification of intangible wealth in this manner is different in some respects from that used by Marshall in the *Principles*. In addition to obviously corporeal wealth, he lists as material goods such things as "rights to hold, or use, or derive benefits from material things . . . the physical gifts of nature, land and water, air and climate . . . mortgages . . . shares . . . all kinds of monopolies, patent rights, copyrights . . . and other rights of usage." Non-material things are internal and external to man. Business ability and professional skill are not wealth because they are internal to man. Good will and business connections of traders and professional men and the organization of their businesses are external to man and are therefore wealth.[18]

[18] Marshall, Alfred, *Principles of Economics* (8th ed., London, 1936), pp. 54–57.

Some of these distinctions are not encountered in current business or accounting practice. It would appear to be more in keeping with existing habit to call privileges of various kinds and monopolies intangible wealth. Shares and mortgages, or debts, are important forms of legal evidences to rights. These we have called tokens.

All corporeal wealth is progressively extinguishable in time, due to natural and human causes. Intangible wealth of an economic nature is also usually extinguishable, but not with equal regularity. Human abilities and skills may reach an optimum point during a life span, after which their usefulness will diminish. Good will and reputation will endure at a maximum only so long as the forces that brought them into being continue to operate. Intangible wealth derived from contracts, patents, and the like may become progressively less valuable as the time of exclusive possession approaches an end.

It will be noted that intangible wealth of economic value is usually associated with special abilities or social privileges that characterize imperfections of competitive markets. It does not follow that there must be an exact or even a close correlation between the degree or imperfection in markets and the proportion of all wealth made up by intangibles. But the embodiments of intangible wealth are, by and large, more specialized than those of corporeal wealth. It may perhaps be said that market imperfections tend to increase as the proportion of intangibles increases, relative to the aggregate of real wealth, of which they are a part.

Depending on the nature of intangibles, titles to them may be easily transferred, or may not be transferable at all. As previously noted, they may possess varying degrees of personality. Generally speaking, intangibles may or may not be divisible, mobile, or convertible to different uses. Their characteristics are too indefinite to permit of more than a broad generalization relative to their liquidity status as a class. Being for the most part unique in character, they are as a class less rather than more liquid than corporeal wealth.

If we can believe the engineers, and there seems to be little reason to doubt them, we may expect to supply our material wants in years to come with increasing ease. This would logically result in a smaller part of available time and energy being devoted to the physical processing of wealth. The tendency may already be discerned. The growth of commercial and service activity in recent years has outdistanced the growth of the producing and processing of physical goods by a considerable margin. Estimates based on data contained in the *General Report on Occupations,* of the Fifteenth Census of the United States,[19] indicate that in the twenty years from 1910 to 1930 the percentage of gainfully employed population engaged in service and trade occupations increased from thirty-six to forty-seven.[20] Professor F. C. Mills, studying the same data, notes the shifts in occupational activity in these terms:

> These three related shifts—an absolute decline in the farm population, a relative decline in the number of industrial employees, and a marked increase in the number of those engaged in mercantile pursuits and in personal service occupations—are important aspects of economic tendencies in the United States during post-war years.[21]

Distributors and those engaged in the service industries are preponderantly concerned with such things as sales forces, types of business organization, personal abilities, contracts, contacts, reputation, good will, copyrights, and other embodiments of what we have called intangible wealth. In future years, perhaps, economists will come to recognize intangible wealth as being of equal importance with corporeal wealth. Among other things, the conscious inclusion of intangible wealth as a significant segment of total wealth may influence our thinking in regard to the future demand for investible funds. Current theories of stagnation may

19 *United States Census, 1930,* Vol. V: *Population,* p. 39, Table 2.

20 In this estimate workers listed by the census under transportation and communication, trade and finance, public service, professional service, domestic and personal service, and clerical occupations are treated as service and trade workers. Those treated as outside of service and trade occupations are workers in agriculture, forestry and fishing, extraction of minerals, and manufacturing and mechanical industries.

21 Mills, *Economic Tendencies in the United States,* p. 419.

need revision. Such a shift of base is not without precedent. The economists of the eighteenth and early nineteenth centuries gave much more attention to agriculture and commerce and less to industry than is now the habit. Intangible wealth has seemingly come to represent an increasingly large segment of the sum total of real wealth, which serves as the object of all property rights.

GLOSSARY

BUYING: The exchange of money for any type of real wealth, either directly or through tokens.

CLAIM: The right to acquire legal ownership of wealth in the course of time.

DEBT:

Money, Anything that represents, as a class, a *general* claim to wealth; a debt of the community to all the holders of money.

Wealth Debt, Debt that is incurred by the passage of title to real wealth, without the concomitant and reverse passage of title to money.

Fiat Debt, Debt that is incurred by the passage of title to money without the concomitant and reverse passage of title to real wealth.

Interest Debt, Debt which accrues by contract on previously established wealth debt and fiat debt, without direct reference to the solitary passage of title to either real wealth or money.

ENTERPRISER: Anyone engaged in productive economic activity.

ESTABLISHMENT: The bringing of wealth into being by individuals or by nature.

EXTINGUISHMENT: The loss of usefulness of wealth due to natural or human causes.

FINAL BUYING: The exchange of money against new wealth output of all descriptions.

HOARDING AND DISHOARDING: The elongation or contraction of the *average* period of holding title to a unit of money.

INTERSTITIAL CIRCULATION: The exchange of money against previously existing wealth-titles and claims in the process of producing and distributing new wealth.

LIQUIDITY:

Of Assets, A quality determined by the exchangeability of things into money in general, but not for a specific amount of money. This ability increases with a narrowing of the range of prices within which it is thought that the asset may be sold and with a shortening of the period of time within which a price can be obtained within this expected range of prices. Liquidity is not a matter of the value of the asset through time.

Of Persons, A quality determined by the liquidity and money amounts of things or assets owned relative to the maturity schedule and money amounts of debts owed; degree of solvency.

LIQUIDITY DESIRES OR PREFERENCES: A want expressed by persons for more or less liquidity in their affairs and effected (1) by a change of the types of assets to which they hold title and (2) by a change in the relation of the nature and amount of their assets to the nature and amount of their liabilities or debts.

NATURAL RESOURCES: Wealth that has accrued as the result of natural agents.

PRIMARY CIRCULATION: Final buying, plus interstitial circulation.

PROFITS:

Individual Money Profits, The net change in money amount of titles and claims to wealth resulting from production, discovery, trading, and forcible appropriation. Decreases in the money amount of titles owned, due to personal use, are not deductible from money profits. Money profits may accrue to everyone engaged in economic activity, regardless of the specific nature of such activity.

Real Profits, or Savings, The difference between establishment and extinguishment of wealth in a period of time. *Money savings* is an ambiguous term not used in the study.

SECONDARY CIRCULATION: The exchange of money against previously existing wealth-titles and claims, without direct reference to the production and distribution of new wealth.

SPENDING: The loss of title or claim to wealth due to extinguishment or other causes. *Consumption* is one source of extinguishment.

STORE: Wealth that has accrued as the result of man-made decisions.

TITLE: Legal ownership of wealth.

TOKENS: Legal instruments evidencing the title or ability to claim real wealth of either a corporeal or intangible nature.

WEALTH:

Real Wealth, Anything that has been appropriated and that contributes, directly or indirectly, to the satisfaction of individual wants. It consists of corporeal and intangible wealth.

Corporeal Wealth, Material or substantive forms of wealth.

Intangible Wealth, Invisible subjects without form, which are nevertheless capable of being appropriated and used to satisfy the wants of mankind.

SELECTED BIBLIOGRAPHY ON LIQUIDITY AND RELATED TOPICS

THE PREPARATION of a bibliography on the subject of liquidity presents a difficult problem. The topic has been typically allotted a place in larger treatments of the subject of banking. Numerous bibliographies of banking are available, and it is not our purpose to duplicate them here.

Those works that have dealt with the subject of liquidity, as such, are few. To limit the bibliography to these would constitute an inadequate coverage of the many ideas of significance to the subject. An additional difficulty arises from the fact that the term "liquidity" has been related to a wider range of economic phenomena in the present work than is generally the case.

We are confronted with the necessity of a compromise involving a somewhat arbitrary selection of materials. The following books and articles, for the most part, but not entirely, are selected from those which have been cited in the preceding text. It is hoped that the sins of omission may be compensated by the virtues of a discriminating and representative brevity. With minor exceptions the bibliography does not cover publications made later than 1938.

Angell, J. W., "The Components of the Circular Velocity of Money," *Quarterly Journal of Economics*, LI (1936–37), 224–72.

——— *The Behavior of Money*. New York, 1936.

——— "The General Dynamics of Money," *Journal of Political Economy*, XLV (1937), 289–346.

Beckhart, B. H., *Qualitative Credit Control*. Chicago, 1936. Commission on Banking Law and Practice, Association of Reserve City Bankers, Bulletin No. 10.

Berle, A. A., Jr., and G. C. Means, *The Modern Corporation and Private Property*. New York, 1932.

Berle, A. A., Jr., and V. Pederson, *Liquid Claims and National Wealth*. New York, 1934.

Bissell, R. M., Jr., "The Rate of Interest," *American Economic Review Supplement*, XXVIII (1938), 23–40.

Bonbright, J. C., *The Valuation of Property*. 2 vols. New York, 1937.

Burns, A. R., *The Decline of Competition*. New York, 1936.
Cannan, Edwin, "The Application of the Theoretical Apparatus of Supply and Demand to Units of Currency," *The Economic Journal*, XXXI (1921), 453–61.
Currie, Lauchlin, "The Decline of the Commercial Loan," *Quarterly Journal of Economics*, XLV (1930–31), 698–709.
——— "The Treatment of Credit in Contemporary Monetary Theory," *Journal of Political Economy*, XLI (1933), 58–79.
——— *The Supply and Control of Money in the United States*. Cambridge, 1934.
Curtis, M., and H. Townshend, *Modern Money*. [American edition.] New York, 1938.
Dunkman, W. E., *Qualitative Credit Control*. New York, 1933.
Durbin, E. F. M., *The Problem of Credit Policy*. New York, 1935.
Ellis, H. S., *German Monetary Theory, 1905–33*. Cambridge, 1934.
Fisher, Irving, *The Nature of Capital and Income*. New York, 1906.
——— *The Theory of Interest*. New York, 1930.
——— "The Debt-Deflation Theory of Great Depressions," *Econometrica*, I (1933), 337–57.
Foreman, C. J., *Efficiency and Scarcity Profits*. Chicago, 1930.
Foster, W. F., and W. Catchings, *Profits*. New York, 1927.
Ghosh, P. C., *The Theory of Profits*. Calcutta, 1933.
Haberler, G., *Prosperity and Depression*. Geneva, 1937.
Hammond, Bray, "Long and Short-Term Credit in Early American Banking," *Quarterly Journal of Economics*, XLIX (1934–35), 79–103.
Hawtrey, *Currency and Credit*. 3d ed. New York, 1928.
——— "Alternative Theories of the Rate of Interest," *Economic Journal*, XLVII (1937), 436–43.
——— *Capital and Employment*. London, 1937.
——— *A Century of Bank Rate*. London, 1938.
Hayek, F. A. von, *Prices and Production*. 2d ed., rev. and enl. London, 1935.
Hicks, J. R., "Mr. Keynes and the 'Classics'; a Suggested Interpretation," *Econometrica*, V (1937), 147–59.
Jones, B., *Debt and Production*. New York, 1933.
Kester, R. B., *Advanced Accounting*. 3d ed. New York, 1935.
Keynes, J. M., *A Tract on Monetary Reform*. New York, 1924.
——— *A Treatise on Money*. 2 vols. New York, 1930.
——— *The General Theory of Employment, Interest and Money*. New York, 1936.
——— "The General Theory of Employment," *Quarterly Journal of Economics*, LI (1936–37), 209–23.

Keynes, J. M. (*continued*), "Alternative Theories of the Rate of Interest," *Economic Journal,* XLVII (1937), 241–52.
Knight, F. H., *Risk, Uncertainty and Profit.* New York, 1921. Hart, Schaffner and Marx Prize Essays, XXXI.
Lange, Oskar, "The Rate of Interest and the Optimum Propensity to Consume," *Economica,* V (n. s., 1938), 12–32.
Lavington, F., "Short and Long Rates of Interest," *Economica,* IV (1924), 291–303.
Machlup, Fritz, "The Liquidity of Short-Term Capital," *Economica,* XII (1932), 271–84.
MacLeod, H. C., *The Theory and Practice of Banking.* 6th ed., 2 vols. London, 1902.
Makower, H., and J. Marschak, "Assets, Prices and Monetary Theory," *Economica,* V (n. s., 1938), 261–88.
Millikan, M., "Liquidity Preference Theory of Interest," *American Economic Review,* XXVIII (1938), 247–60.
Mills, F. C., *Behavior of Prices.* New York, 1927. Publication of the National Bureau of Economic Research, Inc.
——— *Economic Tendencies in the United States.* New York, 1932. Publication of the National Bureau of Economic Research, Inc., in coöperation with the Committee on Recent Economic Changes.
——— *Prices in Recession and Recovery.* New York, 1936. Publication of the National Bureau of Economic Research in coöperation with the Committee on Recent Economic Changes.
Mitchell, W. C., *Business Cycles, the Problem and Its Setting.* New York, 1927. Publication of the National Bureau of Economic Research, Inc.
Mitchell, Waldo F., "Attack upon the Theory of the Liquidity of Bank Earning Assets," *Journal of Political Economy,* XXXI (1923), 243–61.
——— *The Uses of Bank Funds.* Chicago, 1925.
Morton, W. A., "Liquidity and Solvency," *American Economic Review,* XXIX (1939), 272–85.
Moulton, H. G., *Financial Organization and the Economic System.* New York, 1938.
National Resources Committee, *The Structure of the American Economy.* Washington, 1939.
Newman, A. M., "The Doctrine of Liquidity," *Review of Economic Studies,* III (1935–36), 81–99.
Ohlin, B., "Alternative Theories of the Rate of Interest," *Economic Journal,* XLVII (1937), 423–27.
Palyi, Melchoir, *Liquidity.* Minneapolis, 1936. Publication of the Minnesota Bankers Association.

Phillips, C. A., *Bank Credit.* New York, 1920.
Pigou, A. C., *Industrial Fluctuations.* 2d ed. London, 1929.
Riefler, W. W., *Money Rates and Money Markets in the United States.* New York, 1930.
Robertson, D. H., "Saving and Hoarding," *Economic Journal,* XLIII (1933), 399–413.
——— *Banking Policy and the Price Level.* 3d impression, rev. London, 1932.
——— "Notes on Mr. Keynes's Theory of Employment," *Quarterly Journal of Economics,* LI (1936–37), 168–91.
——— "Alternative Theories of the Rate of Interest," *Economic Journal,* XLVII (1937), 428–36.
——— "A Survey of Modern Monetary Theory," *The Manchester School,* IX (1938), 1–20.
Saulnier, R. J., *Contemporary Monetary Theory.* New York, 1938.
Sayers, R. S., *Modern Banking.* London, 1938.
Slichter, S. H., "The Economics of Public Works," in *Current Economic Policies,* ed. by J. B. Hubbard. New York, 1934.
Soddy, Frederick, *Wealth, Virtual Wealth and Debt.* 2d ed. New York, 1933.
Twentieth Century Fund, *The Internal Debts of the United States.* New York, 1933.
——— *Debts and Recovery.* New York, 1938.
Viner, J., "Mr. Keynes on the Causes of Unemployment," *Quarterly Journal of Economics,* LI (1936–37), 147–67.
Watkins, M. W., "The Price System," in the *Encyclopaedia of the Social Sciences,* XII (New York, 1934), 366–75.
Westerfield, R. B., "Liquidity," in the *Encyclopaedia of the Social Sciences,* IX (New York, 1933), 491–95.
Whitney, Caroline, *Experiments in Credit Control.* New York, 1934.
Willis, H. P., *The Theory and Practice of Central Banking.* New York, 1936.
Willis, H. P., J. M. Chapman, and R. W. Robey, *Contemporary Banking.* New York, 1933.

INDEX

Bei Fragen zur Produktsicherheit wenden Sie sich bitte an:
If you have any questions regarding product safety,
please contact:

Walter de Gruyter GmbH
Genthiner Straße 13
10785 Berlin
productsafety@degruyterbrill.com